PACEMAKER®

Pre-Algebra

GLOBE FEARON

Pearson Learning Group

Pacemaker® Pre-Algebra Second Edition

We thank the following educators, who provided valuable comments and suggestions during the development of the First Edition of this book:

REVIEWERS

Melissa Bartolameolli (Curth), Math Teacher, Athens High School, Troy, MI 48098
Jim Geske, Math Special Ed. Chairman, Apple Valley High School, Apple Valley, MN 55124
Lois Lanyard, Resource Center Teacher, Woodbridge High School, Woodbridge NJ 07095

PROJECT STAFF

Executive Editor: Eleanor Ripp; *Supervising Editor*: Stephanie Petron Cahill; *Senior Editor*: Phyllis Dunsay
Editor: Theresa McCarthy; *Production Editor*: Travis Bailey; *Lead Designer*: Susan Brorein
Market Manager: Douglas Falk; *Cover Design*: Susan Brorein, Jennifer Visco
Editorial, Design, and Production Services: GTS Graphics; *Electronic Composition*: Phyllis Rosinsky

About the Cover: Pre-algebra helps people get ready for algebra. The images on the cover represent some of the things you will be learning about in this book. The stopwatch is for measuring time. The line graph is for showing data visually. Balancing a scale reminds us of how we balance an equation. The hot air balloons and snowflakes remind us of positive negative numbers. What other images can you think of to represent pre-algebra?

ISBN: 0-130-23633-0
Printed in the United States of America
7 8 9 10   06 05 04

Globe
Fearon
Pearson Learning Group

1-800-321-3106
www.pearsonlearning.com

Contents

UNIT THREE   143

Chapter 6   Factors and Multiples   144

Chapter 7   Fractions and Mixed Numbers   164

UNIT FOUR · 191

Chapter 8 · Adding and Subtracting Fractions · 192

Chapter 9 · Multiplying and Dividing Fractions · 218

A Note to the Student

Getting ready for algebra is a big step. You may think you don't know anything about algebra, but you do. This book was made to help you prepare for algebra.

The purpose of this book is to make your journey to algebra a success. This journey will be comfortable and interesting. You will build new skills based on what you know already. You will make connections between arithmetic and important skills in algebra. As you work through and review more topics in arithmetic, your skills in algebra will also grow.

Each lesson will present clear models and examples. The lessons will give you a chance to try out your skills in **Try These**. Then, you will go on and use the skills in **Practice**. From lesson to lesson, you will share what you learned with a partner in **Cooperative Learning**. Margin notes are there to give you helpful hints.

Application lessons will show you how you can apply what you know to everyday problems. **Problem Solving** lessons will show you different ways to solve all types of problems. **Calculator** lessons will show you that using a calculator is another way to practice algebra skills. **Math Connections**, **People in Math**, **On-the-Job Math**, and **Math in Your Life** are features that contain interesting information about people and careers in math. They also give you interesting facts about math in other subjects that you might study.

There are many other study aids in the book. At the beginning of every chapter, you will find **Learning Objectives**. They will help you focus on the important points covered in the chapter. You will also find **Words to Know**. This is a look ahead at new vocabulary you will find in the chapter. At the end of each chapter, you will find a **Chapter Review**. This will give you a summary of what you have just learned, vocabulary practice, and a quiz. A **Unit Review** comes after each unit.

Everyone who put this book together worked hard to make it useful, interesting, and enjoyable. The rest is up to you.

We wish you well on your journey to algebra. Our success comes from your success.

 # Unit One

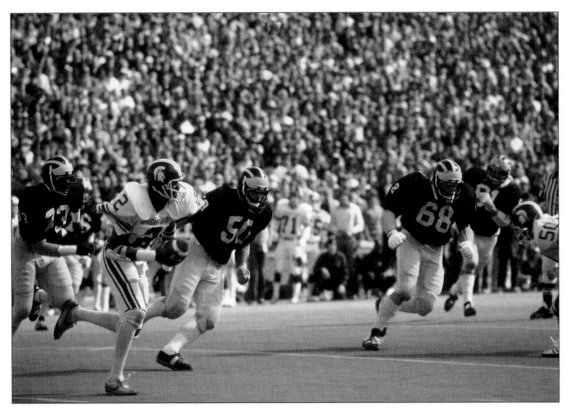

Thousands of fans come to a football game. Before such a big sports event, people who work at the stadium estimate how large the crowd will be. Why do you think they do this?

Learning Objectives

- Use place value.
- Compare whole numbers.
- Round whole numbers.
- Add, subtract, multiply, and divide whole numbers.
- Estimate sums, differences, products, and quotients.
- Use exponents to find powers.
- Use a calculator to add, subtract, multiply, and divide large numbers.
- Guess, check, and revise to solve problems.
- Apply concepts and skills to find perimeter.

Words to Know

digit	one of the ten basic numbers (0, 1, 2, 3, 4, 5, 6, 7, 8, 9)
place value	the value of a place within a number
addend	number added to another number
sum	the answer in addition
difference	the answer in subtraction
estimate	tells you about how large a sum or difference will be
factor	one of the numbers being multiplied
product	the answer in multiplication
base	a factor; in 3^2, 3 is the base; it is used as a factor 2 times
exponent	tells how many times the base is used as a factor
power	the result of multiplying when factors are the same
divisor	the number used to divide
dividend	the number being divided
quotient	the answer in division
remainder	the number left over in division
polygon	a closed figure with three or more sides
perimeter	the sum of the lengths of the sides of a polygon

Population Project

How many people live in your town? How many people live in a nearby town? Record your data in a place-value chart. Which has the greater population? Add to find the total population. Then round your answer. Use a map to report your findings to the class.

Whole numbers are formed from the ten **digits** 0, 1, 2, 3, 4, 5, 6, 7, 8, and 9. The place-value table below shows the value of a digit in a number. The value of a digit in a number has a **place value.** A place-value table is based on groups of tens.

Math Fact
Commas separate millions, thousands, and ones.

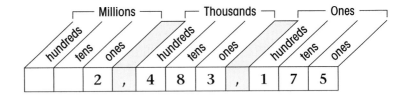

Use the place-value table above. Answer the questions.

▶ **EXAMPLE 1**

What is the value of 2 in 2,483,175?

2 is in the millions place.   2,483,175

2 has a value of 2,000,000.

▶ **EXAMPLE 2**

What is the value of 4 in 2,483,175?

4 is in the hundred-thousands place.   2,483,175

4 has a value of 400,000.

▶ **EXAMPLE 3**

What is the value of 7 in 2,483,175?

7 is in the tens place.   2,483,175

7 has a value of 70.

Try These

Use the place-value table to answer the questions below about the number 9,614,503.

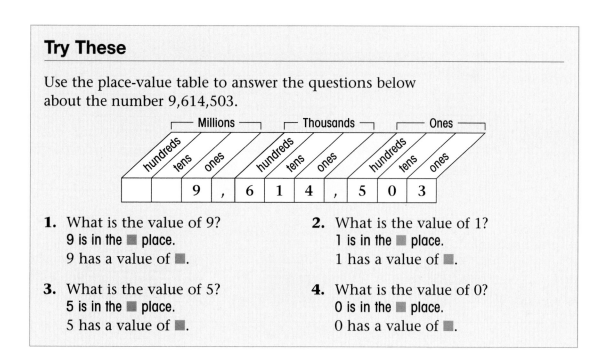

1. What is the value of 9?
   9 is in the ■ place.
   9 has a value of ■.

2. What is the value of 1?
   1 is in the ■ place.
   1 has a value of ■.

3. What is the value of 5?
   5 is in the ■ place.
   5 has a value of ■.

4. What is the value of 0?
   0 is in the ■ place.
   0 has a value of ■.

Practice

1. What is the value of 9 in 365,791?
   What place is 6 in?
   What is the value of 3?

2. What is the value of 5 in 513,648?
   What place is 4 in?
   What is the value of 6?

3. What is the value of 1 in 2,497,178?
   What place is 2 in?
   What is the value of 8?

4. What is the value of 4 in 1,147,563?
   What place is 3 in?
   What is the value of 5?

5. What is the value of 2 in 201,030?
   What place is 1 in?
   What is the value of 3?

6. What is the value of 7 in 6,719,250?
   What place is 2 in?
   What is the value of 1?

Cooperative Learning

7. Write a number with seven digits. Pick out three digits from the number. Have a partner name the place each digit is in.

8. Make up three numbers using the digits 5, 8, 3, 2, 9, and 1 in different orders. Have a partner tell you the value of 8 in each of the three numbers.

You can use place value to compare numbers.

► **EXAMPLE 1**

Compare 8,402 and 453.

Line up the digits by place.

8,402
  453

8,402 has more digits than 453.

Math Facts
> means *is greater than.*
< means *is less than.*

8,402 is greater than 453   or   453 is less than 8,402.

$$8,402 > 453 \quad \text{or} \quad 453 < 8,402$$

► **EXAMPLE 2**

Compare 5,821 and 5,921.

Line up the numbers by place.
5,821 and 5,921 have the
same number of digits.

5,821
5,921

Compare digits place by place
starting on the left.
5 and 5 are equal.

5,821
5,921

8 and 9 are different.

5,821
5,921
$$8 < 9 \text{ or } 9 > 8$$

5,821 is less than 5,921 or 5,921 is greater than 5,821.

$$5,821 < 5,921 \quad \text{or} \quad 5,921 > 5,821$$

► **EXAMPLE 3**

Compare 20,100 and 20,100.

Line up the numbers by place.
20,100 and 20,100 have the
same digits in the same places.

20,100
20,100

20,100 is equal to 20,100.

Math Fact
= means *is equal to.*

$$20,100 = 20,100$$

Try These

Use >, <, or = to compare.

1. Compare 4,602 and 983.

4,602 has ■ digit than 983.   4,602

4,602 is ■ than 983 or 983 is ■ than 4,602 983

■ > 983   or   ■ < 4,602

2. Compare 7,432 and 7,612.

7,432 and 7,612 have the same number of digits. 7,432

7,432 is ■ than 7,612 or 7,612 is ■ than 7,432 7,612

7,432 < ■   or   ■ > ■

3. Compare 392 and 392.

392 and 392 have the same digits in the same places. 392

392 is ■ to 392   392

392 ■ 392

Practice

Use >, <, or = to compare.

1. Compare 3,217 and 2,217.   **2.** Compare 4,999 and 2,999.

3. Compare 2,347 and 7,432.   **4.** Compare 3,219 and 9,003.

5. Compare 670 and 670.   **6.** Compare 544 and 579.

Cooperative Learning

7. Write a pair of numbers. Have a partner compare them. Check the work.

8. Write a number with four digits. Have a partner use the same four digits to write a number greater than the number you wrote. Check the work.

Rounding means changing a number to the nearest ten, hundred, thousand, and so on. Place value is used when rounding numbers.

34 is closer to 30.
34 rounded to the nearest 10 is 30.

580 is closer to 600.
580 rounded to the nearest 100 is 600.

Follow the steps in these examples.

▶ **EXAMPLE 1**

Round 2,472 to the nearest thousand.

1. Find the digit in the rounding place.   2,472

2. Look at the digit to its right.   2,472
   If it is 5 or greater than 5, add 1 to $4 < 5$
   the digit in the rounding place.
   If it is less than 5, leave the digit
   in the rounding place alone.   Leave 2 alone.

3. Change each digit to the right of
   the rounding place to 0.   2,000

2,472 rounded to the nearest thousand is 2,000.

▶ **EXAMPLE 2**

Round 796 to the nearest ten.

1. Find the digit in the rounding place.   796

2. Look at the digit to its right.   796
   If it is 5 or greater than 5, add 1 to $6 > 5$
   the digit in the rounding place.   Increase 9 by 1.

Math Fact
When you are rounding up to a place with the digit 9, you need to round up the place to its left.

3. Since 9 + 1 is 10, increase the digit
   to the left of the rounding place by 1.   Increase 7 by 1.

4. Change both the digit in the
   rounding place and the digit to the
   right of the rounding place to 0.   800

796 rounded to the nearest 10 is 800.

Try These

1. Round 6,231 to the nearest thousand.

Find the digit in the rounding place.	6,231
Look at the digit to its right.	6,231
If it is less than 5, leave the digit in the rounding place alone.	2 ■ 5
	Leave ■ alone.
Change each digit to the right of the rounding place to 0.	6,0■■

    6,231 rounded to the nearest thousand is ■.

2. Round 14,899 to the nearest thousand.

Find the digit in the rounding place.	14,899
Look at the digit to its right.	14,899
If it is 5 or greater than 5, add 1 to the digit in the rounding place.	8 > 5
	Increase ■ by 1.
Change each digit to the right of the rounding place to 0.	■■,■■■

    14,899 rounded to the nearest thousand is ■.

Practice

Round to the nearest ten.

1. 84   **2.** 76   **3.** 385   **4.** 4,764

Round to the nearest hundred.

5. 167   **6.** 258   **7.** 6,739   **8.** 12,849

Round to the nearest thousand.

9. 2,675   **10.** 8,147   **11.** 9,411   **12.** 75,218

Round to the nearest ten thousand.

13. 18,799   **14.** 43,599   **15.** 178,699   **16.** 252,125

Cooperative Learning

17. Explain the rules for rounding numbers to a partner.

18. Write a number with six digits. Have a partner round the number to different places. Check the work.

1·4 Addition

If you have $4 and you earn $3 more, the total you have earned is $7. In this addition example, the 4 and the 3 are called **addends**. The **sum** of 4 and 3 is 7.

$$
\begin{array}{r}
\$4 \quad \leftarrow \text{addend} \\
+\ 3 \quad \leftarrow \text{addend} \\
\hline
\$7 \quad \leftarrow \text{sum}
\end{array}
$$

You add larger numbers by adding the digits within each number place by place. Start with the digits in the ones place. If the total is ten or more, be sure to regroup.

EXAMPLE 1

Add.   435 + 47

Add ones. Regroup.	Add tens.	Add hundreds.
1 4 3 5 + 4 7 ——— 2	1 4 3 5 + 4 7 ——— 8 2	1 4 3 5 + 4 7 ——— 4 8 2

Math Fact
You can regroup 10 ones as 1 ten.

The sum of 435 and 47 is 482.

EXAMPLE 2

Add.   965 + 395

Add ones. Regroup.	Add tens. Regroup.	Add hundreds. Regroup.
1 9 6 5 + 3 9 5 ——— 0	1 1 9 6 5 + 3 9 5 ——— 6 0	1 1 9 6 5 + 3 9 5 ——— 1,3 6 0

Remember
Regroup 10 ones as 1 ten.

Regroup 10 tens as 1 hundred.

Regroup 10 hundreds as 1 thousand.

The sum of 965 and 395 is 1,360.

Try These

1. Add. 43 + 69

Add ones. Regroup.	Add tens. Regroup.
■	■
4 3	4 3
+ 6 9	+ 6 9
■	1 ■ ■

The sum of 43 and 69 is ■.

2. Add. 438 + 697

Add ones. Regroup.	Add tens. Regroup.	Add hundreds. Regroup.
■	■ ■	■ ■
4 3 8	4 3 8	4 3 8
+ 6 9 7	+ 6 9 7	+ 6 9 7
■	■ ■	1,■ ■ ■

The sum of 438 and 697 is ■.

Practice

Add.

1. 27 + 8	**2.** 26 + 45	**3.** 59 + 28	**4.** 73 + 9
5. 38 + 83	**6.** 137 + 48	**7.** 256 + 34	**8.** 367 + 264
9. 687 + 499	**10.** 1,745 + 28	**11.** 2,348 + 176	**12.** 17,345 + 4,896

Cooperative Learning

13. Write an addition problem. Have a partner find the sum. Check the work.

14. Explain to a partner how you would add 897 and 259. Write each step as you work. Have the partner check your work.

If you have $4 and you spend $3, then you have
$1 left. In this subtraction example, $1 is called the
difference between 4 and 3.

$$
\begin{array}{r}
\$4 \\
-\ 3 \\
\hline
\$1
\end{array} \leftarrow \text{difference}
$$

You subtract two whole numbers by subtracting the
digits place by place. Start with the digits in the ones
place. If you cannot subtract, regroup or "borrow" from
the next place. Then, continue to subtract.

▶ **EXAMPLE 1**

Subtract.   885 − 57

Regroup.
Subtract ones.

Subtract tens.

Subtract hundreds.

Math Fact
You can regroup for more ones.
Borrow 1 ten as 10 ones.

$$
\begin{array}{r}
7\ 15 \\
8\ \not{8}\ \not{5} \\
-\ \ 5\ 7 \\
\hline
8
\end{array}
\qquad
\begin{array}{r}
7\ 15 \\
8\ \not{8}\ \not{5} \\
-\ \ 5\ 7 \\
\hline
2\ 8
\end{array}
\qquad
\begin{array}{r}
7\ 15 \\
8\ \not{8}\ \not{5} \\
-\ \ 5\ 7 \\
\hline
8\ 2\ 8
\end{array}
$$

The difference of 885 and 57 is 828.

▶ **EXAMPLE 2**

Subtract.   903 − 256

Regroup.
Subtract ones.

Subtract tens.

Subtract hundreds.

Math Fact
You cannot borrow from 0.
Borrow 1 hundred as 10 tens.
Then borrow 1 ten as 10 ones.

$$
\begin{array}{r}
8\ 9\ 13 \\
\not{9}\ \not{0}\ \not{3} \\
-\ 2\ 5\ 6 \\
\hline
7
\end{array}
\qquad
\begin{array}{r}
8\ 9\ 13 \\
\not{9}\ \not{0}\ \not{3} \\
-\ 2\ 5\ 6 \\
\hline
4\ 7
\end{array}
\qquad
\begin{array}{r}
8\ 9\ 13 \\
\not{9}\ \not{0}\ \not{3} \\
-\ 2\ 5\ 6 \\
\hline
6\ 4\ 7
\end{array}
$$

The difference of 903 and 256 is 647.

Try These

1. Subtract.
638 − 279

The difference of 638 and 279 is ■.

Regroup. Subtract ones.	Regroup. Subtract tens.	Subtract hundreds.
■18	■ ■18	■ ■18
6 $\not3$ $\not8$	$\not6$ $\not3$ $\not8$	$\not6$ $\not3$ $\not8$
− 2 7 9	− 2 7 9	− 2 7 9
■	■ ■ ■	3 ■ ■

2. Subtract.
3,042 − 271

The difference of 3,042 and 271 is ■.

Subtract ones.	Regroup. Subtract tens.	Subtract hundreds, thousands.
	■	■ ■ ■
3,0 4 2	$\not3$,$\not0$ 4 2	$\not3$,$\not0$ 4 2
− 2 7 1	− 2 7 1	− 2 7 1
■	■ ■	2,■ ■ ■

Practice

Subtract.

1.   27
      − 6

2.   46
      − 25

3.   59
      − 28

4.   83
      − 38

5.   367
      − 264

6.   607
      − 499

7.   1,035
      − 967

8.   12,007
      − 3,579

Cooperative Learning

9. Write a subtraction problem. Have a partner find the difference. Check the work.

10. Explain to a partner how you would subtract 89 from 100. Write each step as you work. Have the partner check the work.

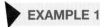

1-6 ► Estimating Sums and Differences

An **estimate** tells you about how large a sum or difference will be. You can use rounding to help you estimate.

► EXAMPLE 1

Math Facts
856 rounds to 900 because 5 in the tens place is equal to or greater than 5.
278 rounds to 300 because 7 in the tens place is equal to or greater than 5.

Estimate the difference of 856 and 278.

Round each number to the nearest hundred.		Subtract the rounded numbers.
856	→	900
− 278	→	− 300
		600

The difference of 856 and 278 is about 600.

► EXAMPLE 2

Math Fact
3,456 rounds to 3,000 because 4 < 5.

Estimate the sum 3,456 + 2,378 + 4,612.

Round each number to the nearest thousand.		Add the rounded addends.
3,456	→	3,000
2,378	→	2,000
+ 4,612	→	+ 5,000
		10,000

The sum 3,456 + 2,378 + 4,612 is about 10,000.

► EXAMPLE 3

You started with $1,920. You spent $279 and $413. Estimate how much you have left.

Remember
Round each number to the nearest hundred.

Estimate how much you spent.	$279	→	$300
	+ 413	→	+ 400
			$700

You spent about $700.

Remember
Round each number to the nearest hundred.

Estimate how much you have left.	$1,920	→	$1,900
	− 700	→	− 700
			$1,200

You have about $1,200 left.

Try These

1. Estimate the sum.
2,556 + 4,378 + 1,712

Round each number to the nearest thousand.	3,000
	■,■■■
	+ ■,■■■
	■,■■■

2,556 + 4,378 + 1,712 is about ■.

2. Estimate the difference.
284 − 122

Round each number to the nearest hundred.	■00
	− 1■■
	■■■

284 − 122 is about ■.

Practice

Round each number to the nearest hundred. Then, estimate the sum.

1. 425 + 137   **2.** 656 + 238   **3.** 596 + 348 + 171

Round each number to the nearest hundred. Then, estimate the difference.

4. 426 − 138   **5.** 756 − 378   **6.** 856 − 128

Round each number to the nearest ten. Then, estimate the difference.

7. 54 − 18   **8.** 76 − 38   **9.** 93 − 28

Cooperative Learning

10. Write two numbers with four digits in each. Have a partner round each to the nearest thousand. Then, estimate the sum.

11. Write two numbers with three digits in each. Have a partner round each number to the nearest hundred. Then, estimate the difference of the larger number and the smaller number.

Multiplying is an easier way to add when the addends are the same.

$$3 + 3 + 3 + 3 = 12 \quad \leftarrow \quad \text{all four addends are the same}$$

Math Fact
The numbers you multiply are factors. The answer is the product.

$$4 \times 3 = 12$$
$$\uparrow \quad \uparrow \qquad \uparrow$$
$$\text{factors} \quad \text{product}$$

$$\begin{array}{r} 4 \leftarrow \text{factor} \\ \times\ 3 \leftarrow \text{factor} \\ \hline 12 \leftarrow \text{product} \end{array}$$

When multiplying a larger number, multiply each place. You may have to rename and add.

 EXAMPLE 1

Multiply. 82×7

Multiply the 2 ones. Rename ones.	Multiply the 8 tens. Add ten.
$\begin{array}{r} 1 \\ 82 \\ \times\ 7 \\ \hline 4 \end{array}$ $2 \times 7 = 14$	$\begin{array}{r} 1 \\ 82 \\ \times\ 7 \\ \hline 574 \end{array}$ $\begin{array}{l} 8 \text{ tens} \times 7 = 56 \text{ tens} \\ 56 \text{ tens} + 1 \text{ ten} = 57 \text{ tens} \end{array}$

The product of 82 and 7 is 574.

Both factors may have more than one digit.

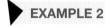 **EXAMPLE 2**

Multiply. 57×36

Multiply by ones.	Multiply by tens.	Add.
$\begin{array}{r} 4 \\ 57 \\ \times\ 36 \\ \hline 342 \end{array}$ ← 6×57	$\begin{array}{r} 2 \\ 4 \\ 57 \\ \times\ 36 \\ \hline 342 \\ 1{,}710 \end{array}$ ← 30×57	$\begin{array}{r} 2 \\ 4 \\ 57 \\ \times\ 36 \\ \hline 342 \\ 1{,}710 \\ \hline 2{,}052 \end{array}$

The product of 57 and 36 is 2,052.

Try These

1. Multiply. 43 × 29

Multiply by ones. Rename ones.	Multiply by tens.	Add.
2 43 × 29 ■■7	2 43 × 29 ■■7 ■■0	2 43 × 29 ■■7 ■■0 ■,■■■

The product of 43 and 29 is ■.

2. Multiply. 538 × 17

Multiply by ones. Rename ones.	Multiply by tens.	Add.
■■ 538 × 17 ■■■6	■■ 538 × 17 ■■■6 ■■■0	■■ 538 × 17 ■■■6 ■■■0 ■,■■■

The product of 538 and 17 is ■.

Practice

Multiply.

1. 27
× 8

2. 36
× 5

3. 59
× 4

4. 73
× 9

5. 67
× 27

6. 87
× 59

7. 78
× 45

8. 35
× 22

9. 45
× 68

10. 48
× 96

11. 169
× 52

12. 374
× 35

Cooperative Learning

13. Write a multiplication problem. Have a partner find the product. Check the work.

14. Ask a partner to explain the steps for finding the product of 198 and 91.

There is a shorter way to show multiplication when the factors are the same.

$$3 \times 3 = 3^2$$

base 3 is a factor 2 times

exponent

$3^2 = 9 \leftarrow$ power

↑ base

In 3^2, 3 is called the **base.** The **exponent** is 2. The exponent tells how many times the base is used as a factor. The exponent also tells the **power** of the base. 9 is the second power of 3. You can use other numbers as exponents. Here are some examples.

$3^1 = 3$	3 is a factor 1 time.
$3^2 = 3 \times 3$	3 is a factor 2 times.
$3^3 = 3 \times 3 \times 3$	3 is a factor 3 times.

▶ EXAMPLE 1

Find the power 5^3.

Use 5 as a factor 3 times.	5^3
Multiply.	$5 \times 5 \times 5$
	125

Remember
Multiply 5×5 first.
$5 \times 5 = 25$
Then, multiply 25×5.

$5^3 = 125$

A base can have more than one digit.

▶ EXAMPLE 2

Find the power 30^2.

Use 30 as a factor 2 times.	30^2
Multiply.	30×30
	900

$30^2 = 900$

Try These

1. Find the power 10^2.

Use 10 as a factor ■ times. 10^2

Multiply. $■ \times ■$

■

$10^2 = ■$.

2. Find the power 6^3.

Use 6 as a factor ■ times. 6^3

Multiply. $■ \times ■ \times ■$

■

$6^3 = ■$.

Practice

Find the power.

1. 6^2	**2.** 9^2	**3.** 11^2	**4.** 60^2
5. 2^3	**6.** 3^3	**7.** 2^4	**8.** 3^4
9. 12^2	**10.** 12^3	**11.** 15^2	**12.** 50^2
13. 5^4	**14.** 2^{10}	**15.** 100^2	**16.** $1,000^2$

Cooperative Learning

17. Explain to a partner how you found the power in number **7** in **Practice**.

18. Write a power. Have a partner find the power. Check the work.

1·9 ▶ Division

The numbers in a division problem have special names. In this problem, the number 4 is the **divisor**. The number 13 is the **dividend**. The number 3 is called the **quotient**. The number 1 is the **remainder**.

Math Fact
3 times 4 is 12. The difference between 13 and 12 is 1. 1 is the remainder.

$$\begin{array}{r} 3 \\ 4\overline{)13} \\ -12 \\ \hline 1 \end{array}$$

quotient
↓
3 R1 ← remainder
divisor → $4\overline{)13}$ ← dividend

When dividing by a 2-digit number, follow these steps:

▶ **EXAMPLE**

Divide. $23\overline{)687}$

STEP 1 Decide where to place the first quotient digit.
23 > 6, but 23 < 68.
Put the first quotient digit over 8.

$23\overline{)687}$

STEP 2 Find the first quotient digit.
3 is too big because 23 × 3 is 69.
69 is too big. Try 2.

$$\begin{array}{r} 2 \\ 23\overline{)687} \\ 46 \end{array}$$

Check
23
× 2
46

STEP 3 Subtract 46 from 68.
Bring down the digit 7.

$$\begin{array}{r} 2 \\ 23\overline{)687} \\ -46 \\ \hline 227 \end{array}$$

Check
68
− 46
22

STEP 4 Find the second quotient digit.
23 × 9 = 207. 207 < 227. Use 9.
Multiply. Then, subtract.
23 > 20.
20 is the remainder.

$$\begin{array}{r} 29 \\ 23\overline{)687} \\ -46 \\ \hline 227 \\ -207 \\ \hline 20 \end{array}$$

$$\begin{array}{r} 29 \text{ R20} \\ 23\overline{)687} \end{array}$$

Try These

1. Divide. $42\overline{)908}$

Begin by finding
the first digit of
the quotient.

$$
\begin{array}{r}
2\blacksquare \\
42\overline{)908} \\
\blacksquare\blacksquare \\
\hline
\blacksquare 8 \\
\blacksquare\blacksquare \\
\hline
26
\end{array}
$$

The quotient of 908 and 42 is $\blacksquare$, with remainder $\blacksquare$.

2. Divide. $61\overline{)1{,}339}$

Begin by finding
the first digit of
the quotient.

$$
\begin{array}{r}
2\blacksquare \\
61\overline{)1{,}339} \\
1\ 22 \\
\hline
11\blacksquare \\
\blacksquare\blacksquare \\
\hline
\blacksquare\blacksquare
\end{array}
$$

The quotient of 1,339 and 61 is $\blacksquare$, with remainder $\blacksquare$.

Practice

Divide.

1. $2\overline{)760}$

2. $3\overline{)679}$

3. $5\overline{)1{,}950}$

4. $7\overline{)3{,}105}$

5. $4\overline{)2{,}094}$

6. $34\overline{)671}$

7. $65\overline{)873}$

8. $44\overline{)284}$

9. $69\overline{)356}$

10. $58\overline{)598}$

11. $87\overline{)3{,}285}$

12. $92\overline{)4{,}314}$

13. $21\overline{)3{,}878}$

14. $53\overline{)8{,}350}$

15. $62\overline{)4{,}350}$

Cooperative Learning

16. Have each member of your group create a division problem. Work each problem. Check each other's work.

17. Ask a partner to explain to you how to divide 4,069 by 128.

When you estimate a product, round each factor and multiply the rounded factors. The zeros in the estimate will equal the total in the rounded factors.

▶ **EXAMPLE 1**

Estimate the product of 56 and 37.

Round each number to
the nearest ten.

$$\begin{array}{r} 60 \\ \times\, 40 \end{array}$$

Multiply the
rounded numbers.
Count zeros
to help.

$$\begin{array}{r} 60 \\ \times\, 40 \\ \hline 2400 \end{array}$$ ← 2 zeros
← 2 zeros
← 2 zeros

The product of 56 and 37 is about 2,400.

When you estimate a quotient, round the dividend and the divisor. Then estimate the quotient digit.

▶ **EXAMPLE 2**

Math Fact
In this problem, 2,786 is the
dividend. 436 is the divisor.

Estimate. $436\overline{)2{,}786}$

$436\overline{)2{,}786}$

436 is rounded to the
nearest hundred.
2,786 is rounded to the
nearest thousand.

$400\overline{)3{,}000}$

Think $4\overline{)30}$.
The quotient is 7.

$400\overline{)3{,}000}$ with quotient 7

$436\overline{)2{,}786}$ is about 7.

Try These

1. Estimate the product of 42 and 47.

   Round each number to the nearest ten.

   $$\begin{array}{r} 40 \\ \times \blacksquare \\ \hline \end{array}$$

   Multiply the rounded factors. Count zeros to help.

   $$\begin{array}{r} 40 \\ \times \blacksquare \\ \hline \blacksquare \end{array}$$

   The product of 42 and 47 is about ■.

2. Estimate. $36\overline{)1{,}678}$

   Round 36 to the nearest 10.

   $40\overline{)\blacksquare}$

   Round 1,678 to the nearest thousand.

   Think $4\overline{)\blacksquare}$.

   $40\overline{)\blacksquare}^{\blacksquare}$

   The quotient is ■.

   $36\overline{)1{,}678}$ is about ■.

Practice

Round each factor to the nearest ten. Then, estimate each product.

1. 56×87
2. 15×32
3. 51×29

4. 42×18
5. 75×37
6. 85×28

Round the dividend to the nearest thousand. Round the divisor to the nearest ten. Then, estimate each quotient.

7. $12\overline{)5{,}418}$
8. $25\overline{)6{,}382}$
9. $34\overline{)6{,}328}$

10. $53\overline{)4{,}425}$
11. $44\overline{)3{,}565}$
12. $17\overline{)6{,}348}$

Cooperative Learning

13. Write a multiplication problem. Have a partner estimate the product. Check the work.

14. Write a division problem. Have a partner estimate the answer. Check the work.

You can add, subtract, multiply, and divide large whole numbers using a calculator. Locate the $+$, $-$, $\times$, $\div$, and $=$ keys on your calculator. Review how to turn on your calculator and how to clear the display. Estimate your answer first. Then, you can compare your calculator answer to your estimate as a check. A check is helpful to be sure you pressed the correct keys.

EXAMPLE 1

Use your calculator to find the sum of 15,459 and 23,635.

Estimate. $15,000 + 24,000 = 39,000$

Math Fact
The display is what you will see on the screen of the calculator.

Enter 15,459
by pressing: [1] [5] [4] [5] [9]

Display
| 15459 |

Then, add 23,635
by pressing: [+] [2] [3] [6] [3] [5] [=]

| 23635 |

The calculator displays 39,094. The sum is close enough to the estimate.

EXAMPLE 2

Use your calculator to find $2,035\overline{)38,665}$.

Estimate.
$$\begin{array}{r} 20 \\ 2,000\overline{)40,000} \end{array}$$

Enter 38,665
by pressing: [3] [8] [6] [6] [5]

Display
| 38665 |

Then, divide by
2,035 by pressing: [÷] [2] [0] [3] [5]

| 2035 |

[=]

| 19 |

The calculator displays 19. This quotient is close enough to the estimate.

Practice

Use your calculator. Find the sum, difference, product, or quotient.

1.   2,743
       + 1,621

2.   4,645
       + 2,556

3.   13,259
       + 8,278

4.   73,456
       − 9,293

5.   367,457
       − 26,493

6.   687,371
       − 19,892

7.   1,785
       × 38

8.   3,993
       × 63

9.   12,435
       × 28

10. $237\overline{)14{,}457}$

11. $623\overline{)175{,}063}$

12. $1{,}827\overline{)244{,}818}$

Math Connection

EARTHQUAKES

An earthquake moves and cracks the earth. Earthquakes happen when rocks deep inside the earth shift. When this happens, energy is released.

A scale was made to measure this energy. It is called the Richter scale. When an earthquake happens, scientists measure the energy. They rate the strength of the earthquake by the amount of energy released. The earthquake is given a rating between 1 and 9. An earthquake rated 1 is the weakest kind of earthquake. An earthquake rated 2 is 10 times more powerful than an earthquake rated 1. An earthquake rated 3 is ten times more powerful than 2, but 100 times more powerful than 1.

Even the weakest earthquake can cause damage. Sections of the earth can rip apart. Buildings may fall. Roads may split. Bridges may crack. Gas lines and electric lines may break. This can cause fires. Fires are the biggest danger in an earthquake.

1·12 Problem Solving: Guess, Check, and Revise

You can guess an answer to a problem. Then check to see if the guess is the answer. If not, revise or change your guess to make it better.

▶ **EXAMPLE**

Ryan is two years older than Jasmine, and Jasmine is one year older than Karlee. The sum of their ages is 34. How old are Ryan, Jasmine, and Karlee?

READ   **What do you need to find out?**
You need to find the ages of Ryan, Jasmine, and Karlee.

PLAN   **What do you need to do?**
You need to guess an age for one of the people. Use your guess to find the other two ages. If your guess is not correct, revise it and check again.

DO   **Follow the plan.**
Guess for Karlee: 5.
Then Jasmine is $5 + 1 = 6$.
Ryan is $6 + 2 = 8$.
Check $5 + 6 + 8 = 19$ *Too small*

Revise guess for Karlee: 9.
Jasmine is $9 + 1 = 10$.
Ryan is $10 + 2 = 12$.
Check $9 + 10 + 12 = 31$ *Too small*

Revise guess for Karlee: 10.
Jasmine is $10 + 1 = 11$.
Ryan is $11 + 2 = 13$.
Check $10 + 11 + 13 = 34$. *Correct sum*

CHECK   **Does the answer make sense?**
Jasmine, 11, is one year older than Karlee, age 10. Ryan, age 13, is two years older than Jasmine, 11. The sum of these ages is $10 + 11 + 13 = 34$. ✓

Karlee is 10, Jasmine is 11, and Ryan is 13.

Try These

1. The sum of Gwen and Irving's monthly earnings is $2,900. Irving earns $450 more than Gwen each month. How much does each earn?

   Guess for Gwen: $1,000
   Irving earns: ■.
   Check $1,000 + ■ = $2,450 *Too small*

   Revise guess for Gwen: $1,225.
   Then Irving earns ■.
   Check $1,225 + ■ = $2,900 *Correct*
   So, Gwen earns $1,225 and Irving earns ■.

2. If you take Derek's jersey number and multiply it by 3 and add 14, you will get 53. What is Derek's jersey number?

   Guess for Derek's jersey number: 10
   Check $10 \times 3 + 14 = $ ■ *Too small*

   Revise guess for the jersey number: 12
   Check $12 \times 3 + 14 = $ ■ *Too small*

   Revise guess for the jersey number: ■
   Check ■ $\times 3 + 14 = 53$ *Correct*
   So, Derek's jersey number is ■.

Practice

Guess, check, and revise to solve the problem.

1. Maria and Lamar are playing a game. Maria noticed that the digits of her score could be reversed to form Lamar's score. Maria's score is 18 more than Lamar's score. Maria's score is a multiple of 5. What is Maria's score?

2. Kim's mom is 47 years old. In 5 years her mother will be 10 years older than twice what Kim's age will be then. How old is Kim now?

3. Denise sold 24 more dresses in January than in February and ten fewer dresses in March than in January. In March she sold 28 dresses. How many dresses did Denise sell in February?

Cooperative Learning

4. Explain to a partner how you find Maria's score in number **1** in **Practice**.

5. Write a problem about the sum of the ages of two students. Make one student three years older than the other. Ask a partner to find the ages of the two students.

A **polygon** is a closed figure with three or more sides. The table below shows the number of sides and the name of the polygon.

Number of Sides	Name
3	Triangle
4	Quadrilateral
5	Pentagon
6	Hexagon
7	Heptagon
8	Octagon

Math Fact

Sides are measured in inches (in.), feet (ft), yards (yd), meters (m), and centimeters (cm).

The **perimeter** is the sum of the lengths of the sides of a polygon.

▸ **EXAMPLE 1**

Find the perimeter.

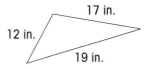

Math Fact

The answer is 48 in. The answer is not 48. Be sure to make in. part of your answer.

The perimeter is the sum of the lengths of the three sides.
12 in. + 17 in. + 19 in. = 48 in.

▸ **EXAMPLE 2**

Find the perimeter.

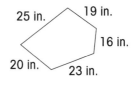

Math Fact

The answer is 103 in. The answer is not 103. Be sure to make in. part of your answer.

The perimeter is the sum of the lengths of the sides.
25 in. + 19 in. + 16 in. + 23 in. + 20 in. = 103 in.

Try These

Find the perimeter.

1.

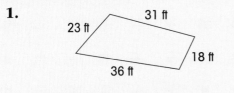

The perimeter is the sum of the lengths of the ▧ sides.

23 ft + 31 ft + 18 ft + 36 ft = ▧

2.

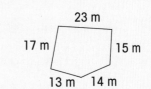

The perimeter is the sum of the lengths of the ▧ sides.

17 m + 23 m + 15 m + 14 m + 13 m = ▧

Practice

Find the perimeter.

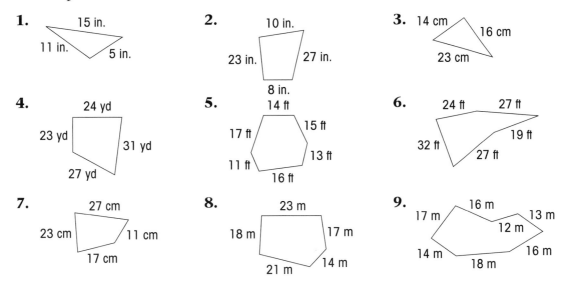

1.
15 in.
11 in.
5 in.

2.
10 in.
23 in.
27 in.
8 in.

3.
14 cm
16 cm
23 cm

4.
24 yd
23 yd
31 yd
27 yd

5.
14 ft
17 ft
15 ft
13 ft
11 ft
16 ft

6.
24 ft
27 ft
32 ft
19 ft
27 ft

7.
27 cm
23 cm
11 cm
17 cm

8.
23 m
18 m
17 m
21 m
14 m

9.
16 m
17 m
13 m
12 m
14 m
18 m
16 m

Cooperative Learning

10. Explain to a partner how you find the perimeter in number **8** in **Practice**.

11. Draw a figure. Label each side with a measurement. Have a partner find the perimeter.

Summary

Addition, subtraction, multiplication, and division are operations on whole numbers.
To round numbers to a place, look at the digit to the right of that place. If the digit is less than five, round down. If the digit is greater than or equal to five, round up.
You can estimate sums, differences, products, and quotients.
Using exponents is a shorter way to show and solve some multiplication problems.
Guess, check, and revise is another way to solve problems.
The perimeter is the sum of the lengths of the sides.

digits

place value

addends

sum

difference

factors

product

base

exponent

power

quotient

divisor

dividend

perimeter

Vocabulary Review

Complete the sentences with words from the box.

1. _____ is the value of a place within a number.

2. The answer in addition is called the _____.

3. The ten basic numbers are called _____.

4. The answer in subtraction is called the _____.

5. Numbers that are added together are called the _____.

6. The _____ is the answer in division.

7. A _____ is the result of multiplying when factors are the same.

8. The _____ is the answer in multiplication.

9. The sum of the lengths of the sides of a polygon is called the _____.

10. In 3^2, 3 is called the _____.

11. The numbers being multiplied are called _____.

12. An _____ tells how many times the base is used as a factor.

13. _____ is the number used to divide.

14. The number being divided is called the _____.

Chapter Quiz

Use 456,812 to find the value of these digits.

1. The digit 4   **2.** The digit 6   **3.** The digit 1

Round the following to the nearest thousand.

4. 4,461   **5.** 911   **6.** 31,769

Add.

7.
$$\begin{array}{r} 38 \\ + 9 \\ \hline \end{array}$$

8.
$$\begin{array}{r} 256 \\ + 153 \\ \hline \end{array}$$

9.
$$\begin{array}{r} 2{,}636 \\ + 328 \\ \hline \end{array}$$

Subtract.

10.
$$\begin{array}{r} 25 \\ - 7 \\ \hline \end{array}$$

11.
$$\begin{array}{r} 256 \\ - 167 \\ \hline \end{array}$$

12.
$$\begin{array}{r} 1{,}735 \\ - 378 \\ \hline \end{array}$$

Multiply.

13.
$$\begin{array}{r} 36 \\ \times 9 \\ \hline \end{array}$$

14.
$$\begin{array}{r} 56 \\ \times 38 \\ \hline \end{array}$$

15.
$$\begin{array}{r} 67 \\ \times 54 \\ \hline \end{array}$$

Divide.

16. $3\overline{)659}$ **17.** $23\overline{)562}$ **18.** $78\overline{)2{,}474}$

Guess, check, and revise to solve the problem.

19. Cameron is three years older than Karlee. Karlee is two years older than Denise. The sum of Cameron, Karlee, and Denise's ages is 49. How old is each person?

Name the figure. Find its perimeter.

20.

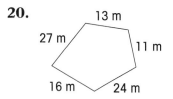

Number Expressions, Equations, Properties

When you play chess, you learn special words like **checkmate**. *You learn rules so players know what to do. In math, you do the same thing. What are some special words and rules we need in math?*

Learning Objectives

- Recognize a number expression.
- Simplify number expressions.
- Tell whether two number expressions are equal.
- Recognize a number equation.
- Tell whether a number equation is true or false.
- Explain the properties of operations and numbers.
- Use a calculator to simplify number expressions.
- Write number equations for word statements.
- Apply concepts and skills to find area.

Words to Know

number expression	a number or numbers together with operation symbols
parentheses	a pair of grouping symbols ( ); may also mean multiplication
simplify	carry out the operations; find the value
equivalent	having the same value; equal
number equation	a statement that two number expressions are equal
property	a fact that is true for addition and for multiplication
Commutative Properties	two numbers can be added in any order; two numbers can be multiplied in any order
Associative Properties	more than two numbers can be added or multiplied in groups of two; the way the numbers are grouped does not matter
Identity Properties	adding 0 to a number does not change the number; multiplying a number by 1 does not change the number
Zero Property	a number multiplied by 0 is 0
Distributive Property	to multiply a sum or difference by a number, multiply each number of the sum or difference
Division Properties	a number divided by itself is 1; a number divided by 1 is the same number; 0 divided by any number that is not 0 is 0
area	the number of squares needed to cover a closed figure

Perimeter and Area Project

Terry has 20 feet of fencing to fence in a rectangular garden. Draw and label two possible rectangles to represent her garden. Write a number expression to represent the perimeter of each garden. Then find the area of each garden. Which garden has the greater area? With your classmates, find all the possible rectangles with a perimeter of 20 feet. Which garden has the greatest area?

Number Expressions

Numbers and operation signs are used to write number expressions. A single number is also an expression. Here are some **number expressions.**

$$6 \quad 9 + 7 \quad 10 \div 2 \quad 5 \times 3 \quad 8 - 4$$

Math Fact
$10 \div 2$ means
10 divided by 2.

To find the value of a number expression, do the operation. The value of 6 is 6.

▶ **EXAMPLE 1**

Find the value of $9 + 7$.

Add.
$$9 + 7$$
$$16$$

The value of $9 + 7$ is 16.

▶ **EXAMPLE 2**

Find the value of $10 \div 2$.

Divide.
Think $2\overline{)10}$.
$$10 \div 2$$
$$5$$

The value of $10 \div 2$ is 5.

There are other ways to show multiplication. You can use a dot. You can also use **parentheses.**

$$5 \times 3 \quad \longrightarrow \quad 5 \bullet 3 \quad \text{or} \quad 5(3) \quad \text{or} \quad (5)3$$
$$\uparrow \uparrow$$
parentheses

▶ **EXAMPLE 3**

Find the value of $5(3)$.

Multiply.
$$5 \times 3$$
$$15$$

The value of $5(3)$ is 15.

Try These

1. Find the value of 8 − 4.

Subtract.   8 − ■

■

The value of 8 − 4 is ■.

2. Find the value of 5 • 3.

Multiply.   5 × ■

■

The value of 5 • 3 is ■.

Practice

Find the value of each number expression.

1. 12 ÷ 4

2. 9 − 3

3. 9

4. 2 • 6

5. 10 − 9

6. (8)2

7. 14 + 6

8. 5 ÷ 1

9. 4 × 1

10. 12

11. 11 − 5

12. 9 × 2

13. 10 + 3

14. (7)2

15. 20 ÷ 10

16. 30 − 10

17. 100 + 20

18. 25

19. 2(10)

20. 25 ÷ 5

Cooperative Learning

21. Write a number expression using addition. Have a partner find the value of the expression. Check the work.

22. Write a number expression using parentheses to show multiplication. Have a partner find the value of the expression. Check the work.

23. Explain to a partner how you found the value of the expression in number **15** in **Practice**.

When you find the value of an expression, you **simplify** the expression. You have already simplified number expressions with one operation. You can also simplify a number expression with more than one operation. You must follow The Order of Operations:

1. Multiply and divide from left to right.
2. Then, add and subtract from left to right.

▶ **EXAMPLE 1**

Simplify. $18 - 5 \times 2$

Multiply first.
$$18 - \underline{5 \times 2}$$

Subtract next.
$$\underline{18 - 10}$$
$$8$$

The value of $18 - 5 \times 2$ is 8.

▶ **EXAMPLE 2**

Math Fact
Start with $12 \div 3$.

Simplify. $2 + 12 \div 3 - 4$

Divide first.
$$2 + \underline{12 \div 3} - 4$$

Add next.
$$\underline{2 + 4} - 4$$

Subtract.
$$\underline{6 - 4}$$
$$2$$

The value of $2 + 12 \div 3 - 4$ is 2.

▶ **EXAMPLE 3**

Math Fact
Work from left to right.
Start with 2^3.

Simplify. $13 + 2^3 \div 4$

2^3 means $2 \times 2 \times 2$.
$$13 + 2^3 \div 4$$

Multiply first.
$$13 + \underline{2 \times 2 \times 2} \div 4$$

Divide next.
$$13 + \underline{8 \div 4}$$

Add.
$$\underline{13 + 2}$$
$$15$$

The value of $13 + 2^3 \div 4$ is 15.

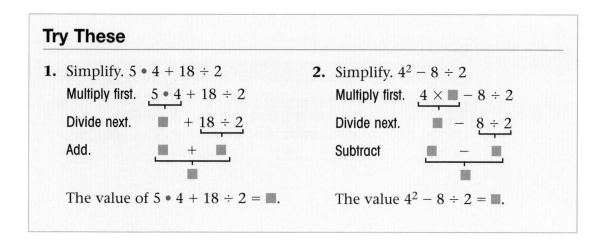

Try These

1. Simplify. $5 \cdot 4 + 18 \div 2$

Multiply first. $\underline{5 \cdot 4} + 18 \div 2$

Divide next.   ■ $+ \underline{18 \div 2}$

Add. $\underline{■ \quad + \quad ■}$
                ■

The value of $5 \cdot 4 + 18 \div 2 = $ ■.

2. Simplify. $4^2 - 8 \div 2$

Multiply first. $\underline{4 \times ■} - 8 \div 2$

Divide next.   ■ $- \underline{8 \div 2}$

Subtract $\underline{■ \quad - \quad ■}$
                ■

The value $4^2 - 8 \div 2 = $ ■.

Practice

Simplify.

1. $7 - 5 + 2$

2. $20 + 10 - 6$

3. $10 + 3 - 6 + 2$

4. $8 + 2^2 - 10 \div 5$

5. $15 - 5 \times 2$

6. $2^3 \times 2 \div 2 \times 4$

7. $28 \div 7 \cdot 2$

8. $9 + 4 \times 1$

9. $24 - 20 \div 5$

10. $4^2 + 3^2 \div 3$

11. $27 - 5 \times 2$

12. $3^3 \div 9 + 2$

13. $8 \cdot 4 \div 2$

14. $4^2 \times 2 - 20$

15. $10 \div 2 + 8$

16. $9 + 15 \div 15 - 10$

17. $2 + 25 \times 2 \div 5^2$

18. $32 + 30 \div 10$

Cooperative Learning

19. Work with a partner to simplify $8 \cdot 6 \div 12 - 3$. Take turns doing the steps. Check each other's work.

20. Make up a number expression using addition and multiplication. Ask a partner to simplify it. Check the work.

You have seen parentheses used to show multiplication. **Parentheses** can also be used to group numbers and operations in an expression.

$$2(4 + 9) \qquad (1 + 3)2 \qquad 16 \div (2 + 2)$$

When expressions contain parentheses, do the operations in the parentheses first. Then follow the special order of operations.

▸ **EXAMPLE 1**

Simplify. $24 \div (6 - 3)$

Do the subtraction
in parentheses first. $24 \div (6 - 3)$

Divide. $24 \div 3$

                          8

The value of $24 \div (6 - 3)$ is 8.

▸ **EXAMPLE 2**

Simplify. $(2^3 - 2) \times 4 - 1$

Do the operations
in parentheses first. $(2^3 - 2) \times 4 - 1$

                    $(2 \times 2 \times 2 - 2) \times 4 - 1$

                           $(8 - 2) \times 4 - 1$

Multiply next. $6 \times 4 - 1$

Subtract. $24 - 1$

                              23

The value of $(2^3 - 2) \times 4 - 1$ is 23.

Practice

Simplify.

1. $2(5 - 2)$

2. $8 \div (2 + 2)$

3. $(6 - 4) + 3$

4. $13 - (4 + 2)$

5. $18 \div (6 - 5)$

6. $(9 + 1) - 2^2$

7. $(33 - 3) \div 3$

8. $(2 + 7) \times 2 - 4$

9. $42 + (8 - 6)$

10. $(2^2 + 2) - 4$

11. $(5 + 1)2$

12. $8 \times (4 \div 2)$

13. $(2^2 + 4) \div 4$

14. $(4 + 2)^2$

15. $(42 + 1) - 4$

16. $(20 + 10) \div 5$

17. $(10 - 3) \times 2 + 1$

18. $(45 \div 9) \times 2 - 3$

19. $2^2(10 - 8)$

20. $(5 + 8) - 3 \times 2$

Cooperative Learning

21. Simplify $3 \times 4 + 2$. Have a partner simplify $3(4 + 2)$. Compare your answers. Why are they different?

22. Make up a number expression that contains parentheses to group numbers and operations. Use multiplication and addition. Have a partner simplify the expression. Check the work.

2·4 ▶ Equivalent Number Expressions

Two number expressions are equivalent if they both have the same value. The expressions may have different numbers and operations. You can simplify each expression to see if the two values are equal.

▶ **EXAMPLE 1**

Tell whether $3 + 5$ and $12 - 4$ are equivalent.

Simplify each expression.

$$\underbrace{3 + 5}_{8} \text{ and } \underbrace{12 - 4}_{8}$$

Check
8 is equal to 8.

The value of $3 + 5$ is 8.
The value of $12 - 4$ is 8.
$3 + 5$ and $12 - 4$ are equivalent.

▶ **EXAMPLE 2**

Tell whether $5(4 - 2)$ and $5 \bullet 4 - 2$ are equivalent.

Simplify each expression.

$$\underbrace{5(4 - 2)}_{\underbrace{5(2)}_{10}} \text{ and } \underbrace{5 \bullet 4 - 2}_{\underbrace{20 - 2}_{18}}$$

Check
10 does not equal 18.

The value of $5(4 - 2)$ is 10.
The value of $5 \bullet 4 - 2$ is 18.
$5(4 - 2)$ and $5 \bullet 4 - 2$ are not equivalent.

▶ **EXAMPLE 3**

Tell whether $(9 + 1) + 6$ and $9 + (1 + 6)$ are equivalent.

Simplify each expression.

$$\underbrace{(9 + 1) + 6}_{\underbrace{10 + 6}_{16}} \text{ and } \underbrace{9 + (1 + 6)}_{\underbrace{9 + 7}_{16}}$$

Check
16 is equal to 16.

The value of $(9 + 1) + 6$ is 16.
The value of $9 + (1 + 6)$ is 16.
$(9 + 1) + 6$ and $9 + (1 + 6)$ are equivalent.

Try These

1. Tell whether $8 \div 8 \times 8$ and $16 \div 2$ are equivalent.

   The value of $8 \div 8 \times 8$ is ■.

   The value of $16 \div 2$ is 8.

   Are $8 \div 8 \times 8$ and $16 \div 2$ equivalent? ■

2. Tell whether $(3 \times 2)^4$ and $3 \times 2(4)$ are equivalent.

   The value of $(3 \times 2)^4$ is ■.

   The value of $3 \times 2(4)$ is ■.

   Are $(3 \times 2)^4$ and $3 \times 2(4)$ equivalent? ■

Practice

Tell whether the expressions are equivalent. Write *yes* or *no*.

1. $27 \div 3$ and $5 + 4$

2. $3 \bullet 6$ and $13 - 5$

3. $6 + 3$ and $3 \bullet 4$

4. $4 \bullet 2$ and $16 \div 2$

5. $9 - 2$ and $21 + 3$

6. $6 \bullet 4$ and $11 + 13$

7. $(5 + 4) + 1$ and $5 + (4 + 1)$

8. $(5 - 2) - 1$ and $5 - (2 - 1)$

9. $8 \bullet 2 \bullet 4$ and $8 \bullet 4 \bullet 2$

10. $7 \div 7$ and $9 \div 9$

11. $16 \div 4$ and 4

12. 20 and 20

13. $(5 + 1) - 1$ and $5 + (1 - 1)$

14. $3^2 + 2^2$ and $(3 + 2)^2$

15. $2 \bullet 2 \div 2$ and $2 \div 2 \bullet 2$

16. $6 - 6 + 6$ and $6 + 6 - 6$

17. $0 + 9$ and 3^2

18. $(4 - 1)^2$ and $4^2 - 1^2$

Cooperative Learning

19. Explain to a partner how you are able to tell whether or not the expressions in number **18** in **Practice** are equivalent.

20. Write a number expression using addition and multiplication. Have a partner write an equivalent expression using multiplication and division. Check the work.

Number expressions can be used to write number equations. A **number equation** is a statement that two expressions are equivalent. You can use an equal sign to write an equation. Here are some number equations.

$$7 = 7 \qquad 5 + 1 = 1 + 5 \qquad 9 \div 3 = 3$$
$$\text{true} \qquad\qquad \text{true} \qquad\qquad\qquad \text{true}$$

A number equation is true if the expressions on both sides of the equal sign have the same value. If the two expressions have different values, you do not have an equation.

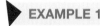

Math Fact
5 + 4 is on the left side.
12 − 3 is on the right side.

Tell whether $5 + 4$ and $12 - 3$ are equivalent.

The value of 5 + 4 is 9.

The value of 12 − 3 is 9.

$$\underbrace{5 + 4}_{9} = \underbrace{12 - 3}_{9}$$

5 + 4 and 12 − 3 are equivalent.

Math Fact
6 is not equal to 4.
≠ means "is not equal to."

Tell whether $3 \bullet 2$ is equal to $20 \div 5$.

The value of 3 • 2 is 6.

The value of 20 ÷ 5 is 4.

$$\underbrace{3 \bullet 2}_{6} \; ? \; \underbrace{20 \div 5}_{4}$$

$3 \bullet 2 \neq 20 \div 5$.

Tell whether $17 - 9$ and 2^3 form an equation.

The value of 17 − 9 is 8.

The value of 2^3 is 8.

$$\underbrace{17 - 9}_{8} \; ? \; \underbrace{2^3}_{\underbrace{2 \times 2 \times 2}_{8}}$$

$17 - 9 = 2^3$. The expressions form an equation.

Practice

Tell whether the expressions are equivalent. Write *yes* or *no*.
If yes, write an equation.

1. $28 \div 4$ and $5 + 2$

2. $4 \cdot 7$ and $33 - 5$

3. 14 and 14

4. $2 \cdot 9$ and $24 - 5$

5. $26 + 13$ and $3 \cdot 13$

6. $4 \cdot 2$ and $16 \div 2$

7. $19 - 7$ and $36 \div 12$

8. $42 \cdot 2$ and $21 + 12$

9. $19 - 12$ and $14 \div 2$

10. $17 + 14$ and $5 \cdot 5$

11. $27 \div 3$ and $5 + 4$

12. 5 and 5

13. $7 - 5$ and $2^3 - 6$

14. $3 + 23$ and $7 \cdot 4$

15. $7 + 3$ and $(10 + 3) - 2$

16. $(10 + 20) \div 6$ and $2 + 3$

17. $9 - 2$ and $3^2 - 2$

18. $5 + 1$ and $36 \div 9$

19. 10 and 10

20. $2 \cdot 4$ and $24 \div 3$

Cooperative Learning

23. Explain to a partner how you are able to tell whether the expressions in number **16** in **Practice** form an equation.

24. Write an equation using addition and multiplication. Have a partner tell whether it is true or false. Check the work.

2·6 Addition Properties

You can add 2 and 3 in any order. The sum is the same. These number equations show this **property** of addition. Both equations are true.

$$2 + 3 = 5 \qquad\qquad 3 + 2 = 5$$

This is the **Commutative Property of Addition.**

There are other properties of addition. These properties will help you perform operations quickly.

Associative Property of Addition
Sometimes you have to add more than two numbers. The way the numbers are grouped does not matter. You can add the numbers in groups of two.

$$(6 + 2) + 1 = 6 + (2 + 1)$$

Identity Property of Addition
Adding 0 to any number does not change the number.

$$3 + 0 = 3 \qquad 0 + 5 = 5 \qquad 9 + 0 = 9$$

▶ **EXAMPLE 1**

Name the property shown by $(5 + 7) + 8 = 5 + (7 + 8)$.

The sum of three numbers $\qquad (5 + 7) + 8 = 5 + (7 + 8)$
Adding the numbers in groups of two

$(5 + 7) + 8 = 5 + (7 + 8)$ shows the Associative Property of Addition.

▶ **EXAMPLE 2**

Use the Commutative Property of Addition to complete. $8 + 9 = ? + 8$

Adding two numbers in any order $\quad 8 + 9 = 9 + 8$

9 is the missing number on the right side.

Try These

1. Name the property shown by
   $0 + 10 = 10$.

   Adding ▦ to any number
   doesn't change the number.

   ▦ Property of Addition

2. Use a property of addition to
   complete.

   $(2 + 8) + 4 = ▦ + (8 + 4)$

   This is the sum of three numbers.
   Use the Associative Property.

   ▦ is the number missing on the
   right side.

Practice

Name the property shown.

1. $5 + 3 = 3 + 5$

2. $(6 + 9) + 4 = 6 + (9 + 4)$

3. $10 + 0 = 10$

4. $8 + 1 = 1 + 8$

5. $(8 + 2) + 1 = 8 + (2 + 1)$

6. $7 + (2 + 3) = (7 + 2) + 3$

Use a property to complete.

7. $4 + 8 = 8 + ▦$

8. $7 + ▦ = 7$

9. $(6 + 4) + 2 = 6 + (▦ + 2)$

10. $▦ + 11 = 11$

11. $6 + 15 = ▦ + 6$

12. $2 + (3 + ▦) = (2 + 3) + 5$

Cooperative Learning

13. Write a number equation that shows one of the properties of
    addition. Have a partner name the property.

14. Explain to a partner how you used a property to complete
    number **12** in **Practice**.

2·7 Multiplication Properties

You can multiply 2 and 3 in any order. The product is the same. These equations show this property of multiplication. Both equations are true.

$$2 \times 3 = 6 \qquad 3 \times 2 = 6$$

This is called the **Commutative Property of Multiplication.**

There are other properties of multiplication.

Associative Property of Multiplication
When you have to multiply more than two numbers, multiply them in groups of two. The way the numbers are grouped does not matter.

$$(2 \bullet 3) \bullet 4 \;=\; 2 \bullet (3 \bullet 4)$$

Identity Property of Multiplication
Multiplying a number by 1 does not change the number.

$$3 \times 1 = 3 \qquad 1 \times 5 = 5 \qquad 9 \times 1 = 9$$

Zero Property of Multiplication
Multiplying a number by 0 is 0.

$$3 \times 0 = 0 \qquad 0 \times 5 = 0 \qquad 9 \times 0 = 0$$

EXAMPLE 1

Name the property shown by $(5 \bullet 7) \bullet 8 = 5 \bullet (7 \bullet 8)$.

This is the product of three numbers. $\quad (5 \bullet 7) \bullet 8 = 5 \bullet (7 \bullet 8)$
Multiplying the numbers in groups of two.

$(5 \bullet 7) \bullet 8 = 5 \bullet (7 \bullet 8)$ shows the Associative Property of Multiplication.

EXAMPLE 2

Use the Commutative Property of Multiplication to complete $8 \times 9 = ? \times 8$.

This shows multiplying two numbers in any order. $\quad 8 \times 9 = ? \times 8$

9 is missing on the right side.

Try These

1. Name the property shown by: $1 \times 10 = 10$.

   Multiplying any number by ■ does not change the number.

   ■ Property of Multiplication

2. Use a property of multiplication to complete:

   $(2 \cdot 8) \cdot 4 = ■ \cdot (8 \cdot 4)$

   This is the product of three numbers. Use the Associative Property.

   ■ is the number missing on the right side.

Practice

Name the property shown.

1. $5 \times 3 = 3 \times 5$

2. $(6 \cdot 9) \cdot 4 = 6 \cdot (9 \cdot 4)$

3. $10 \times 0 = 0$

4. $8 \times 1 = 8$

5. $(8 \cdot 2) \cdot 1 = 8 \cdot (2 \cdot 1)$

6. $4 \times 10 = 10 \times 4$

Use a property to complete.

7. $4 \times 8 = 8 \times ■$

8. $7 \times ■ = 7$

9. $(6 \cdot 4) \cdot 2 = 6 \cdot (■ \cdot 2)$

10. $1 \times ■ = 12$

11. $■ \times 9 = 0$

12. $5 \times 9 = ■ \times 5$

Cooperative Learning

13. Write a number equation that shows one of the properties of multiplication. Have a partner name the property.

14. Explain to a partner how you used a property to complete number 12 in **Practice**.

The **Distributive Property** uses two operations. Here, multiplication and addition are being used.

$$2(3 + 4) = 2 \bullet 3 + 2 \bullet 4$$

You distribute 2 over each number in the parentheses. Do this by multiplying each number by 2.

The Distributive Property also uses multiplication and subtraction.

$$5(7 - 2) = 5 \bullet 7 - 5 \bullet 2$$

Multiply each number in the parentheses by 5.

▶ **EXAMPLE 1**

Use the Distributive Property to complete.

$$3(5 - 2) = ? - ?$$

Multiply 5 and 2 by 3. $3 \bullet 5 - 3 \bullet 2$

$$3(5 - 2) = 3 \bullet 5 - 3 \bullet 2$$

▶ **EXAMPLE 2**

Use the Distributive Property to complete.

$$2 \bullet 5 + 2 \bullet 6 = ? \, (? + ?)$$

5 and 6 are both multiplied by 2. $2(5 + 6)$

$$2 \bullet 5 + 2 \bullet 6 = 2(5 + 6)$$

▶ **EXAMPLE 3**

There are three **Division Properties.**

A number divided by itself is 1.

$$3\overline{)3}^{\,1} \quad \longrightarrow \quad 3 \div 3 = 1$$

A number divided by 1 is the same number.

$$1\overline{)3}^{\,3} \quad \longrightarrow \quad 3 \div 1 = 3$$

0 divided by any number that is not 0 is 0.

$$3\overline{)0}^{\,0} \quad \longrightarrow \quad 0 \div 3 = 0$$

Try These

1. Use the Distributive Property to complete.

   $2(7 + 3) = 2 \cdot \blacksquare + 2 \cdot \blacksquare$

2. Use the Distributive Property to complete.

   $6 \cdot 5 - 6 \cdot 4 = 6(\blacksquare - \blacksquare)$

Use the Division Properties to complete.

3. $5\overline{)5} \rightarrow 5 \div 5 = \blacksquare$

4. $1\overline{)7} \rightarrow 7 \div 1 = \blacksquare$

5. $9\overline{)\blacksquare}^{\,0} \rightarrow \blacksquare \div 9 = \blacksquare$

Practice

Use a property to complete.

1. $5(3 - 2) = 5 \cdot \blacksquare - 5 \cdot \blacksquare$

2. $\blacksquare(3 + 1) = 7 \cdot 3 + 7 \cdot 1$

3. $5 \cdot 6 - 5 \cdot 2 = 5(\blacksquare - \blacksquare)$

4. $\blacksquare \cdot 2 + \blacksquare \cdot 2 = 4(2 + 2)$

5. $8(\blacksquare - 2) = 8 \cdot 3 - 8 \cdot 2$

6. $3 \cdot 2 + \blacksquare \cdot 1 = 3(2 + 1)$

7. $8\overline{)0}^{\,\blacksquare} \rightarrow 0 \div 8 = \blacksquare$

8. $\blacksquare\overline{)6}^{\,6} \rightarrow 6 \div \blacksquare = 6$

9. $4\overline{)\blacksquare}^{\,1} \rightarrow \blacksquare \div 4 = \blacksquare$

Cooperative Learning

10. Explain to a partner how you used the Distributive Property to complete number **5** in **Practice**.

11. Explain to a partner how you used a Division Property to complete number **9** in **Practice**.

Calculator: Simplifying Expressions

You can use your calculator to simplify expressions. First, decide which operation to do first. It will be helpful to write some of your answers on paper as you work with the calculator.

▶ **EXAMPLE 1**

Use your calculator to simplify the expression $26 - 4 \cdot 6 + 5$.

Display

Multiply first.	$26 - 4 \cdot 6 + 5$	
Enter 4 × 6 by pressing:	[4] [×] [6] [=]	24
Write this on paper:	$26 - 24 + 5$	
Clear the display.		
Subtract next.	$26 - 24 + 5$	
Enter 26 − 24.	[2] [6] [−] [2] [4] [=]	2
Add 5.	[+] [5] [=]	7

The value of $26 - 4 \cdot 6 + 5$ is 7.

▶ **EXAMPLE 2**

Use your calculator to simplify the expression $5(3 + 14)$.

Display

Remember
Do the operation inside the parentheses first.

Add first.	$5(3 + 14)$	
Enter 3 + 14 by pressing:	[3] [+] [1] [4] [=]	17
Write this on paper:	$5(17)$	
Clear the display.		
Multiply.	$5(17)$	
Enter 5 × 17 by pressing:	[5] [×] [1] [7] [=]	85

The value of $5(3 + 14)$ is 85.

Practice

Use your calculator to simplify each expression.

1. $29 - 16 + 48 \div 3$

2. $26 + 14 \div 7 - 15$

3. $12 \times 13 - 23$

4. $28 \times 13 - 27$

5. $368 \div 4 - 22$

6. $(45 + 67) \div 7$

7. $5(23 + 14)$

8. $(196 - 8) \div 4$

9. $18 \times 12 - 3$

10. $30(15 - 3)$

11. $120 \div 10 + 2$

12. $22 + 35 \div 7$

On-the-Job Math

PHARMACY ASSISTANT

Have you ever had a prescription filled? If so, you probably watched a pharmacy assistant at work.

Pharmacy assistants do many jobs. First, they take a doctor's prescription from a customer. They check the person's name and address. They ask if the person is allergic to any medicine. Many times assistants count the pills. The doctor wants the person to have a certain number of pills, so the count must be exact. The pharmacist checks the work before it is given to the customer. Then, the customer pays for the medicine. Assistants take the money to a cash register and make change.

Pharmacy assistants keep busy all the time. Sometimes, the shelves need to be cleaned up and large orders of medicine need to be put away. The assistants fill out insurance forms. Sometimes, the information is put into a computer. Pharmacy assistants have to be very careful. Even a small mistake could be a problem for a customer.

If you like details and enjoy working with people, you might like to work as a pharmacy assistant.

You can write number equations for word statements. This will be a useful tool in solving problems.

Addition is used to find the total.
Twice means 2 times as much.
How much left means subtraction.
Separate into equal amounts means division.

EXAMPLE

A manufacturer shipped 72 mugs separated into 3 cases. There are 24 mugs in each case. Write a number equation to show this.

READ   **What do you need to find out?**
You need to find the number equation for the word statement.

PLAN   **What do you need to do?**
Choose the correct operation. Write an equation. Use the symbol for the operation, the numbers given, and the equal sign.

DO   **Carry out the plan.**

Choose the operation.	division
Divide 72 by 3.	$72 \div 3$
Write the equation.	$72 \div 3 = 24$

CHECK   **Does your answer make sense?**
72 mugs are separated into 3 cases. This means $72 \div 3$. Each case holds 24 mugs. ✓

The number equation for the problem is $72 \div 3 = 24$.

Practice

Write a number equation for each.

1. Hector makes $50 each week at a part-time job. He just got a raise of $5. He now makes $55 each week.

2. Rosa bought 3 pairs of shoes. Each pair cost $40. She paid $120 for all three pairs.

3. Wade had 25 packages to deliver at the start of the day. Before lunch, he delivered 14 packages. He had 11 left to deliver after lunch.

4. Jose uses 3 pans to make 36 muffins. Each pan holds 12 muffins.

5. Margarita walks 3 miles each day. She walks 5 days each week. In one week she walks 15 miles.

6. Jamal plans to spend 12 hours painting his apartment. He wants to spend 3 hours a day doing the painting. It will take Jamal 4 days to paint his apartment.

7. Rita made 12 car payments last year. She paid a total of $1,200. Her payments were $100 each month.

Cooperative Learning

8. Explain to a partner how you wrote the number equation for number 7 in **Practice**.

9. Write word statements. Look at numbers **1–7** in **Practice** for some ideas. Have a partner write a number equation for what you wrote. Check the work.

Area is the number of squares needed to cover a closed figure. This rectangle is covered by 6 squares. It has an area of 6 square meters.

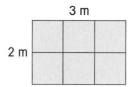

You can also find the area of a rectangle by multiplying the length by the width. The length of the rectangle is 3 meters. The width of the rectangle is 2 meters.

Area of a Rectangle = length • width
6 square meters = 3 m • 2 m

▶ **EXAMPLE**

Find the area of the rectangle.

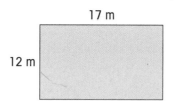

Area of a Rectangle = length • width

204 square meters = 12m • 17m

The length and width of a rectangle can be in any unit of measure. Feet, yards, inches, and centimeters are some of the units you will see. Remember that the area is a number of squares. So area is given in square units. Square feet, square yards, square inches, and square centimeters are some of the units for area.

Try These

Find the area of the rectangles.

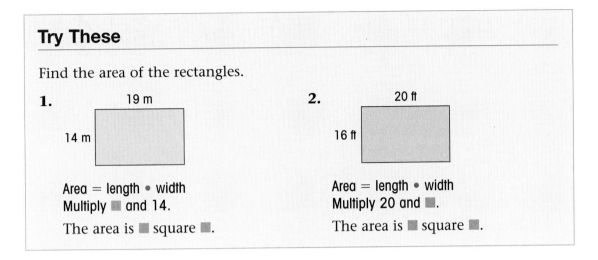

1.

19 m

14 m

Area = length • width
Multiply ■ and 14.

The area is ■ square ■.

2.

20 ft

16 ft

Area = length • width
Multiply 20 and ■.

The area is ■ square ■.

Practice

Find the area.

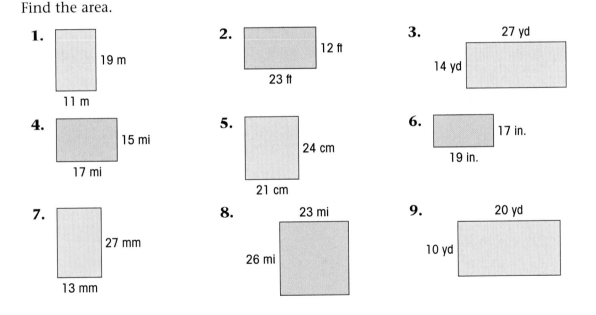

1.

19 m

11 m

2.

12 ft

23 ft

3.

27 yd

14 yd

4.

15 mi

17 mi

5.

24 cm

21 cm

6.

17 in.

19 in.

7.

27 mm

13 mm

8.

23 mi

26 mi

9.

20 yd

10 yd

Cooperative Learning

10. Ask a partner to explain how to find the area in number 3 in **Practice**. Check the work.

11. Explain to a partner how to find the area of the rectangle in number 9 in **Practice**.

Chapter 2 ▷ Review

Summary

Numbers and operations are used to write number expressions.
To simplify a number expression with more than one operation, multiply and divide from left to right. Then, add and subtract from left to right.
When an expression contains parentheses, do the operations in the parentheses first.
You can simplify each expression to see if the values are equal.
An equation is true if the expressions on both sides of the equal sign have the same value.
Properties for operations and numbers will help you perform operations quickly.
Writing a number equation for a word statement is a useful problem-solving skill.
You can use multiplication to find area.

number expression

simplify

parentheses

equivalent

number equation

property

Associative Property

Zero Property

Distributive Property

Division Property

area

Vocabulary Review

Complete the sentences with words from the box.

1. When you carry out the operations you _____.
2. Numbers together with operation symbols form a _____.
3. When a number multiplied by 0 is 0, it is called the _____.
4. A fact that is true for all numbers is a _____.
5. The _____ is when a number divided by 1 is the same number.
6. _____ are grouping symbols.
7. The _____ is used to multiply a sum or difference by a number.
8. _____ is the number of squares needed to cover a closed figure.
9. More than two numbers multiplied in groups of two is an example of an _____.
10. A statement that two number expressions are equal is called a _____.
11. Numbers having the same value are _____.

Chapter Quiz

Find the value of each number expression.

1. $14 - 8$ **2.** $30 + 11$ **3.** $22 - 1$

4. 10×3 **5.** $42 \div 6$ **6.** $18 \div 1$

Simplify.

7. $15 - 4 \cdot 3$ **8.** $2 \cdot 3^2$ **9.** $2(2 + 3) - 1$

Tell whether the expressions are equivalent. Write *yes* or *no*. If yes, write an equation.

10. 12×3 and 9 **11.** $27 \div 9$ and 3 **12.** $4^3 + 3^3$ and $(4 + 3)^3$

13. $12 \div 3$ and $2 \cdot 2$ **14.** $3 \cdot 6$ and $23 - 5$ **15.** $24 \div 4$ and $5 + 2$

Name the property shown.

16. $5 + 3 = 3 + 5$ **17.** $(6 \cdot 9) \cdot 4 = 6 \cdot (9 \cdot 4)$ **18.** $11 \times 0 = 0$

Write a number equation for each.

19. Luisa sold 4 sweatshirts. Each sweatshirt costs $20. She sold a total of $80.

20. Ed drives 15 miles each day. He drives 7 days a week. In one week, he drives 105 miles.

Find the area.

21. **22.**

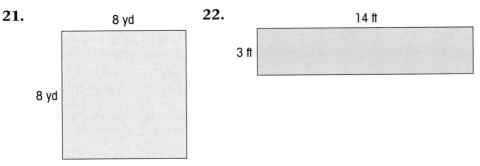

Unit 1 **Review**

Choose the letter for the correct answer.

Use the chart to answer Questions 1–2.

Regular polygon	Number of Sides	Length of each side
triangle	3	2 in.
pentagon	5	5 in.
hexagon	6	3 in.
heptagon	7	1 in.

1. Find the perimeter of the hexagon.

   A. 6 in.
   B. 7 in.
   C. 18 in.
   D. 25 in.

2. Which has the greatest perimeter?

   A. Triangle
   B. Pentagon
   C. Hexagon
   D. Heptagon

3. Philip is twice as old as Maria. Maria is two years younger than Pedro. The sum of their ages is 26. How old is Pedro?

   A. 6 years
   B. 8 years
   C. 12 years
   D. 15 years

4. Find the area of a rectangle that is 20 miles long and 5 miles wide.

   A. 50 miles
   B. 100 miles
   C. 50 square miles
   D. 100 square miles

5. Which expression would you use to find the area of this square?

2 in.

2 in. ⬜ 2 in.

2 in.

   A. 2 in. $\times$ 2 in.
   B. 2 in. + 2 in.
   C. 2 in. + 2 in. + 2 in. + 2 in.
   D. 2 in. $\times$ 2 in. $\times$ 2 in. $\times$ 2 in.

6. Rosita baked 48 cookies. She put the cookies onto 6 plates. How many cookies are on each plate? Which number equation solves the problem?

   A. $6 \times 8 = 48$
   B. $48 \div 8 = 6$
   C. $48 \div 6 = 8$
   D. None of the above

Critical Thinking

Jake spends 60 hours each month practicing sports. He spends 16 more hours practicing skateboarding than playing basketball. How much time does he spend playing basketball? **CHALLENGE** Write a number equation to show the number of hours spent each week playing basketball.

Unit Two

In this sound studio, the engineer uses a mixing board to put together a song. His understanding of math helps him give the music its beat. What are the symbols for the different beats in music?

Learning Objectives

- Identify variable expressions.
- Identify like terms.
- Simplify variable expressions.
- Evaluate variable expressions.
- Use a calculator to evaluate variable expressions.
- Solve problems by drawing a picture.
- Apply concepts and skills to find volume.

Words to Know

variable	a letter that represents a number
variable expression	an expression containing operations with variables or with variables and numbers
terms	parts of an expression separated by a + or − sign
constant	a term that is a number
coefficient	a number that multiplies a variable
like terms	numbers or terms that have the same variables with the same exponent
simplify a variable expression	combine like terms
combine like terms	add or subtract the coefficients of the variables
substitute	replace a variable with a number
evaluate a variable expression	find the value by substituting numbers for the variables
volume	the number of cubes needed to fill a space

Volume Project

Bring in four small to medium-sized boxes. In your math journal, record what you think is the volume of each box. Then measure the length, width, and height of each box. Round each measure to the nearest whole number. Calculate the volume of the box. You can use the expression $l \times w \times h$ for the volume. Record the results in your math journal. Compare your results with your guesses to see how close each guess is to the actual volume.

3·1 ▶ Variable Expressions

Here are a basketball team's final scores for its first three games: 48, 76, 59. You can use a variable to represent the scores. A **variable** is a letter that represents any number. Use s to represent the scores. Then s means 48, 76, or 59. In the fourth game, the team scores 80 points. You can use s to mean 80 or any other score.

A **variable expression** contains operations, numbers, and variables. These expressions contain addition and subtraction.

$$4 + 7 \qquad x - y \qquad t + 4 \qquad 8 - c + d$$

▶ **EXAMPLE 1**

Name the variables in $s - t + 4$.

The variables are the letters. $s - t + 4$
s and t are the variables.

Variable expressions that contain multiplication or division can be written in different ways.

$$2 \times a \rightarrow 2 \bullet a \quad \text{or} \quad 2a \qquad \text{or} \quad 2(a) \quad \text{or} \quad (2)a$$
$$cd \quad \rightarrow c \bullet d \quad \text{or} \quad c \times d \quad \text{or} \quad (c)d \quad \text{or} \quad c(d)$$
$$\frac{3x}{5} \quad \rightarrow 3x \div 5$$

▶ **EXAMPLE 2**

Complete. $4a^2 = 4 \bullet a \bullet ?$

$$4a^2 = 4 \bullet a \bullet ?$$
$4a^2$ means 4 times a times a. $4a^2 = 4 \bullet a \bullet a$

▶ **EXAMPLE 3**

Complete. $abc = a \bullet ? \bullet c$

$$abc = a \bullet ? \bullet c$$
abc means a times b times c. $abc = a \bullet b \bullet c$

▶ **EXAMPLE 4**

Complete. $\frac{5t}{8} = ? \div 8$

$$\frac{5t}{8} = ? \div 8$$
$\frac{5t}{8}$ means $5t$ divided by 8. $\frac{5t}{8} = 5t \div 8$

Name the variable or variables in each.

1. $4(x - y)$

The letters are x and ■.
The variables are x and ■.

2. $5 - 2a^2 + b^2$

The letters are a and ■.
The variables are a and ■.

Complete.

3. $xy = x \cdot$ ■

xy means x times ■.

4. $\frac{5n}{4} = 5n \div$ ■

$\frac{5n}{4}$ means $5n$ divided by ■.

Practice

Name the variable or variables in each.

1. $20 - 2x$

2. $\frac{3a}{8}$

3. $ab - c$

4. c^3

5. $2(l + w)$

6. $4(r + s)$

7. $\frac{y}{9}$

8. s^3

9. $2d - 4g$

10. $b \cdot b$

11. lwh

12. $y \cdot y \cdot y$

Complete.

13. $9y = 9 \cdot ?$

14. $rs = ? \cdot s$

15. $\frac{d}{4} = ? \div 4$

16. $s^3 = s \cdot s \cdot ?$

17. $8r = 8(?)$

18. $4x^2 + 1 = 4 \cdot x \cdot ? + 1$

Cooperative Learning

19. Explain to a partner how to complete number **17** in **Practice**.

20. Write a variable expression using addition and multiplication. Have a partner name the variables. Check the work.

The parts of an expression have special names. The **terms** of an expression are the parts separated by a + sign or a − sign. A term that is a number is called a constant term or **constant**.

$$2x - 5y + xy + 3$$

▶ **EXAMPLE 1**

Four terms are $2x$, $5y$, xy, and 3. The constant is 3.

Name the terms in $4x^3 - 2x + 7$.

Math Fact
7 is the constant.

Look for the parts separated by a + or −. $4x^3 - 2x + 7$

There are three terms, $4x^3$, $2x$, and 7

A **coefficient** is a number that multiplies a variable.

$$2a^3 \rightarrow 2 \bullet a^3 \qquad \text{2 is the coefficient of } a^3.$$
$$s \rightarrow 1 \bullet s \qquad \text{1 is the coefficient of } s.$$
$$6xy \rightarrow 6 \bullet xy \qquad \text{6 is the coefficient of } xy.$$

▶ **EXAMPLE 2**

Name the coefficient in $10ab$.

Look for a number $10ab = 10 \bullet ab$
times variables.

10 is the coefficient of ab.

Math Fact
$2ab$ and $4ba$ have the same variables. $4ba$ means $4ab$.

Like terms have the same variables or the same exponent. All numbers are like terms.

Like Terms	Unlike Terms
$2ab$ and $4ba$	x and y
$4x$ and $9x$	y^3 and y^2
a^2 and $12a^2$	ab and bc
5 and 7	9 and $9x$

▶ **EXAMPLE 3**

Are $4x^2y$ and $8x^2y$ like or unlike?

Same variables with $4x^2y$ and $8x^2y$
same exponents

$4x^2y$ and $8x^2y$ are like terms.

Try These

1. Name the terms in
$x^3 + y^2 - x + 12$.

Look for the parts separated by + or −.
The terms are x^3, ■, x, 12.
The constant is ■.

2. Name the coefficient in
$8x^2y$.

Look for a number times variables.
$8x^2y = ■ \cdot x^2y$
■ is the coefficient of x^2y.

Are the terms like or unlike?

3. $10x^2y$ and $2yx^2$

Terms have the same variables with the same exponents.
$10x^2y$ and $2yx^2$ are ■ terms.

4. $5x^2$ and $5x$

Variables have different exponents.
$5x^2$ and $5x$ are ■ terms.

Practice

Name the terms in each.

1. $2x + 7y + 8$

2. $-3xy + 9x$

3. 12

Name the coefficient in each.

4. $3a^2$

5. $12w$

6. ab

Are the terms like or unlike?

7. $3x^3$ and $3x^2$

8. ab and $2ab$

9. 5 and 8

Cooperative Learning

10. Explain to a partner how you find the coefficient in number 6 in **Practice**.

11. Write a variable expression with some like terms. Have a partner name the terms, the coefficients, and the like terms. Check the work.

3·3 Combining Like Terms

In the last chapter, you simplified number expressions by performing the operations. You can also **simplify a variable expression** by **combining like terms**.

$$\underbrace{x + x}_{} \ + \ \underbrace{x + x + x}_{} \text{ is the same as } \underbrace{x + x + x + x + x}_{}.$$

So $2x$ + $3x$ is the same as $5x$
because 2 + 3 is the same as 5.

Combining like terms means adding or subtracting the coefficients of the variables. For number terms, just add or subtract the numbers.

▶ **EXAMPLE 1**

Think 10 − 2 = 8.

Simplify. $10x - 2x$

Combine like terms. $\underbrace{10x - 2x}_{}$

$8x$

Sometimes, you need to combine more than two like terms. Combine them two at a time.

▶ **EXAMPLE 2**

Math Fact
a means $1a$.

Simplify. $4a + 2a - a$

Combine like terms. $\underbrace{4a + 2a}_{} - a$

$\underbrace{6a - 1a}_{}$

$5a$

You may have to change the order of terms so that like terms are together. Be sure to move the + or − sign.

▶ **EXAMPLE 3**

Math Fact
y means $1y$.

Simplify. $3y + 7x - y - 2x$

Change the order. $\underbrace{3y - 1y}_{} + \underbrace{7x - 2x}_{}$

Combine like terms. $2y \ \ + \ \ 5x$

▶ **EXAMPLE 4**

Simplify. $a + ab + bc + a^2$

All terms are unlike. Stop!

Try These

Simplify.

1. $2xy + 9 + 8xy - 1$

Change the order. $\qquad 2xy + 8xy + 9 - 1$

Combine like terms. $\qquad \blacksquare\, xy + \blacksquare$

2. $4a^2 + a + 3 - a^2 - 1$

Change the order. $\qquad 4a^2 - a^2 + a + 3 - 1$

Combine like terms. $\qquad \blacksquare\, a^2 + a + \blacksquare$

Practice

Simplify.

1. $a + a + 2a$

2. $5x + x + 8 - 6$

3. $2x^2 + 2 + 9x^2$

4. $c + 2d$

5. $5 + 2y + 8$

6. $6a + 7 - 5a + 3$

7. $2xy + xy$

8. $3w + 7 - 7s - w$

9. $5b^2 - 2b + 3b^2$

10. $1 + 2ab + 7a + 9$

11. $6 + 9d - 2$

12. $10 - 2 + 4x^2 + y^2$

13. $5t + 8 - t + 2$

14. $r^2 + s^2$

15. $x^2 - x$

16. $6x + x^2 + x + 3x^2$

Cooperative Learning

17. Explain to a partner how to simplify the expression in number **8** in **Practice**.

18. Write a variable expression containing + signs. Have a partner simplify it. Check the work.

3·4 ▶ Evaluating Variable Expressions

You have already found the value of a number expression by performing its operations. You can find the value of a variable expression by **substituting** or replacing the variable with a number. By doing this, you will get a number expression. Then, perform the operation in the number expression. This process is called **evaluating a variable expression**.

▶ **EXAMPLE 1**

Evaluate $14 - a$ when $a = 8$.

Replace a with 8.	$14 - a$
Subtract.	$14 - 8$
	6

The value of $14 - a$ is 6 when $a = 8$.

▶ **EXAMPLE 2**

Find the value of $2x$ when $x = 10$.

Math Fact
$2x$ means 2 times x.

	$2x$
Replace x with 10.	$2 \cdot x$
Multiply.	$2 \cdot 10$
	20

The value of $2x$ is 20 when $x = 10$.

▶ **EXAMPLE 3**

Find the value of $b \div 4$ when $b = 20$.

Replace b with 20.	$b \div 4$
Divide.	$20 \div 4$
	5

The value of $b \div 4$ is 5 when $b = 20$.

▶ **EXAMPLE 4**

Evaluate c^2 when $c = 3$.

Math Fact
c^2 means $c \times c$.

	c^2
Replace c with 3.	$c \cdot c$
Multiply.	$3 \cdot 3$
	9

The value of c^2 is 9 when $c = 3$.

Try These

Evaluate each variable expression.

1. $a + 9$ when $a = 3$

| Replace a with 3. | $a + 9$ |
| Add. | $\blacksquare + 9 = \blacksquare$ |

The value of $a + 9$ is $\blacksquare$ when $a = 3$.

2. $6y$ when $y = 4$

| Replace y with 4. | $6y$ |
| Multiply. | $6 \cdot \blacksquare = \blacksquare$ |

The value of $6y$ is $\blacksquare$ when $y = 4$.

3. $w \div 5$ when $w = 15$

| Replace w with 15. | $w \div 5$ |
| Divide. | $\blacksquare \div 5 = \blacksquare$ |

The value of $w \div 5$ is $\blacksquare$ when $w = 15$.

4. s^3 when $s = 7$

Rewrite s^3.	$s \cdot s \cdot s$
Replace s with 7.	
Multiply.	$\blacksquare \cdot \blacksquare \cdot \blacksquare = \blacksquare$

The value of s^3 is $\blacksquare$ when $s = 7$.

Practice

Evaluate each variable expression.

1. $L + 4$ when $L = 10$

2. $9 + t$ when $t = 2$

3. $8 - c$ when $c = 1$

4. $20 - d$ when $d = 12$

5. $6b$ when $b = 4$

6. $5a$ when $a = 3$

7. $P \div 4$ when $P = 28$

8. $r \div 10$ when $r = 20$

9. h^2 when $h = 9$

10. z^2 when $z = 1$

11. b^3 when $b = 2$

12. d^3 when $d = 3$

Cooperative Learning

13. Pick three numbers for v. Ask a partner to evaluate $v + 5$ for each of the numbers. Check the work.

14. Pick three numbers for x. Ask a partner to evaluate $4x$ for each of the numbers. Check the work.

You have just found the value of variable expressions that contain one operation. Now you will find the value of variable expressions that contain more than one operation.

 EXAMPLE 1

Remember

Order of Operations

1. Multiply or divide from left to right.
2. Then add or subtract from left to right.

Evaluate $5a + 2$ when $a = 10$.

Replace a with 10.
Perform the operations.

$$5a + 2$$
$$5 \bullet a + 2$$
$$5 \bullet 10 + 2$$
$$50 + 2$$
$$52$$

The value of $5a + 2$ is 52 when $a = 10$.

 EXAMPLE 2

Evaluate $3x^2 \div x$ when $x = 2$.

Replace x with 2.
Perform the operations.

$$3x^2 \div x$$
$$3 \bullet x \bullet x \div x$$
$$3 \bullet 2 \bullet 2 \div 2$$
$$6 \bullet 2 \div 2$$
$$12 \div 2$$
$$6$$

The value of $3x^2 \div x$ is 6 when $x = 2$.

Variable expressions may contain parentheses. After you replace the variable with a number, remember to do the operations in parentheses first.

▶ **EXAMPLE 3**

Evaluate $2(10 - y)$ when $y = 6$.

Replace y with 6.
Perform the operations.

$$2(10 - y)$$
$$2(10 - 6)$$
$$2(4)$$
$$8$$

The value of $2(10 - y)$ is 8 when $y = 6$.

Try These

Evaluate each variable expression.

1. $4b \div 3$ when $b = 6$

$$4b \div 3$$

Replace b with 6. $4 \cdot b \div 3$
Perform the $4 \cdot 6 \div 3$
operations. $\blacksquare \div 3$
                       $\blacksquare$

The value of $4b \div 3$ is $\blacksquare$
when $b = 6$.

2. $10(3 + n^2)$ when $n = 2$

$$10(3 + n^2)$$

Replace n with 2. $10(3 + n \cdot n)$
Perform the $10(3 + 2 \cdot \blacksquare)$
operations. $10(3 + \blacksquare)$
                       $10(\blacksquare)$
                       $\blacksquare$

The value of $10(3 + n^2)$ is $\blacksquare$
when $\blacksquare = 2$.

Practice

Evaluate each variable expression.

1. $2d + 9$ when $d = 1$

2. $12 \div 3x$ when $x = 1$

3. $s^2 \div 2s$ when $s = 4$

4. $r^2 - r$ when $r = 6$

5. $8(a + 1)$ when $a = 5$

6. $6(y - 2)$ when $y = 12$

7. $x(2 + x)$ when $x = 2$

8. $(15 \div a)a$ when $a = 5$

9. $x^2 + 2x + 1$ when $x = 4$

10. $d^3 + 2d - 1$ when $d = 2$

11. $s^2 + 3s - 1$ when $s = 1$

12. $4 + 2r + r^2$ when $r = 5$

Cooperative Learning

13. Explain to a partner how you find the value of the variable expression in number **8** in **Practice**.

14. Use x to write a variable expression that contains addition, multiplication, and exponents. Have a partner find the value of the expression when the value of x is 2.

Using More Variables

A variable expression may contain more than one variable. You can find the value of expressions with more than one variable by replacing each variable with a number. You will get a number expression. Perform the operations in the number expression.

▶ **EXAMPLE 1**

Evaluate $2x + y + 4$ when $x = 3$ and $y = 1$.

$$2x + y + 4$$

Replace x with 3 and y with 1.
$$2 \cdot x + y + 4$$
Perform the operations.
$$2 \cdot 3 + 1 + 4$$

$$6 + 1 + 4$$

$$7 + 4$$

$$11$$

The value of $2x + y + 4$ is 11 when $x = 3$ and $y = 1$.

▶ **EXAMPLE 2**

Evaluate $10nz^2$ when $n = 3$ and $z = 2$.

$$10nz^2$$

Replace n with 3 and z with 2.
$$10 \cdot n \cdot z \cdot z$$
Perform the operations.
$$10 \cdot 3 \cdot 2 \cdot 2$$

$$30 \cdot 2 \cdot 2$$

$$60 \cdot 2$$

$$120$$

The value of $10nz^2$ is 120 when $n = 3$ and $z = 2$.

▶ **EXAMPLE 3**

Evaluate $s(8 \div r)$ when $s = 4$ and $r = 2$.

Replace s with 4 and r with 2.
$$s(8 \div r)$$
Perform the operations.
$$4(8 \div 2)$$

$$4(4)$$

$$16$$

The value of $s(8 \div r)$ is 16 when $s = 4$ and $r = 2$.

Try These

Evaluate each variable expression.

1. $8d - m$ when $d = 6$ and $m = 8$

Replace d with 6 and m with 8. $8d - m$

Perform the operations. $8(6) - ∎$

     $∎ - ∎$

     $∎$

The value of $8d - m$ is $∎$ when $d = 6$ and $m = 8$.

2. $y ÷ (6 + 2f)$ when $y = 20$ and $f = 2$

Replace y with 20 and f with 2. $y ÷ (6 + 2f)$

Perform the operations. $∎ ÷ (6 + 2 • 2)$

     $∎ ÷ (6 + 4)$

     $∎ ÷ ∎$

     $∎$

The value of $y ÷ (6 + 2f)$ is $∎$ when $y = 20$ and $f = 2$.

Practice

Evaluate each variable expression.

1. $3h + r^2 + 6$ when $h = 3$ and $r = 4$

2. $4s - 8t$ when $s = 7$ and $t = 2$

3. $6m + 9 ÷ g$ when $m = 5$ and $g = 3$

4. $8 - x + 5y$ when $x = 2$ and $y = 3$

5. $4s + 3r^2$ when $s = 3$ and $r = 2$

6. $(x + 3k) ÷ 2$ when $x = 2$ and $k = 6$

7. $2(l + w)$ when $l = 8$ and $w = 4$

8. lwh when $l = 2$, $w = 3$, and $h = 5$

9. $a(b - 2)$ when $a = 10$ and $b = 8$

10. $s - 3d + 5$ when $s = 9$ and $d = 2$

Cooperative Learning

11. Explain to a partner how you evaluate the variable expression in number **8** in **Practice**.

12. Write a variable expression with x and y. Use multiplication and addition in the expression. Have a partner evaluate the expression when $x = 2$ and $y = 1$. Check the work.

You can use a calculator to evaluate an expression. Replace variables with their values. Then, use your calculator to perform the operations.

▶ **EXAMPLE**

Use your calculator to evaluate the expression $22x + 116 + 31y$ when x is 32 and y is 25.

Math Fact
Remember the order of operations when working with your calculator. Work left to right. Do multiplication and division first. Then, add and subtract.

Display

		Display
Enter 22 by pressing:	2 2	22
Multiply by 32 by pressing:	× 3 2	32
	=	704
Enter 31 by pressing:	3 1	31
Multiply by 25 by pressing:	× 2 5	25
	=	775

The expression becomes $704 + 116 + 775$.

Enter 704 by pressing:	7 0 4	704
Add 116 by pressing:	+ 1 1 6	116
	=	820
Add 775 by pressing:	+ 7 7 5	775
	=	1595

The value of $22x + 116 + 31y$ is 1,595 when x is 32 and y is 25.

Practice

Use your calculator to evaluate each expression.

1. $132k + r + 267$ when k is 13 and r is 342

2. $4j - 8p$ when j is 231 and p is 57

3. $56m + 322 \div g$ when m is 25 and g is 14

4. $148 - x - 15y$ when x is 67 and y is 4

5. $234s + 15r$ when s is 13 and r is 79

6. $x + 113k$ when x is 223 and k is 16

7. $\dfrac{n}{17} - 13$ when n is 952

8. $s - 23d + 315$ when s is 469 and d is 19

Math Connection

THE GREAT PYRAMID

About 4,500 years ago, the Egyptians built pyramids. These large, triangular-shaped buildings were tombs for kings and queens.

The Great Pyramid is one of the most famous pyramids. It is made of more than two million stone blocks. The blocks were cut from stone. Workers had to drag the blocks to the building site. The workers used ramps to place the blocks on top of each other and to move them one at a time. When finished, the Great Pyramid was almost 500 feet tall.

Pyramids amaze us. The Egyptians did not have modern tools. They did not have cars or machines. They did not have computers to help design the building. The Egyptians made pyramids with simple tools like chisels and saws. They used about 100,000 workers. They relied on their understanding of math to design the building. They did a good job. The Great Pyramid and many others are still standing in Egypt today.

Problem Solving: Draw a Diagram

Tanya wants to put a fence around a garden. She draws a picture to help her see what she needs.

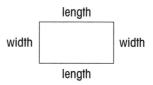

length

width | | width

length

The amount of fencing Tanya needs is:

width + length + width + length

Now Tanya can write a variable expression.

Use w for width and l for length. $w + l + w + l$
Combine like terms. $w + w + l + l$
        $2w + 2l$

Tanya can use this expression to find the amount of fencing she needs around the garden.

▶ **EXAMPLE**

Tanya wants her garden to be 6 feet wide and 10 feet long. How much fencing does she need?

READ **What do you need to find out?**
The amount of fencing needed for a garden 6 feet wide and 10 feet long

PLAN **What do you need to do?**
Evaluate the expression $2w + 2l$ for $w = 6$ and $l = 10$.

DO **Follow the plan.**
Replace w with 6 and l with 10. $2 \cdot w + 2 \cdot l$
Perform the operations. $2 \cdot 6 + 2 \cdot 10$
   $12 + 20$
   32

Tanya will need 32 feet of fencing.

CHECK **Does the answer make sense?**
Add the lengths of the sides $6 + 6 + 10 + 10$
of the fenced-in garden. $32 ✓$

10 ft

6 ft | | 6 ft

10 ft

Try These

Solve each problem.

1. How much rope does Tanya need if she makes the garden 5 feet wide and 8 feet long?

Replace *w* with 5 and *l* with 8. $2l + 2w$

Perform the operations.

$2 \cdot \blacksquare + 2 \cdot \blacksquare$

$\blacksquare + \blacksquare$

$\blacksquare$

Tanya needs ■ feet of rope if the width of the garden is 5 feet and the length is 8 feet.

2. How much rope does Tanya need if she makes the garden 10 feet wide and 15 feet long?

Replace *w* with 10 and *l* with 15. $2l + 2w$

Perform the operations.

$2 \cdot \blacksquare + 2 \cdot \blacksquare$

$\blacksquare + \blacksquare$

$\blacksquare$

Tanya needs ■ feet of rope if the width of the garden is 10 feet and the length is 15 feet.

Practice

Solve each problem.

1. How much rope is needed for a garden that is 20 feet wide and 40 feet long?

2. A square is a rectangle. All of its sides have the same length. How much rope is needed to close in a square garden with each side 20 feet long?

3. How much rope is needed to close in a square garden when each side is 15 feet long?

4. Tanya has 50 feet of rope to close in a garden. The width of the garden is 10 feet. How long is the garden?

5. Tanya can close in a square garden with 60 feet of rope. How long should she make the length of each side?

Cooperative Learning

6. Explain to a partner how you solved the problem in number **4** in **Practice**.

7. Ask a partner to draw a picture of a garden. The garden will have five sides of the same length. Then ask how much rope is needed to close in the garden, if each side is 8 feet long. Check the work.

3-9 ▶ Application: Volume

Volume is the number of cubes needed to fill space. You can find volume by counting the cubes. You can also find volume by using multiplication.

▶ **EXAMPLE 1**

Here is a box with a length of 4 inches, width of 3 inches, and height of 2 inches. To find the volume of the box, you can find how many cubes are needed to fill it.

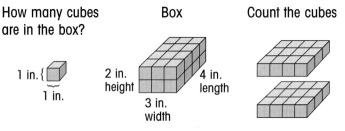

You can count 24 cubes. The volume of the box is 24 cubes. Each cube is a cubic inch. The volume can be written as 24 cubic inches or 24 in.^{3}.

You can also find the volume by multiplying the length, the width, and the height.

$$\text{length} \times \text{width} \times \text{height}$$
$$\underline{4 \times 3} \times 2$$
$$\underline{12 \ \times 2}$$
$$24$$

The volume is 24 in.^{3}.

▶ **EXAMPLE 2**

Find the volume of a box with a height of 3 feet, width of 3 feet, and length of 3 feet.

Multiply to find the volume.

$$3 \times 3 \times 3$$
$$\underline{9 \times 3}$$
$$27$$

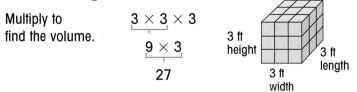

The volume is 27 cubic feet or 27ft^3.

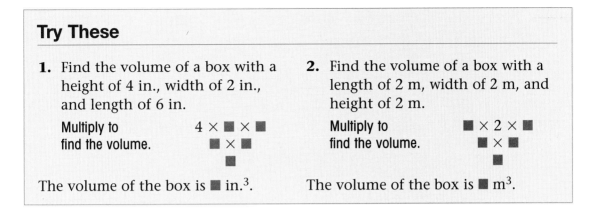

Try These

1. Find the volume of a box with a height of 4 in., width of 2 in., and length of 6 in.

   Multiply to find the volume.

   $4 \times \blacksquare \times \blacksquare$
   $\blacksquare \times \blacksquare$
   $\blacksquare$

   The volume of the box is $\blacksquare$ in.^{3}.

2. Find the volume of a box with a length of 2 m, width of 2 m, and height of 2 m.

   Multiply to find the volume.

   $\blacksquare \times 2 \times \blacksquare$
   $\blacksquare \times \blacksquare$
   $\blacksquare$

   The volume of the box is $\blacksquare$ m^3.

Practice

Find the volume of each box.

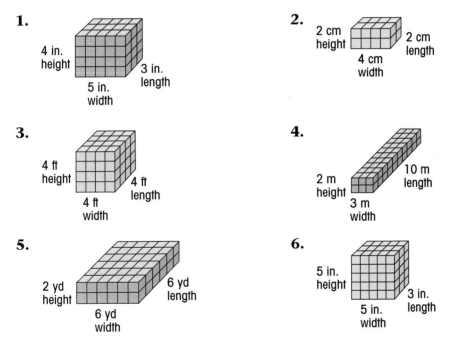

1. 4 in. height, 5 in. width, 3 in. length

2. 2 cm height, 4 cm width, 2 cm length

3. 4 ft height, 4 ft width, 4 ft length

4. 2 m height, 3 m width, 10 m length

5. 2 yd height, 6 yd width, 6 yd length

6. 5 in. height, 5 in. width, 3 in. length

Cooperative Learning

7. Explain to a partner how you find the volume of the box in number 5 in **Practice**.

8. Write the length, width, and height of a box. Have a partner find the volume of the box. Check the work.

Summary

Variable expressions contain operations, numbers, and variables.
Multiplication and division can be written in different ways.
The terms of an expression are parts of a variable expression.
Combining like terms means adding or subtracting the coefficients of the same variables.
Replace the variables in an expression with numbers to evaluate expression.
Drawing a picture can help you solve problems.
You can find volume by counting cubes or by using multiplication.

variable

variable expression

coefficient

terms

constant

like terms

combine like terms

simplify

substitute

evaluate

volume

Vocabulary Review

Complete the sentences with words from the box.

1. An expression containing operations with variables or with variables and numbers is called a ＿＿.

2. A ＿＿ is a number that multiplies a variable.

3. A letter that represents a number is called a ＿＿.

4. ＿＿ are parts of an expression separated by a + or − sign.

5. A term that is a number is called a ＿＿.

6. If you replace a variable with a number you ＿＿.

7. The number of cubes needed to fill a space is called ＿＿.

8. ＿＿ are terms with the same variables and the same exponents.

9. When you add or subtract the coefficients of the variables you ＿＿.

10. When you ＿＿ a variable expression you combine like terms.

11. When you ＿＿ a variable expression you find the value by substituting numbers for the variables.

Chapter Quiz

Name the variable or variables in each.

1. $12x - 4y$ **2.** $2(x + y)$ **3.** $2ab + 3c$

Are the terms like or unlike?

4. $2x^2$ and $2x^4$ **5.** $5ab$ and $2ab$ **6.** 12 and 18

Simplify.

7. $2a + 2a + 42a$ **8.** $10y + y + 12 - 4$ **9.** $3x^2 + 3 + 9x^2$

Evaluate each variable expression.

10. $L + 8$ when $L = 16$ **11.** $12 + t$ when $t = 3$

12. $4 - c$ when $c = 1$ **13.** lwh when $l = 5$, $w = 8$, and $h = 8$

14. $a(b - 1)$ when $a = 12$ and $b = 4$

Solve each problem.

15. How much rope is needed to close in a garden that is 100 feet wide and 60 feet long?

16. A square is a rectangle. All of its sides have the same length. How much rope is needed to close in a square garden with each side 40 feet long?

17. Find the volume of the box.

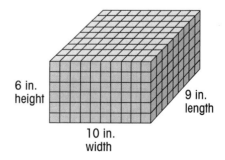

6 in. height

9 in. length

10 in. width

An equation is always in balance. What is on one side must equal what is on the other side. How does a tightrope walker keep his balance?

Learning Objectives

- Identify a variable equation.
- Tell whether two equations are equivalent.
- Find the solution of an equation.
- Solve equations by adding, subtracting, multiplying, and dividing.
- Solve equations using more than one operation.
- Check solutions to equations by using a calculator.
- Find number patterns.
- Apply concepts and skills to solve geometry formulas.

Words to Know

variable equation	an equation containing a variable
solution	a value of the variable that makes a variable equation true
solve	find the solution of an equation
equivalent equations	variable equations with the same solutions
properties of equality	adding, subtracting, multiplying, or dividing both sides of an equation by the same number gives an equivalent equation
inverse operations	operations that "undo" each other; addition and subtraction are inverse operations, and multiplication and division are inverse operations

Patterns Project

Mathematical patterns follow a rule. Look for the rule in this pattern. Then complete the pattern.

2, 5, 8, __, 14, __, __, 23   2, 5, 8, **11**, 14, **17**, **20**, 23

Write an equation to show how to go from the first number to the second number in the pattern above. Use an inverse operation to reverse the pattern.

23, __, __, 14, __, 8, 5, 2   23, **20**, **17**, 14, **11**, 8, 5, 2

Create your own mathematical patterns. Use different operations. Have your classmates find the rules. See if your patterns can be linked to any others in the class. Make a display.

4·1 Variable Equations

Can you balance this scale? How many pounds is x?

The scale is balanced only when x is 10 lb.

Math Fact

$\neq$ means *is not equal to.*

A **variable equation** is an equation that contains a variable. The variable equation $x = 10$ shows the scale problem.

| $x = 10$ | $x = 10$ | $x = 10$ |
| $8 \neq 10$ | $10 = 10$ true | $11 \neq 10$ |

The **solution** of $x = 10$ is 10. The solution is the value of the variable that makes the equation true. To **solve** an equation is to find its solution.

 **EXAMPLE 1**

Check

By looking, you can tell 7 is the solution of $y = 7$.

Solve. Then, check the solution. $y = 7$

Solution: 7

Check. **Replace *y* with 7.** $y = 7$
                                  $7 = 7$ true

7 is the solution of $y = 7$.

A variable equation may contain many operations.

 **EXAMPLE 2**

Is 5 the solution of $2x - 4 = 6$?

$$2x - 4 = 6$$

Replace x with 5. $2 \cdot 5 - 4 = 6$

Multiply. Then, subtract. $\underline{10 - 4} = 6$

                                  $6 \ = 6$ true

5 is the solution of $2x - 4 = 6$.

Try These

1. Solve. Then, check the solution.

$x = 4$

The solution is ■.

Check. Replace x with ■.

$■ = 4$

  true

■ is the solution of $x = 4$.

2. Is 2 the solution of $5 + 3y = 12$?

Replace y with 2.

$5 + 3(■) = 12$

$5 + ■ = 12$

$■ \neq 12$

2 is not the solution of $5 + 3y = 12$.

Practice

Solve. Then, check the solution.

1. $s = 15$ **2.** $m = 0$ **3.** $x = 3$

4. $y = 5$ **5.** $n = 12$ **6.** $a = 8$

7. $b = 1$ **8.** $x = 2$ **9.** $y = 20$

Tell whether or not the number is a solution of the equation.

10. 3; $20 - y = 17$ **11.** 6; $n \bullet 7 = 56$

12. 20; $x \div 2 = 10$ **13.** 13; $r - 9 = 4$

14. 0; $2x + 5 = 5$ **15.** 2; $9 - 3d = 3$

16. 3; $4(x + 1) = 16$ **17.** 4; $8s = 24$

Cooperative Learning

18. Explain to a partner how you are able to tell whether or not 2 is the solution of the equation in number **15** in **Practice.**

19. Write a variable equation using addition. Then write three numbers. Ask a partner to check each number to see if it is a solution of your equation.

The solution of $x = 10$ is easy to find. Only the variable x is on the left side. Only the number 10 is on the right side. The solution of $x - 1 = 9$ and $x + 1 = 11$ are not as easy to find. They also have 10 as a solution.

$$x = 10$$

Solution: 10

Check: $x = 10$

$$10 = 10$$

true

$$x - 1 = 9$$

Solution: 10

Check: $x - 1 = 9$

$$10 - 1 = 9$$

$$9 = 9$$

true

$$x + 1 = 11$$

Solution: 10

Check: $x + 1 = 11$

$$10 + 1 = 11$$

$$11 = 11$$

true

Equations with the same solution are **equivalent equations**. These are equivalent equations:

$$x = 10 \qquad x - 1 = 9 \qquad x + 1 = 11$$

▶ **EXAMPLE 1**

Show that $x = 6$ and $\frac{x}{2} = 3$ are equivalent.

$$x = 6 \qquad\qquad\qquad \frac{x}{2} = 3$$

Solution: 6   → Replace x with 6. $x \div 2 = 3$

Check: $x = 6$ $6 \div 2 = 3$

$$6 = 6 \qquad\qquad\qquad\qquad 3 = 3$$

true   true

$x = 6$ and $\frac{x}{2} = 3$ are equivalent.

▶ **EXAMPLE 2**

Show that $x = 5$ and $2x - 6 = 4$ are equivalent.

$$x = 5 \qquad\qquad\qquad\qquad 2x - 6 = 4$$

Solution: 5   → Replace x with 5. $2 \bullet 5 - 6 = 4$

Check: $x = 5$ $10 - 6 = 4$

$$5 = 5 \qquad\qquad\qquad\qquad 4 = 4$$

true   true

$x = 5$ and $2x - 6 = 4$ are equivalent.

Try These

1. Show that $y = 2$ and $2y = 4$ are equivalent.

$$y = 2 \qquad\qquad\qquad 2y = 4$$

Solution: ▨   → Replace y with ▨. $2 \cdot ▨ = 4$

Check: $y = 2$ $▨ = 4$

        $▨ = 2$ true

$y = 2$ and $2y = 4$ are equivalent.

2. Show that $x = 1$ and $3(x + 1) = 6$ are equivalent.

$$x = 1 \qquad\qquad\qquad 3(x + 1) = 6$$

Solution: ▨   → Replace x with ▨. $3(▨ + 1) = 6$

Check: $x = 1$ $3(▨) = 6$

        $▨ = 1$ $▨ = 6$

         true   true

$x = 1$ and $3(x + 1) = 6$ are equivalent.

Practice

Show that each pair of equations is equivalent.

1. $y = 5$ and $y - 2 = 3$ **2.** $y = 8$ and $y \div 4 = 2$

3. $x = 9$ and $x + 3 = 12$ **4.** $b = 6$ and $3b = 18$

5. $x = 4$ and $5 = 3x - 7$ **6.** $y = 4$ and $4 = 2(y - 2)$

7. $a = 10$ and $20 = a + 10$ **8.** $b = 5$ and $18 = 3 + 3b$

Cooperative Learning

9. Explain to a partner how you show that the equations in number **6** in **Practice** are equivalent.

10. Write an equation that is equivalent to $x = 5$. Ask a partner to show that $x = 5$ and your equation are equivalent.

These three equations are equivalent. They show facts or **properties of equality.** Later, you will use these facts to solve equations.

$x = 8$

Solution: 8

Check: $x = 8$

$8 = 8$

$x + 2 = 8 + 2$

Solution: 8

Check: $x + 2 = 8 + 2$

$8 + 2 = 8 + 2$

$10 = 10$

$x - 3 = 8 - 3$

Solution: 8

Check: $x - 3 = 8 - 3$

$8 - 3 = 8 - 3$

$5 = 5$

Adding the same number to both sides or subtracting the same number from both sides of an equation gives an equivalent equation.

▶ **EXAMPLE 1**

$x = 9$ and $x + 5 = 9 + ?$ are equivalent.

5 is added to left side. $x + 5 = 9 + ?$

Add 5 to the right side. $x + 5 = 9 + 5$

$x = 9$ and $x + 5 = 9 + 5$ are equivalent.

These three equivalent equations show other properties.

$x = 12$

Solution: 12

Check: $x = 12$

$12 = 12$

$2 \bullet x = 2 \bullet 12$

Solution: 12

Check: $2 \bullet x = 2 \bullet 12$

$2 \bullet 12 = 2 \bullet 12$

$24 = 24$

$x \div 2 = 12 \div 2$

Solution: 12

Check: $x \div 2 = 12 \div 2$

$12 \div 2 = 12 \div 2$

$6 = 6$

Multiplying or dividing both sides of an equation by the same number gives an equivalent equation.

▶ **EXAMPLE 2**

$x = 16$ and $x \div 4 = 16 \div ?$ are equivalent.

Left side divided by 4. $x \div 4 = 16 \div ?$

Divide right side by 4. $x \div 4 = 16 \div 4$

$x = 16$ and $x \div 4 = 16 \div 4$ are equivalent.

Complete to have equivalent equations.

1. $x = 5$

$x - \blacksquare = 5 - 2$

$x = 5$ and $x - \blacksquare = 5 - 2$
are equivalent.

2. $y = 10$

$\blacksquare \bullet y = 2 \bullet 10$

$y = 10$ and $\blacksquare \bullet y = 2 \bullet 10$
are equivalent.

Practice

Complete to have equivalent equations.

1. $7 = x$
$7 - 2 = x - ?$

2. $a = 30$
$a \div ? = 30 \div 10$

3. $t = 6$
$t \times ? = 6 \times 3$

4. $y = 5$
$y + ? = 5 + 2$

5. $y = 20$
$? \times y = 3 \times 20$

6. $x = 9$
$x \div ? = 9 \div 3$

7. $z = 12$
$3 + z = 12 + ?$

8. $w = 5$
$? + w = 5 + 7$

9. $b = 10$
$b \div ? = 10 \div 2$

10. $c = 13$
$c - ? = 13 - 3$

Cooperative Learning

11. Explain to a partner how you complete the equation in **6**
in **Practice.**

12. Write an equation equivalent to $a = 5$. Then remove a number
from your equation. Ask a partner to fill in the missing number.

To solve equations you will need to "undo" operations. Try to remember what you know about addition and subtraction to see what this means.

$$\underline{(5 - 2)} + 2 \qquad \underline{(5 + 2)} - 2$$
$$\underline{3 + 2} \qquad \underline{7 - 2}$$
$$5 \qquad \qquad 5$$

Adding and subtracting the same number from 5 does not change 5. Addition "undoes" subtraction. Subtraction "undoes" addition. Addition and subtraction are **inverse operations.**

> **EXAMPLE 1**

Complete. $(8 + 3) - ? = 8$

Undo addition. $(8 + 3) - ? = 8$

Subtract 3. $(8 + 3) - 3 = 8$

$(8 + 3) - 3 = 8$

Multiplication undoes division. Division undoes multiplication. Multiplication and division are **inverse operations.**

$$\underline{(6 \times 3)} \div 3 \qquad \underline{(6 \div 3)} \times 3$$
$$\underline{18 \div 3} \qquad \underline{2 \times 3}$$
$$6 \qquad \qquad 6$$

Multiplying and dividing by the same number does not change 6.

> **EXAMPLE 2**

Complete. $(15 \div 5) \times ? = 15$

Undo division. $(15 \div 5) \times ? = 15$

Multiply by 5. $(15 \div 5) \times 5 = 15$

$(15 \div 5) \times 5 = 15$

Try These

Complete.

1. $(10 \times 4) \div \blacksquare = 10$

Undo multiplication.

Divide by $\blacksquare$.

$(10 \times 4) \div \blacksquare = 10$

2. $(20 - 10) + \blacksquare = 20$

Undo subtraction.

Add $\blacksquare$.

$(20 - 10) + \blacksquare = 20$

Practice

Complete.

1. $(9 \times 7) \div \, ? = 9$

2. $(12 + 8) - \, ? = 12$

3. $(16 - 7) + \, ? = 16$

4. $(4 \div 2) \times \, ? = 4$

5. $(36 \div 9) \times \, ? = 36$

6. $(10 \times 5) \div \, ? = 10$

7. $(50 \times 2) \div \, ? = 50$

8. $(20 \div 10) \times \, ? = 20$

9. $(13 - 8) + \, ? = 13$

10. $(25 \times 3) \div \, ? = 25$

11. $(30 - 20) + \, ? = 30$

12. $(50 + 15) - \, ? = 50$

Cooperative Learning

13. Explain to a partner how to complete number **8** in **Practice**.

14. Write an example to show how multiplication "undoes" division. Remove a number from your example. Ask a partner to fill in the missing part.

Solving Equations by Subtracting

The equation $x = 6$ can be solved just by looking at it. The equation $x + 4 = 9$ is not as easy to solve. You can use subtraction to undo the addition. This will give an equivalent equation that is easier to solve.

 **EXAMPLE 1**

Solve. Then, check the solution. $x + 4 = 9$

Undo addition with subtraction. $\qquad x + 4 = 9$

Subtract 4 from both sides. $\qquad x + 4 - 4 = 9 - 4$

Remember
To simplify means to perform the operations.

Simplify each side. $\qquad x + 0 = 5$

$$x = 5$$

Solution: $\quad$ 5

Check. Replace x with 5. $\qquad x + 4 = 9$

$$5 + 4 = 9$$

$$9 = 9 \quad \text{true}$$

The variable may be on the right side of the equation. Be careful when you subtract the same number from both sides.

 **EXAMPLE 2**

Solve. Then, check the solution. $\quad 12 = 10 + t$

Math Fact
Subtracting the same number from both sides of an equation gives an equivalent equation.

Undo addition with subtraction. $\qquad 12 = 10 + t$

Subtract 10 from both sides. $\qquad 12 - 10 = 10 - 10 + t$

Simplify each side. $\qquad 2 = 0 + t$

$$2 = t$$

Solution: $\quad$ 2

Check. Replace t with 2. $\qquad 12 = 10 + t$

$$12 = 10 + 2$$

$$12 = 12 \quad \text{true}$$

Try These

Solve. Then, check the solution.

1. $13 = b + 3$

$$13 = b + 3$$

Subtract ▓ from both sides. $13 - ▓ = b + 3 - ▓$

Simplify each side. $▓ = b + ▓$
$▓ = b$

Solution: ▓

Check. Replace b with ▓.
$$13 = b + 3$$
$$13 = ▓ + 3$$
$$13 = ▓$$
true

2. $n + 8 = 21$

$$n + 8 = 21$$

Subtract ▓ from both sides. $n + 8 - ▓ = 21 - ▓$

Simplify each side. $n + ▓ = ▓$
$n = ▓$

Solution: ▓

Check. Replace n with ▓.
$$n + 8 = 21$$
$$▓ + 8 = 21$$
$$▓ = 21$$
true

Practice

Solve. Then, check the solution.

1. $h + 5 = 9$

2. $c + 6 = 9$

3. $n + 4 = 15$

4. $20 = s + 4$

5. $10 = t + 7$

6. $12 = v + 0$

7. $b + 15 = 17$

8. $11 = x + 9$

9. $x + 5 = 20$

10. $6 + c = 14$

11. $10 = 9 + t$

12. $7 = s + 4$

Cooperative Learning

13. Explain to a partner how you solve the equation in number **8** in **Practice**.

14. Think of a number less than 10. Add this number to the left side of $x = 10$. Ask a partner to solve this new equation. Check the solution.

Solving Equations by Adding

Some equations contain subtraction. You can solve these equations by using addition to undo subtraction. This will give an equivalent equation that is easier to solve.

▶ **EXAMPLE 1**

Math Fact
Adding the same number to both sides of an equation gives an equivalent equation.

Solve. Then, check the solution. $x - 5 = 8$

Undo subtraction with addition.　$x - 5 = 8$
Add 5 to both sides.　　　$x - 5 + 5 = 8 + 5$
Simplify each side.　　　　　$x + 0 = 13$
　　　　　　　　　　　　　　　$x = 13$
　　　　　　　　Solution:　　13
Check. Replace x with 13.　　$x - 5 = 8$
　　　　　　　　　　　　　　$13 - 5 = 8$
　　　　　　　　　　　　　　$8 = 8$　true

▶ **EXAMPLE 2**

Solve. Then, check the solution.　　$9 = y - 2$

Undo subtraction with addition.　　　$9 = y - 2$
Add 2 to both sides.　　　　$9 + 2 = y - 2 + 2$
Simplify each side.　　　　　　$11 = y - 0$
　　　　　　　　　　　　　　　$11 = y$
　　　　　　　　Solution:　　11
Check. Replace y with 11.　　　$9 = y - 2$
　　　　　　　　　　　　　　$9 = 11 - 2$
　　　　　　　　　　　　　　$9 = 9$　true

▶ **EXAMPLE 3**

Math Fact
An equation may contain 0. Solve the equation just as you do with other numbers.

Solve. Then check the solution.　$x - 7 = 0$

Undo subtraction with addition.　　$x - 7 = 0$
Add 7 to both sides.　　　$x - 7 + 7 = 0 + 7$
Simplify each side.　　　　　$x + 0 = 7$
　　　　　　　　　　　　　　　$x = 7$
　　　　　　　　Solution:　　7
Check. Replace x with 7.　　　$x - 7 = 0$
　　　　　　　　　　　　　　$7 - 7 = 0$
　　　　　　　　　　　　　　$0 = 0$　true

Try These

Solve. Then, check the solution.

1. $n - 5 = 20$

$$n - 5 = 20$$

Add ■ to both sides. $\quad n - 5 + ■ = 20 + ■$

Simplify each side. $\qquad n - ■ = ■$

$$n = ■$$

Solution: $\quad$ ■

Check. Replace $n - 5 = 20$
n with ■. $\qquad ■ - 5 = 20$

$$■ = 20$$

true

2. $6 = b - 3$

$$6 = b - 3$$

Add ■ to both sides. $\quad 6 + ■ = b - 3 + ■$

Simplify each side. $\qquad ■ = b - ■$

$$■ = b$$

Solution: $\quad$ ■

Check. Replace $6 = b - 3$
b with ■. $\qquad 6 = ■ - 3$

$$6 = ■$$

true

Practice

Solve. Then, check the solution.

1. $k - 30 = 10$

2. $c - 4 = 16$

3. $n - 8 = 22$

4. $8 = s - 5$

5. $a - 0 = 5$

6. $2 = f - 2$

7. $b - 15 = 20$

8. $40 = x - 20$

9. $c - 7 = 21$

10. $12 = b - 24$

11. $0 = x - 8$

12. $n - 5 = 25$

Cooperative Learning

13. Explain to a partner how you solve the equation in number **7** in **Practice**.

14. Think of a number less than 20. Subtract that number from the left side of $y = 20$. Ask a partner to solve your equation. Check the solution.

Solving Equations by Multiplying

The equation $x \div 3 = 10$ contains division. The variable x is divided by 3. Multiplication by 3 can be used to undo this division. This will give an equivalent equation. The equivalent equation will be easier to solve.

EXAMPLE 1

Math Fact
Multiplying both sides of an equation by the same number gives an equivalent equation.

Solve. Then, check the solution. $x \div 3 = 10$

Undo division with multiplication.	$x \div 3 = 10$
Multiply both sides by 3.	$x \div 3 \times 3 = 10 \times 3$
Simplify each side.	$x = 30$

Solution: 30

Check. Replace x with 30.

$$x \div 3 = 10$$
$$30 \div 3 = 10$$
$$10 = 10 \quad \text{true}$$

EXAMPLE 2

Solve. Then, check the solution. $9 = y \div 2$

Undo division with multiplication.	$9 = y \div 2$
Multiply both sides by 2.	$9 \bullet 2 = y \div 2 \bullet 2$
Simplify each side.	$18 = y$

Solution: 18

Check. Replace y with 18.

$$9 = y \div 2$$
$$9 = 18 \div 2$$
$$9 = 9 \quad \text{true}$$

EXAMPLE 3

Math Fact
$\frac{m}{5}$ means $m \div 5$.

Solve. Then, check the solution. $\frac{m}{5} = 4$

Undo division with multiplication.	$m \div 5 = 4$
Multiply both sides by 5.	$m \div 5 \bullet 5 = 4 \bullet 5$
Simplify each side.	$m = 20$

Solution: 20

Check. Replace m with 20.

$$\frac{m}{5} = 4$$
$$\frac{20}{5} = 4$$
$$20 \div 5 = 4$$
$$4 = 4 \quad \text{true}$$

Try These

Solve. Then, check the solution.

1. $n \div 6 = 5$

	$n \div 6 = 5$
Multiply both sides by ▦.	$n \div 6 \cdot ▦ = 5 \cdot ▦$
Simplify each side.	$n = ▦$
Solution:	▦
Check. Replace n with ▦.	$n \div 6 = 5$
	$▦ \div 6 = 5$
	$▦ = 5$
	true

2. $3 = b \div 6$

	$3 = b \div 6$
Multiply both sides by ▦.	$3 \cdot ▦ = b \div 6 \cdot ▦$
Simplify each side.	$▦ = b$
Solution:	▦
Check. Replace b with ▦.	$3 = b \div 6$
	$3 = ▦ \div 6$
	$3 = ▦$
	true

Practice

Solve. Then, check the solution.

1. $x \div 3 = 5$

2. $t \div 4 = 6$

3. $10 = n \div 4$

4. $2 = s \div 20$

5. $9 = t \div 3$

6. $0 = c \div 10$

7. $m \div 5 = 4$

8. $5 = y \div 8$

9. $d \div 2 = 10$

10. $\frac{n}{5} = 2$

11. $\frac{a}{2} = 6$

12. $y \div 20 = 1$

Cooperative Learning

13. Explain to a partner how you solve the equation in number **11** in **Practice**.

14. Write an equation with $x \div 2$ as the left side. Use any number for the right side. Ask a partner to solve your equation. Check the solution.

The equation $x = 5$ has x or $1 \cdot x$ on the left side and 5 on the right side. This is why it is easy to see that $x = 5$ has a solution of 5. The equation $6x = 18$ has $6x$ or $6 \cdot x$ on the left side. You can undo the multiplication so that the left side is just x. Use division to undo multiplication.

▶ **EXAMPLE 1**

Math Fact
Dividing both sides of an equation by the same number gives an equivalent equation.

Solve. Then, check. $6x = 18$

Undo multiplication with division.	$6x = 18$
Divide both sides by 6.	$6x \div 6 = 18 \div 6$
Simplify each side.	$x = 3$
	Solution: 3
Check. Replace x with 3.	$6x = 18$
	$6 \cdot 3 = 18$
	$18 = 18$ true

▶ **EXAMPLE 2**

Solve. Then, check. $35 = 7y$

Undo multiplication with division.	$35 = 7y$
Divide both sides by 7.	$35 \div 7 = 7y \div 7$
Simplify each side.	$5 = y$
	Solution: 5
Check. Replace y with 7.	$35 = 7y$
	$35 = 7 \cdot 5$
	$35 = 35$ true

▶ **EXAMPLE 3**

Remember
Parentheses in an equation can be used to show multiplication.

Solve. Then, check. $x(9) = 36$

Undo multiplication with division.	$x(9) = 36$
Divide both sides by 9.	$x(9) \div 9 = 36 \div 9$
Simplify each side.	$x = 4$
	Solution: 4
Check. Replace x with 4.	$x(9) = 36$
	$4(9) = 36$
	$36 = 36$ true

Try These

Solve. Then, check the solution.

1. $n \cdot 8 = 56$

	$n \cdot 8 = 56$
Divide both sides by ■.	$n \cdot 8 \div ■ = 56 \div ■$
Simplify each side.	$n = ■$
Solution:	■
Check. Replace n with ■.	$n \cdot 8 = 56$
	$■ \cdot 8 = 56$
	$■ = 56$
	true

2. $30 = 3b$

	$30 = 3b$
Divide both sides by ■.	$30 \div ■ = 3b \div ■$
Simplify each side.	$■ = b$
Solution:	■
Check. Replace b with ■.	$30 = 3b$
	$30 = 3 \cdot ■$
	$30 = ■$
	true

Practice

Solve. Then, check the solution.

1. $5x = 45$ **2.** $4c = 52$ **3.** $9n = 72$

4. $8s = 24$ **5.** $8t = 16$ **6.** $3 = 3f$

7. $2 \cdot b = 20$ **8.** $50 = 5 \cdot y$ **9.** $14 = 7n$

10. $48 = s(4)$ **11.** $5c = 10$ **12.** $0 = 2x$

Cooperative Learning

13. Explain to a partner how to solve the equation in number **10** in **Practice**.

14. Write an equation with *2n* on the right side. Use any even number on the left side. Ask a partner to solve your equation. Check the solution.

Some equations contain more than one operation. You must undo more than one operation to solve these equations. Follow a special order when you do this. First, undo addition or subtraction. Then, undo multiplication or division.

► **EXAMPLE 1**

Solve. Then, check the solution. $3x - 5 = 16$

Undo subtraction by addition.	$3x - 5 = 16$
Add 5 to both sides.	$3x - 5 + 5 = 16 + 5$
Simplify each side.	$3x - 0 = 21$
Undo multiplication by division.	$3x = 21$
Divide both sides by 3.	$3x \div 3 = 21 \div 3$
Simplify each side.	$x = 7$

Solution: 7

Check. Replace x with 7.

$$3x - 5 = 16$$
$$3 \bullet 7 - 5 = 16$$
$$21 - 5 = 16$$
$$16 = 16 \quad \text{true}$$

► **EXAMPLE 2**

Solve. Then, check the solution. $20 = \frac{y}{2} + 4$

$$20 = \frac{y}{2} + 4$$

Undo addition by subtraction.	$20 = y \div 2 + 4$
Subtract 4 from both sides.	$20 - 4 = y \div 2 + 4 - 4$
Simplify each side.	$16 = y \div 2 + 0$
Undo division with multiplication.	$16 = y \div 2$
Multiply both sides by 2.	$16 \times 2 = y \div 2 \times 2$
	$32 = y$

Solution: 32

Check. Replace y with 32.

$$20 = \frac{y}{2} + 4$$
$$20 = y \div 2 + 4$$
$$20 = 32 \div 2 + 4$$
$$20 = 16 + 4$$
$$20 = 20 \quad \text{true}$$

Try These

Solve. Then, check the solution.

1. $4z + 3 = 23$

$$4z + 3 = 23$$

Subtract ■ from both sides.
$$4z + 3 - ■ = 23 - ■$$

Simplify each side.
$$4z + 0 = ■$$
$$4z = ■$$

Divide both sides by ■.
$$4z ÷ ■ = ■ ÷ 4$$
$$z = ■$$

Solution: ■

Check. Replace z with ■.
$$4z + 3 = 23$$
$$4 • ■ + 3 = 23$$
$$■ + 3 = 23$$
$$■ = 23$$
true

2. $2 = r ÷ 3 - 4$

$$2 = r ÷ 3 - 4$$

Add ■ to both sides.
$$2 + ■ = r ÷ 3 - 4 + ■$$

Simplify each side.
$$■ = r ÷ 3 + 0$$
$$■ = r ÷ 3$$

Multiply both sides by ■.
$$■ • ■ = r ÷ 3 • ■$$
$$■ = r$$

Solution: ■

Check. Replace r with ■.
$$2 = r ÷ 3 - 4$$
$$2 = ■ ÷ 3 - 4$$
$$2 = ■ - 4$$
$$2 = ■$$
true

Practice

Solve. Then, check the solution.

1. $16 = 2x - 8$

2. $18 = 2x + 6$

3. $c ÷ 3 - 5 = 21$

4. $20 = 6 + 7h$

5. $4n - 11 = 17$

6. $w ÷ 7 + 2 = 5$

7. $\frac{n}{2} + 2 = 5$

8. $9 = 4n - 15$

9. $2a - 4 = 132$

Cooperative Learning

10. Explain to a partner how you solve the equation in number **6** in **Practice**.

11. Write the equation $2a = 20$. Think of an even number less than 10. Subtract it from the left side of $2a = 20$. Ask a partner to solve your equation. Check the solution.

Calculator: Checking Solutions

Some equations have large numbers. You can check their solutions with your calculator.

▶ **EXAMPLE 1**

Check if 23 is the solution of $19x - 301 = 136$.

Write the equation. $\qquad$ $19x - 301 = 136$

Replace x with 23. $\qquad$ $19 \cdot 23 - 301 = 136$

Use your calculator to simplify the left side.

		Display
Enter 19 by pressing:	①⑨	*19*
Multiply 23 by pressing:	✕②③	*23*
	⊟	*437*
Subtract 301 by pressing:	⊟③⓪①	*301*
	⊟	*136*

$136 = 136$ is true. 23 is the solution of $19x - 301 = 136$.

▶ **EXAMPLE 2**

Check if 896 is the solution of $42 = 27 + \dfrac{n}{56}$

Write the equation. $\qquad$ $42 = 27 + \dfrac{n}{56}$

Replace n with 896. $\qquad$ $42 = 27 + \dfrac{896}{56}$

Use your calculator to simplify the right side.

		Display
Enter 896 by pressing:	⑧⑨⑥	*896*
Divide by 56 by pressing:	⊟⑤⑥	*56*
	⊟	*16*
Enter 27 by pressing:	②⑦	*27*
Add 16 by pressing:	⊞①⑥	*16*
	⊟	*43*

$42 = 43$ is not true. 896 is **not** the solution of $42 = 27 + \dfrac{n}{56}$.

Practice

Check whether the value of the variable is the solution of the equation.

1. $972 = 27z$ when z is 36

2. $\frac{x}{497} = 29$ when x is 14,413

3. $8c - 67 = 37$ when c is 12

4. $188 = 4r + 8$ when r is 54

5. $37x - 111 = 1554$ when x is 45

6. $351n - 351 = 702$ when n is 4

People in Math

BENJAMIN BANNEKER

Benjamin Banneker

Black Heritage USA 15c

As a young boy in the early 1700s, Benjamin Banneker became interested in math and science. Even though he had no formal schooling, he learned as much as he could on his own. Once, he built a clock out of wood. He used math to help him figure out how to carve each gear. People came from all over to see his clock.

As Banneker grew older, he wanted to study stars and planets. He became so interested in astronomy that he would stay awake all night writing down what he saw. Soon, he taught himself about astronomy, too.

Banneker knew so much about math and science that he was asked to help plan the nation's capital. He helped measure the land's shape, size, and boundaries of what is now Washington, D.C.

Banneker also used his skills to help predict the weather for farmers and sailors. His writing was published in almanacs and books about the weather, the moon, the sun, and the tides. He once sent a copy of his almanac to Thomas Jefferson. Even the future president of the United States was impressed.

One method for solving a problem is to find a pattern. Sometimes the pattern is a number pattern. Look to see how numbers change or repeat to find the pattern.

▶ **EXAMPLE**

Find the pattern. Then, find the next two numbers.
4, 7, 10, 13, _?_, _?_,

READ **What do you need to find out?**
You need to find the next two numbers in the pattern.

PLAN **What do you need to do?**
You need to find how you go from the first number to the second number. Continue until you see a pattern. Then, use it to find the next two numbers.

DO **Follow the plan.**
The numbers are getting larger. 4, 7, 10, 13, _?_, _?_
4 + 3 = 7,   7 + 3 = 10,
10 + 3 = 13   +3 +3 +3 +3 +3

Add 3 to 13 to find the   4, 7, 10, 13, _16_, _?_
next number. 13 + 3 = 16
                                          +3

Add 3 to 16 to find the   4, 7, 10, 13, _16_, _19_
next number. 16 + 3 = 19
                                          +3

CHECK **Does your answer make sense?**
To check the pattern, subtract 3. Start at 19.
4, 7, 10, 13, _16_, _19_   ✓

−3 −3 −3 −3 −3

The next two numbers in the pattern are 16 and 19.

Try These

Find the pattern. Then, find the next two numbers.

1. 2, 6, 18, 54, _?_ , _?_

   The second number is ■ times the first.
   The third number is ■ times the second.
   The fourth number is ■ times the third.
   The next number is ■ × 54.   2, 6, 18, 54, ■ , _?_
   The last number is ■ × ■.   2, 6, 18, 54, ■ , ■
   2, 6, 18, 54, ■, ■

2. 1, 0, 3, 0, 5, 0, _?_ , _?_

   The first number is ■. It is followed by 0.
   The third number is ■. It is followed by 0.
   The fifth number is ■. It is followed by 0.
   The seventh number is ■.   1, 0, 3, 0, 5, 0, ■ , _?_
   It is followed by ■.   1, 0, 3, 0, 5, 0, ■ , ■
   1, 0, 3, 0, 5, 0, ■, ■

Practice

Find the pattern. Then, find the next two numbers.

1. 2, 4, 6, 8, _?_ , _?_   2. 1, 4, 9, 16, _?_ , _?_

3. 32, 16, 8, 4, _?_ , _?_   4. 6, 11, 16, 21, _?_ , _?_

5. 1, 0, 2, 0, 4, 0, 8, _?_ , _?_   6. 6, 9, 5, 8, 4, _?_ , _?_

Cooperative Learning

7. Explain to a partner how to find the pattern and the next two numbers in number 6 in **Practice**.

8. Write a number pattern. Ask a partner to find the next two numbers.

You can use what you know about solving equations to solve formulas. Here are the formulas you will need.

Perimeter of a rectangle = 2 • length + 2 • width
$$P = 2 \bullet l + 2 \bullet w$$

Area of a rectangle = length × width
$$A = l \times w$$

Volume of a box = length × width × height
$$V = l \times w \times h$$

▶ **EXAMPLE 1**

Find the width of a rectangle that has an area of 18 cm² and a length of 6 cm.

Use the area formula.	$A = l \bullet w$
Area is 18. Length is 6.	$A = l \bullet w$
Use 18 for A and 6 for l.	$18 = 6 \bullet w$

Now solve this equation for w.

Divide both sides by 6. $18 \div 6 = 6 \bullet w \div 6$
$$3 = w$$

Solution: 3

Check
$A = lw$
$18 = 6 \bullet 3$
$18 = 18$ true

The width of the rectangle is 3 cm.

▶ **EXAMPLE 2**

Find the length of a rectangle with a perimeter of 14 in. and width of 3 in.

Use the perimeter formula.	$P = 2l + 2w$
Use 14 for P and 3 for w.	$P = 2l + 2w$
Simplify each side.	$14 = 2l + 2 \bullet 3$

Now solve the equation for l.	$14 = 2l + 6$
Subtract 6 from both sides.	$14 - 6 = 2l + 6 - 6$
Simplify each side.	$8 = 2l + 0$
	$8 = 2l$
Divide each side by 2.	$8 \div 2 = 2l \div 2$
	$4 = l$

Solution: 4

Check
$P = 2l + 2w$
$14 = 2 \bullet 4 + 2 \bullet 3$
$14 = 8 + 6$
$14 = 14$ true

The length of the rectangle is 4 in.

Try These

1. Find the height of a box with a volume of 48 in.^{3}, a length of 6 in., and a width of 2 in.

Select the formula.	$V = lwh$
Replace V with ▨ , l with ▨ , and w with ▨.	▨ $=$ ▨ • ▨ • h
Simplify the right side.	▨ $=$ ▨ • h
Divide both sides by ▨.	▨ $= h$
Solution:	▨

The height of the box is ▨ in.

2. Find the width of a rectangle with area of 20 cm^2 and length of 5 cm.

Select the formula.	$A = l • w$
Replace A with ▨ and l with ▨.	▨ $=$ ▨ • w
Divide both sides by ▨.	▨ $= w$
Solution:	▨

The width of the rectangle is ▨ cm.

Practice

Use the formulas.

1. Find the width of a rectangle with a length of 6 yd and a perimeter of 18 yd.

2. Find the width of a rectangle with a length of 10 m and a perimeter of 30 m.

3. Find the width of a rectangle with an area of 24 cm^2 and length of 8 cm.

4. Find the length of a rectangle with an area of 16 in.^{2} and a width of 2 in.

5. Find the height of a box with a volume of 40 in.^{3}, a length of 5 in., and a width of 2 in.

Cooperative Learning

6. Explain to a partner how you find the length of the rectangle in number **4** in **Practice**.

7. The area of a rectangle is 100 cm^2. Ask a partner to find a length and a width for the rectangle that would give this area. Check the numbers in the formula.

Summary

A variable equation is like a balance scale. Each side must be the same number.
Equations are equivalent when they have the same solution.
Adding the same number to both sides of an equation gives an equivalent equation.
Subtracting the same number from both sides of an equation gives an equivalent equation.
Multiplying or dividing both sides of an equation by the same number gives an equivalent equation.
To solve an equation you need to "undo" operations.
You can solve equations by adding, subtracting, multiplying, or dividing.
You must undo more than one operation to solve equations that contain more than one operation.
Finding a pattern is one method for solving problems.
You can use what you know about solving equations to solve formulas.

variable equation

solution

solve

equivalent equations

properties of equality

inverse operations

Vocabulary Review

Complete the sentences with words from the box.

1. To _____ an equation means to find the solution of the equation.

2. An equation containing a variable is called a _____.

3. Variable equations with the same solutions are _____.

4. The value for the variable that makes a variable equation true is the _____.

5. Operations that "undo" each other are _____.

6. The _____ let you add, subtract, multiply, or divide both sides of an equation by the same number to get an equivalent equation.

Chapter Quiz

Tell whether or not the number is a solution of the equation.

1. $22; w - 11 = 11$

2. $2; 2(5 + y) = 10$

Show that each pair of equations is equivalent.

3. $c = 3$ and $8 = 20 - 4c$

4. $d = 40$ and $4 = d \div 10$

Complete to have equivalent equations.

5. $14 = y$
$14 \times 2 = y \times ?$

6. $20 = t$
$2 + 20 = ? + t$

Complete.

7. $(50 \div 10) \times ? = 50$

8. $(50 \times 25) \div ? = 50$

Solve. Then, check the solution.

9. $12 + y = 15$

10. $4 = 1 + r$

11. $c - 40 = 10$

12. $5 = t - 15$

13. $t \div 8 = 8$

14. $10 = \frac{x}{3}$

15. $28 = 4y$

16. $16 = y(2)$

17. $10t - 10 = 60$

18. $50 = 20 + 3a$

Find the pattern. Then, find the next two numbers.

19. 3, 1, 4, 2, 5, _?_ , _?_

20. 1, 3, 6, 10, 15, _?_ , _?_

Use the formula.

21. Find the width of a box with a volume of 36 ft^3, a length of 6 ft, and a height of 3 ft.

Chapter 5

Decimals and Algebra

Think about how short a second in time is. How would you like to win or lose a race by one hundredth of a second?

Learning Objectives

- Use place value in decimals.
- Round decimals.
- Add, subtract, multiply, and divide decimals.
- Learn how to move the decimal point.
- Use scientific notation.
- Simplify expressions with decimals.
- Evaluate expressions with decimals.
- Solve equations containing decimals.
- Use a calculator for estimating with decimals.
- Work backward to make a plan and solve problems.
- Apply concepts and skills using frequency tables.

Words to Know

decimal	a number written with a dot; values of places to the left of the dot are greater than 1. Values of places to the right are less than 1.
decimal point	the dot in a decimal; it separates the part greater than 1 from the part less than 1.
scientific notation	a number written as the product of two factors; the first factor is a decimal and the second factor is a power of ten.
tally	a way to keep a count
frequency table	a table that shows counts of items in different groups

Decimal Project

Research newspapers and on-line for results of the 2000 Summer Olympics in Australia. Choose three timed events. Then find the top three winners in each event. Record their times on a place-value chart. Give the time differences among the three in each category. Present your results to the class.

You can use what you know about whole numbers and place value to find the place value of **decimals.**

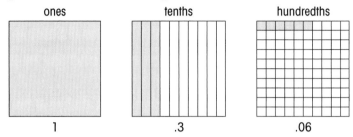

ones   tenths   hundredths

1   .3   .06

1.36 is read 1 and 36 hundredths.

EXAMPLE 1

Give the value of each digit in 1.36.
    1 is in the ones place. 1 has a value of 1.
    3 is in the tenths place. It has a value of .3 or 3 tenths.
    6 is in the hundredths place. It has a value of .06 or 6 hundredths.

Digits to the left of the **decimal point** have a value of 1 or greater. Digits to the right of the decimal point have a value less than 1.

ones		tenths	hundredths	thousandths	← Read
3	.	0	1	7	← 3 and 17 thousandths
3	.	2			← 3 and 2 tenths

EXAMPLE 2

Compare 3.017 and 3.2.
Line up the decimal points.   3.017
                                    3.2

Math Fact
> means *is greater than.*

Compare digits left to right. $2 > 0$
So, $3.2 > 3.017$.

EXAMPLE 3

Compare 7.2 and 7.20.   ← This zero has no value.
Line up the decimal points.   7.2
                                      7.20

Compare digits left to right. $2 = 2$

$7.2 = 7.20$

Try These

1. Give the value of each digit in 21.45

2 is in the tens place.
2 has a value of 20.

1 is in the ■ place.
1 has a value of ■.

■ is in the tenths place.
It has a value of ■ tenths.

5 is in the ■ place.
It has a value of ■.

2. Compare 9.301 and 9.31.

Line up the decimal points.

9.301
9.31

Compare digits left to right.   3 = 3

Compare the next digits to the right.   ■ < 1

Is 9.301 less than 9.31? Yes or no?   ■

9.301 ■ 9.31

Practice

Give the value of each digit.

1. 9.5

2. 7.70

3. 15.95

4. 122.5

5. 0.11

6. 10.87

Compare the numbers.

7. 1.0 and 1.1

8. 2.3 and 2.30

9. 50.5 and 55.0

10. 33.912 and 33.902

11. 215.4 and 215.41

12. 67.4 and 67.40

Cooperative Learning

13. Write a decimal, and have a partner read it. Then, have the partner give the value of each digit.

14. Write a pair of decimals. Have a partner compare them.

5·2 ▸ Rounding Decimals

Rounding decimals means changing a decimal to the nearest tenth, hundredth, thousandth, and so on. Place value is used when rounding decimals. This number line can help you round decimals.

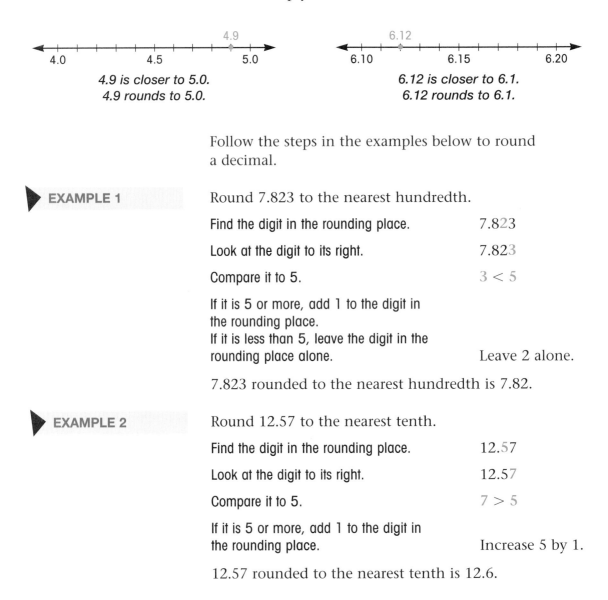

4.9 is closer to 5.0.
4.9 rounds to 5.0.

6.12 is closer to 6.1.
6.12 rounds to 6.1.

Follow the steps in the examples below to round a decimal.

▶ **EXAMPLE 1**

Round 7.823 to the nearest hundredth.

Find the digit in the rounding place.	7.823
Look at the digit to its right.	7.823
Compare it to 5.	3 < 5
If it is 5 or more, add 1 to the digit in the rounding place. If it is less than 5, leave the digit in the rounding place alone.	Leave 2 alone.

7.823 rounded to the nearest hundredth is 7.82.

▶ **EXAMPLE 2**

Round 12.57 to the nearest tenth.

Find the digit in the rounding place.	12.57
Look at the digit to its right.	12.57
Compare it to 5.	7 > 5
If it is 5 or more, add 1 to the digit in the rounding place.	Increase 5 by 1.

12.57 rounded to the nearest tenth is 12.6.

Try These

1. Round 6.237 to the nearest hundredth.

Find the digit in the rounding place.	6.237
Look at the digit to its right.	6.237
Compare it to 5.	7 ▇ 5
If it is 5 or more, add 1 to the digit in the rounding place.	Increase 3 by 1.

6.237 rounded to the nearest hundredth is ▇.

2. Round 7.326 to the nearest hundredth.

Find the digit in the rounding place.	7.326
Look at the digit to its right.	7.326
Compare it to 5.	6 ▇ 5
If it is 5 or more, add 1 to the digit in the rounding place.	Increase 2 by 1.

7.326 rounded to the nearest hundredth is ▇.

Practice

Round to the nearest hundredth.

1. 0.123   **2.** 1.465   **3.** 12.897

4. 6.029   **5.** 7.909   **6.** 8.222

Round to the nearest tenth.

7. 3.211   **8.** 6.554   **9.** 19.127

10. 4.087   **11.** 8.99   **12.** 1.111

Cooperative Learning

13. As a class, write numbers with decimals. Write the name of each place above the numbers.

14. Work with a partner. Write a decimal with place values of hundredths and thousandths. Round to the nearest tenth. Then, round to the nearest hundredth.

5·3 ▶ Adding and Subtracting Decimals

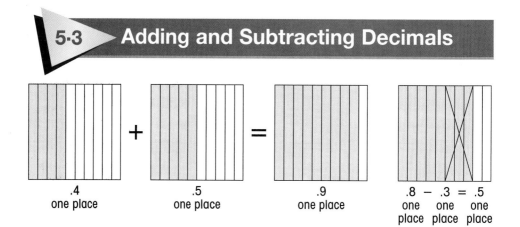

| .4 | .5 | .9 | .8 − .3 = .5 |
| one place | one place | one place | one one one place place place |

There are the same number of places in the sum as in the decimals you are adding. There are the same number of places in the difference as in the decimals you are subtracting.

▶ **EXAMPLE 1**

Add.   16.25 + 8.12

Line up the decimal points.
$$16.25$$
$$+\ 8.12$$

Add.
Place the decimal point in the sum.
$$\overset{1}{}$$
$$16.25$$
$$+\ 8.12$$
$$\overline{24.37}$$

▶ **EXAMPLE 2**

Subtract. 5.29 − 1.75

Line up the decimal points.
$$5.29$$
$$-\ 1.75$$

Subtract.
Place the decimal point in the difference.
$$\overset{4}{}\overset{12}{}$$
$$5.29$$
$$-\ 1.75$$
$$\overline{3.54}$$

Sometimes you have to write zeros before you add or subtract so that all decimals will have the same number of places.

▶ **EXAMPLE 3**

Add. 9 + 1.05 + 20.3

Write zeros and line up the decimal points.
$$9.00$$
$$1.05$$
$$+\ 20.30$$

Add.
Place the decimal point in the sum.
$$9.00$$
$$11.05$$
$$+\ 20.30$$
$$\overline{30.35}$$

Try These

1. Add. $39 + 2.13$

Write zeros and line up the decimal points.

$$\begin{array}{r} 39.00 \\ +\ 2.13 \end{array}$$

Add.
Place the decimal point in the sum.

$$\begin{array}{r} ■ \\ 39.00 \\ +\ 2.13 \\ \hline ■■.■■ \end{array}$$

The sum of 39 and 2.13 is ■.

2. Subtract. $67 - 6.92$

Write zeros and line up the decimal points.

$$\begin{array}{r} 67.■■ \\ -\ 6.92 \end{array}$$

Subtract.
Place the decimal point in the difference.

$$\begin{array}{r} ■\ ■■ \\ 67.■■ \\ -\ 6.92 \\ \hline ■■.■■ \end{array}$$

The difference of 67 and 6.92 is ■.

Practice

Add or subtract.

1. $2.7 + 8.4$

2. $3.67 + 4.83$

3. $1.745 + 2.8$

4. $7.6 - 4.5$

5. $6.87 - 4.99$

6. $2.348 - 1.76$

7. $5 + 2.8$

8. $3.78 + 25$

9. $1.639 + .967$

10. $9.3 + 12$

11. $10 - 8.63$

12. $.05 - .007$

Cooperative Learning

13. Work with a partner. Use decimals to write an addition problem. Have your partner find the sum. Check the work.

14. Work with a partner. Use decimals to write a subtraction problem. Have your partner find the difference. Check the work.

5·4 Multiplying Decimals

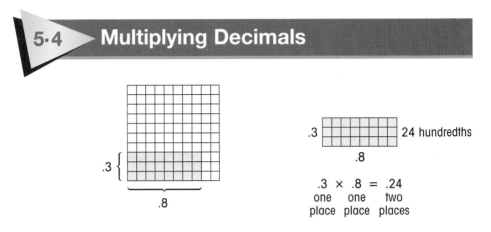

.3 ☐☐☐☐ 24 hundredths
.8

.3 × .8 = .24
one   one   two
place place places

When you multiply, the number of decimal places in the product is equal to the sum of the decimal places in the factors.

▶ **EXAMPLE 1**

Multiply. 4.25×1.5

Multiply.

```
  1  2
  4 . 2 5
× 1 . 5
  2 1 2 5
  4 2 5 0
  6 3 7 5
```

Place the decimal point.

```
  1  2
  4 . 2 5   ←    2 places
× 1 . 5     ← + 1 place
  2 1 2 5          3 places
  4 2 5 0
  6 . 3 7 5  ←
```

$4.25 \times 1.5 = 6.375$

Sometimes you have to write zeros in the product before you can place the decimal point.

▶ **EXAMPLE 2**

Multiply. $.03 \times 1.002$

Multiply.

```
  1 . 0 0 2
×     . 0 3
  3 0 0 6
```

Place the decimal point.

```
  1 . 0 0 2 ←    3 places
×     . 0 3 ← + 2 places
. 0 3 0 0 6 ←    5 places
```

$.03 \times 1.002 = .03006$

Try These

1. Multiply. 5.24×5.1

Multiply.	Place the decimal point.	
■ ■	■ ■	
5 . 2 4	5 . 2 4	2 places
× 5 . 1	× 5 . 1	+ 1 place
5 2 4	5 2 4	■ places
2 6 2 0 0	2 6 2 0 0	
■■■■■	■■■■■	

The product of 5.24 and 5.1 is ■.

2. Multiply. 4×3.49

Multiply.	Place the decimal point.	
4 . 0 0	4 . 0 0	■ places
× 3 . 4 9	× 3 . 4 9	+ ■ places
3 6 0 0	3 6 0 0	■ places
1 6 0 0 0	1 6 0 0 0	
1 2 0 0 0 0	1 2 0 0 0 0	
■■■■■■	1 3 . 9 6 0 0	

The product of 4 and 3.49 is ■.

Practice

Multiply.

1. $.7 \times 3.25$

2. $.4 \times 4.57$

3. 2.7×5.68

4. $5.6 \times .25$

5. $6.8 \times .425$

6. $.48 \times 23.5$

7. 9×6.87

8. 2.1×4.08

9. $.40 \times 1.052$

10. 8×1.25

11. 3.4×5.2

12. 1.75×10.5

Cooperative Learning

13. Explain to a partner how to find the product in number **6** in **Practice**.

14. Create a multiplication problem involving decimals. Ask a partner to find the product. Check the work.

5-5 ▶ Multiplying by Moving the Decimal Point

You can use what you know about multiplying by 10, 100, or 1,000 to learn a shortcut.

3.75	3.75	3.75
× 10	× 100	× 1,000
37.50	375.00	3,750.00

Now look at this:

$$3.75 \times 10 = 3\,7\,.\,5 = 37.5$$

1 zero   1 place to the right

$$3.75 \times 100 = 3\,7\,5\,. = 375$$

2 zeros   2 places to the right

$$3.75 \times 1,000 = 3\,7\,5\,0\,. = 3\,7\,5\,0$$

3 zeros   3 places to the right

To multiply by 10, 100, or 1,000, move the decimal point to the right.

EXAMPLE 1

Multiply. 42.4×100

$$42.4 \times 100 = 4\,2\,4\,0\,. = 4{,}240$$

2 zeros   2 places to the right

EXAMPLE 2

Multiply. $42.4 \times 1,000$

$$42.4 \times 1,000 = 4\,2\,4\,0\,0\,. = 42{,}400$$

3 zeros   3 places to the right

Try These

1. Multiply. 62.4×10

Move the decimal point to the right.

How many places? ▦

$62.4 \times 10 =$ ▦.

2. Multiply. $5.1 \times 1,000$

Move the decimal point to the right.

How many places? ▦

$5.1 \times 1,000 =$ ▦.

Practice

Multiply by moving the decimal point.

1. $.723 \times 10$

2. $.478 \times 1,000$

3. 2.79×10

4. 8.92×100

5. 9.52×100

6. $13.24 \times 1,000$

7. $.743 \times 100$

8. $.467 \times 1,000$

9. 2.71×10

10. 8.92×100

11. $9.52 \times 1,000$

12. 1.32×10

13. 1.4×100

14. 2.92×10

15. $3.47 \times 1,000$

16. $.54 \times 10$

17. 1.87×100

18. $1.650 \times 1,000$

19. 1.5×100

20. $.25 \times 1,000$

21. $2.95 \times 1,000$

Cooperative Learning

22. Explain to a partner how you find the product in number **18** in **Practice**.

23. Write a number. Ask a partner to move the decimal point to multiply the number by 10, by 100, and by 1,000. Check the work.

5·6 Dividing Decimals

When dividing decimals, you may need to divide a decimal by a whole number.

EXAMPLE 1

Divide. $38.1 \div 6$

Place the decimal point in the quotient over the decimal point in the dividend.

Divide as with whole numbers. You may need to place zeros in the dividend to continue.

Math Fact
The divisor is 6.
38.1 is the dividend.

$$6)\overset{.}{38.1}$$

$\longrightarrow$

$$\begin{array}{r} 6.35 \\ 6)\overline{38.10} \\ -36 \\ \hline 2\,1 \\ -1\,8 \\ \hline 30 \\ -30 \\ \hline 0 \end{array}$$

$38.1 \div 6 = 6.35$

Multiplying the divisor and the dividend by 10, 100, or 1,000 will not change the quotient.

$$2)\overset{.2}{\overline{.4}} \qquad 20)\overset{.\,2}{\overline{4\,0\,.\,0}} \qquad 200)\overset{.\,2}{\overline{4\,0\,.\,0}} \qquad 2,000)\overset{.\,2}{\overline{4\,0\,0\,.\,0}}$$

When the divisor is a decimal, multiply the divisor and the dividend by 10, 100, or 1,000. Then, your divisor becomes a whole number.

EXAMPLE 2

Divide. $.465 \div .15$

$$1\,5\,.)\overset{.}{4\,6\,.\,5}$$

$\longrightarrow$

$$\begin{array}{r} 3.1 \\ 15)\overline{46.5} \\ -45 \\ \hline 1\,5 \\ -1\,5 \\ \hline 0 \end{array}$$

$.465 \div .15 = 3.1$

Try These

Divide.

1. 24.3 ÷ 9

Place the decimal point.
Then, divide.

```
      2.■
  9)24.3
   −18
    ■■
  −■■
      0
```

24.3 ÷ 9 = 2.■

2. .828 ÷ .23

Multiply the divisor and dividend by ■.

8 2 . 8 ÷ 2 3 .

```
       3.■
  23)82.8
    −69
     ■■■
   −■■■
```

.828 ÷ .23 = 3.■

Practice

Divide.

1. 21.6 ÷ 2.7

2. 37.2 ÷ 3.1

3. 8.61 ÷ .7

4. 8.92 ÷ .4

5. 9.52 ÷ .17

6. 132 ÷ 3.3

7. 4.6 ÷ 23

8. 30.02 ÷ 7.9

9. 27 ÷ 4.5

10. 47.12 ÷ 15.2

11. 22.5 ÷ 1.5

12. 9.63 ÷ .3

13. 3.94 ÷ .4

14. 13.16 ÷ .8

15. 6.125 ÷ .25

Cooperative Learning

16. Explain to a partner how you divide in number **3** in **Practice**.

17. Create a division problem involving decimals. Ask a partner to do the division. Check the work.

5-7 Dividing by Moving the Decimal Point

You can use what you know about multiplying or dividing by powers of ten to learn a shortcut.

$$\begin{array}{r} .08 \\ 10\overline{)\,.80} \\ -80 \\ \hline 0 \end{array} \qquad \begin{array}{r} .008 \\ 100\overline{)\,.800} \\ -800 \\ \hline 0 \end{array} \qquad \begin{array}{r} .0008 \\ 1{,}000\overline{)\,.8000} \\ -8000 \\ \hline 0 \end{array}$$

Now look at this:

$$.8 \div 10 = .0\,8 = .08$$

1 zero   1 place to the left

$$.8 \div 100 = .0\,0\,8 = .008$$

2 zeros   2 places to the left

$$.8 \div 1{,}000 = .0\,0\,0\,8 = .0008$$

3 zeros   3 places to the left

To divide by 10, 100, or 1,000, move the decimal point to the left.

EXAMPLE 1

Divide. $56.7 \div 100$

$$56.7 \div 100 = .5\,6\,7 = .567$$

2 zeros   2 places to the left

EXAMPLE 2

Divide. $56.7 \div 1{,}000$

$$56.7 \div 1{,}000 = .0\,5\,6\,7 = .0567$$

3 zeros   3 places to the left

Try These

1. Divide. $14.9 \div 10$

   Move the decimal point to the left.

   How many places? ▦

   $14.9 \div 10 =$ ▦

2. Divide. $28.7 \div 1,000$

   Move the decimal point to the left.

   How many places? ▦

   $28.7 \div 1,000 =$ ▦

Practice

Divide by moving the decimal point.

1. $8.32 \div 10$
2. $49.8 \div 1,000$
3. $1.68 \div 10$

4. $7.81 \div 100$
5. $84.1 \div 100$
6. $243.5 \div 1,000$

7. $96.5 \div 100$
8. $3.78 \div 1,000$
9. $46.2 \div 10$

10. $10.81 \div 10$
11. $7.46 \div 1,000$
12. $2.48 \div 1,000$

13. $252.2 \div 100$
14. $1.83 \div 10$
15. $2.69 \div 1,000$

16. $.57 \div 100$
17. $64.2 \div 100$
18. $25.54 \div 1,000$

19. $700 \div 1,000$
20. $29 \div 10$
21. $.50 \div 10$

Cooperative Learning

22. Explain to a partner how you find the quotient in number **16** in **Practice**.

23. Write a number. Have a partner move the decimal point to divide by 10, by 100, and by 1,000. Check the work.

5-8 ▶ Scientific Notation

Scientists often use **scientific notation** to name large numbers. A number in scientific notation has two factors.

$$2.495 \qquad \times \qquad 10^3$$

first factor   second factor

a number between 1 and 10   a power of 10

3 decimal places   power is 3

Math Fact

10^3
$= 10 \times 10 \times 10$
$= 1,000$

You can find the large number by doing the multiplication.

$$2.495 \times 10^3 = 2.495 \times 1,000 = 2\ 4\ 9\ 5\ . = 2,495$$

▶ **EXAMPLE 1**

Find the number named by 4.19×10^2.

$$4.19 \times 10^2$$

10^2 is equal to 100. 4.19×100

Move the decimal point. $4\ 1\ 9\ .$

$$4.19 \times 10^2 = 419$$

▶ **EXAMPLE 2**

Write scientific notation for 8,432.

Find the first factor.   8,432

Move the decimal point 3 places to the left. $8\ .\ 4\ 3\ 2$

3 places to the left means multiply by 1,000.

Find the second factor. 10^3

$$8,432 = 8.432 \times 10^3$$

Try These

1. Find the number named by 3.46×10^3.

$$3.46 \times 10^3 = 3.46 \times \blacksquare$$

Move the decimal point. $3\ 4\ 6\ 0$

$3.46 \times 10^3 = \blacksquare$

2. Write 687 in scientific notation.

Find the first factor. $\blacksquare$

Find the second factor. 10^2

$687 = \blacksquare \times 10^2$

Practice

Find the number named by each.

1. 3.4×10^1

2. 4.6×10^2

3. 5.39×10^2

4. 2.537×10^3

5. 4.564×10^2

6. 1.364×10^4

7. 3.774×10^3

8. 2.509×10^5

9. 8.2×10^4

Write each number in scientific notation.

10. 67

11. 476

12. 6,894

13. 387

14. 49,673

15. 6,297

16. 54,972

17. 349,237

18. 25,025

Cooperative Learning

19. Use scientific notation to name a large number. Have a partner write the number. Check the work.

20. Write a large number. Have a partner write scientific notation for the number. Check the work.

When you work with whole numbers, you simplify variable expressions by combining like terms. You do this by adding or subtracting the numbers that are coefficients of the variables. You do the same thing when the coefficients are decimals. Add or subtract the decimal coefficients.

EXAMPLE 1

Remember
Think: 1.5 + 2.1

Simplify. $1.5x + 2.1x$

Combine like terms. $\underbrace{1.5x + 2.1x}$
$3.6x$

When you combine more than two like terms, combine them two at a time.

EXAMPLE 2

Simplify. $7.4b - 3.1b + b$

Combine like terms. $\underbrace{7.4b - 3.1b} + b$

b means $1b$. $\underbrace{4.3b \quad + 1b}$
$5.3b$

You may have to change the order of terms so that like terms go together. Be sure to move the + or − sign.

EXAMPLE 3

Simplify. $2.25y^2 + 4.5x + 1.05y^2 - 2.2x$

Change the order. $\underbrace{2.25y^2 + 1.05y^2} + \underbrace{4.5x - 2.2x}$
$3.30y^2 \quad + \quad 2.3x$

EXAMPLE 4

Math Fact
Sometimes, only the numbers can be combined.

Simplify. $4.1c + 9.3cd - 8d + 1.2 + 5.7$

Combine like terms. $4.1c + 9.3cd - 8d + \underbrace{1.2 + 5.7}$

$4.1c + 9.3cd - 8d + \quad 6.9$

Practice

Simplify.

1. $9.2a + a + 2.49$

2. $10.6y + y + 9.1 - 6$

3. $2.2c^2 + 5 + 8.4c^2$

4. $x + 2.9y$

5. $7.4 + 3.3c - 2.3$

6. $5.2r + 8.1 - 5r + 3.2$

7. $12.5xy + xy$

8. $3.2v + 6.1 - 1.5s - v$

9. $4.2b^2 - 1.6b + 2.4b^2$

10. $2.25 + .4xy + .5x + 9.3$

11. $5.5 + 12.1r - 2$

12. $15.25 - 2.5 + .5x^2 - .7y$

13. $10.7s + 20.5 - s + 2.3$

14. $.5c^2 + .5d^2$

Cooperative Learning

15. Explain to a partner how to simplify the expression in number **12** in **Practice**.

16. Write a variable expression containing a + sign. Make decimals the coefficients of the variables. Ask a partner to simplify your expression. Check the work.

5·10 Evaluating Expressions

You can find the value of a variable expression with decimals just as you do with whole numbers. Replace the variables with their decimal values. This will give you a number expression. Then perform the operations in the number expressions.

 **EXAMPLE 1**

Evaluate $2.25 - x$ when $x = 1.24$.

Replace x with 1.24.	$2.25 - x$
Subtract.	$2.25 - 1.24$
	1.01

The value of $2.25 - x$ is 1.01 when $x = 1.24$.

 **EXAMPLE 2**

Math Fact
b^2 means b times b.

Evaluate $b^2 + 2.1b$ when $b = 3.1$.

$$b^2 + 2.1b$$

Replace b with 3.1 $b \cdot b + 2.1b$

Perform the operations. $\underline{(3.1)(3.1)} + \underline{2.1(3.1)}$

$$\underbrace{9.61 \quad + \quad 6.51}$$

$$16.12$$

The value of $b^2 + 2.1b$ is 16.12 when $b = 3.1$.

A variable expression may contain more than one variable. Replace each variable with its value when you evaluate the expression.

▶ **EXAMPLE 3**

Remember
Work inside parentheses first.

Evaluate $r(s - 1)$ when $r = 5.2$ and $s = 8.1$.

Replace r with 5.2 and $r(s - 1)$
s with 8.1. $5.2\underbrace{(8.1 - 1)}$

Perform the operations. $5.2(7.1)$

$$36.92$$

The value of $r(s - 1)$ is 36.92 when $r = 5.2$ and $s = 8.1$.

Try These

Evaluate each variable expression.

1. $4.2x \div 2$ when $x = 2.1$

	$4.2x \div 2$
Replace x with 2.1.	$4.2 \cdot x \div 2$
Perform the operations.	$4.2 \cdot \blacksquare \div 2$
	$\blacksquare \div 2$
	$\blacksquare$

The value of $4.2x \div 2$ is $\blacksquare$ when $x = 2.1$.

2. $6c - d$ when $c = 2.1$ and $d = 3.4$

	$6c - d$
Replace c with 2.1 and d with 3.4.	$6 \cdot c - d$
	$6 \cdot 2.1 - \blacksquare$
Perform the operations.	$\blacksquare - \blacksquare$
	$\blacksquare$

The value of $6c - d$ is $\blacksquare$ when $c = 2.1$ and $d = 3.4$.

Practice

Evaluate each variable expression.

1. $1.5y$ when $y = 6.3$

2. $8(b + 1)$ when $b = 2.2$

3. $2a(b + 1)$ when $a = 2.4$ and $b = 1.1$

4. $2l + 2w$ when $l = 5.7$ and $w = 2.3$

5. $9.8 \div m$ when $m = .4$

6. $4.3(x - 2)$ when $x = 5.7$

7. $s^2 + s$ when $s = 2.1$

8. lw when $l = 12.5$ and $w = 6.5$

9. $x + 3y + 4.5$ when $x = 2.5$ and $y = 5.5$

10. $a^2 + b$ when $a = .5$ and $b = 2.2$

Cooperative Learning

11. Explain to a partner how to evaluate the variable expression in number **10** in **Practice**.

12. Write a variable expression with c and d. Use addition and multiplication in the expression. Have a partner evaluate the expression when $c = 2.5$ and $d = 1.25$. Check the work.

5·11 ▶ Solving Equations with Decimals

You solve equations with decimals just as you solve equations with whole numbers. Remember that addition and subtraction undo each other. Multiplication and division undo each other.

▶ **EXAMPLE 1**

Solve. Then, check the solution. $y - 6.2 = 7.9$

Undo subtraction with addition. $y - 6.2 + 6.2 = 7.9 + 6.2$

Add 6.2 to both sides.

Simplify each side.
$$y - 0 = 14.1$$
$$y = 14.1$$

Solution: 14.1

Check. Replace y with 14.1.
$$y - 6.2 = 7.9$$
$$14.1 - 6.2 = 7.9$$
$$7.9 = 7.9 \text{ true}$$

Sometimes you have to undo more than one operation to solve an equation.

▶ **EXAMPLE 2**

Math Fact
Undo addition or subtraction first. Then, undo multiplication or division.

Solve. Then, check. $10.1 = 2.2x + 1.3$

Undo addition with subtraction. $10.1 - 1.3 = 2.2x + 1.3 - 1.3$

Subtract 1.3 from both sides.

Simplify each side. $8.8 = 2.2x$

Undo multiplication with division.

Divide both sides by 2.2. $8.8 \div 2.2 = 2.2x \div 2.2$
$$4 = x$$

Solution: 4

Check. Replace x with 4.
$$10.1 = 2.2x + 1.3$$
$$10.1 = 2.2(4) + 1.3$$
$$10.1 = 8.8 + 1.3$$
$$10.1 = 10.1 \text{ true}$$

Try These

Solve. Then, check.

1. $18.2 = 9.1y$

Undo multiplication
with division. $\quad 18.2 = 9.1y$

Divide both sides
by ■. $\qquad 18.2 \div ■ = 9.1y \div ■$

Simplify each side. $\qquad ■ = y$

$\qquad\qquad$ Solution: $\quad ■$

Check.

Replace y with ■. $\quad 18.2 = 9.1y$
$\qquad\qquad\qquad 18.2 = 9.1(■)$
$\qquad\qquad\qquad 18.2 = ■$ true

2. $3x - 2.1 = 4.8$

Undo subtraction
with addition. $\quad 3x - 2.1 = 4.8$

Add ■ to $\quad 3x - 2.1 + ■ = 4.8 + ■$
both sides. $\qquad\qquad 3x + 0 = ■$

Undo multiplication
with division. $\qquad\qquad 3x = ■$

Divide both
sides by ■. $\qquad 3x \div ■ = ■ \div 3$

Simplify each side. $\qquad x = 2.3$

$\qquad\qquad$ Solution: $\quad ■$

Check.

Replace x
with ■. $\qquad\qquad 3x - 2.1 = 4.8$
$\qquad\qquad\qquad 3(■) - 2.1 = 4.8$
$\qquad\qquad\qquad ■ - 2.1 = 4.8$
$\qquad\qquad\qquad ■ = 4.8$ true

Practice

Solve. Then, check.

1. $x - 2.7 = 10.1$

2. $4.3 = y + 2.1$

3. $2.4m = 4.8$

4. $5.7 = x \div .3$

5. $8.25 = 4a + 1.25$

6. $x \div 2 - 1 = 6.4$

7. $5x - 10.5 = 20.5$

8. $\frac{y}{7} = 1.4$

9. $2l + .5 = 12.9$

10. $5w = 50.25$

Cooperative Learning

11. Explain to a partner how you solve the equation in number **10** in **Practice**.

12. Write the equation $2.4 = 2y$. Add any whole number to both sides. Ask a partner to solve your equation. Check the work.

Calculator: Estimating with Decimals

You may want to estimate an answer to operations with decimals before you do the operations on a calculator. Then, compare your estimate to the calculator answer. This will let you check your calculator answer to be sure you pressed the correct keys.

EXAMPLE 1

Add. 38.92 + 10.4 + 18.9

Estimate first. Round each number to the nearest ten.
Then, add.   40 + 10 + 20 = 70
Your calculator answer should be close to 70.

		Display
Enter 38.92 by pressing:	3 8 . 9 2	38.92
Then, add 10.4 by pressing:	+ 1 0 . 4 =	49.32
Then, add 18.9 by pressing:	+ 1 8 . 9 =	68.22

The calculator displays 68.22. This is close to your estimate of 70.

EXAMPLE 2

Subtract. 1.8872 − .6423

Estimate first. Round each number to the nearest tenth.
Then, subtract.   1.9 − .6 = 1.3
Your calculator answer should be close to 1.3.

		Display
Enter 1.8872 by pressing:	1 . 8 8 7 2	1.8872
Then, subtract .6423 by pressing:	− . 6 4 2 3	
	=	1.2449

The calculator displays 1.2449. This is close to your estimate of 1.3.

Practice

Round each decimal to the nearest whole number to estimate the answer. Compare your calculator answer to your estimate.

1. 90.45 + 78.8

2. 13.547 − 11.2

3. 19.15 × 2.1

4. 15.45 ÷ 3.3

5. 47.147 + 19.5

6. 36.7 − 10.92

Round each decimal to the nearest tenth to estimate the answer. Compare your calculator answer to your estimate.

7. 3.426 + .1387

8. 1.756 − .3789

9. 3.456 × 2.18

10. 1.762 ÷ .251

11. .6759 + .237 + .1958

12. 5.585 − 1.1289

On-the-Job Math

FASHION DESIGNER

Do you enjoy buying new clothes? Do you like putting new outfits together? Can you measure carefully? If so, you might enjoy a career as a fashion designer.

A fashion designer designs and makes clothing. A good understanding of color, fabric, and sizes is needed. Using math is very important, too.

Today, a fashion designer may use a computer to help design a piece of clothing. The fashion designer can choose different fabrics and colors from the computer and see the design before it is made. Then, a pattern is drawn. The pattern is used to cut and sew the fabric.

A fashion designer must be able to estimate the amount of fabric it will take to make a piece of clothing. A good estimate will save a lot of fabric from being wasted. A fashion designer also has to be able to measure carefully. If the measurements are wrong, the piece of clothing will not fit. Then, it cannot be sold.

Problem Solving: Working Backward

You may have to make a plan to solve a problem. Before you use your plan, you may need more information. First, find the information. Then, go back and use your plan.

EXAMPLE

Inez earned $20.00. She received $10.00 as a gift. Then she spent $8.00 for a CD. How much does she have left?

READ **What do you need to find out?**
You need to find how much money Inez has left.

PLAN **What do you need to do?**
You need to work backward, using the information you already have.

DO **Follow the plan.**
Money left = Money in all − Money spent
? = ? − $8.00

Find money in all.
Money in all = Money earned + Gift
= $20.00 + $10.00
= $30.00

Now go back. Use $30.00 for money in all.
Money Left = Money in all − Money spent
$22.00 = $30.00 − $8.00

CHECK **Does your answer make sense?**
If Inez had $30.00 to begin with, then $22.00 left makes sense. ✓

Inez has $22.00 left.

Try These

Solve.

1. Josh bought 4 books at $15.00 each. He also bought a bookcase for $150. How much did he spend in all?

Spent in all =
       Cost of books + Cost of bookcase
   ?   =   ?   +   ■

Cost of books = 4 • ■

Spent in all =
       Cost of books + Cost of bookcase
   ?   =   ■   +   ■

Spent in all = ■

2. The Kim family traveled 550 miles on the first day of their vacation and 525 miles on the second day. They must go a total of 1,500 miles to reach a resort. How far do they still have to go after the two days?

Still to go = Total − Traveled so far
   ?   = 1,500 −   ?

Traveled so far = 550 + ■

Still to go = Total − Traveled so far
   ?   = 1,500 −   ■

Still to go = ■

Practice

1. A store had 250 videotapes at the start of a month. The store received a shipment of 144 tapes during the month. A total of 280 were sold during the month. How many tapes did the store have at the end of the month?

2. Pam has 750 stamps in her collection. She bought 50 more. Then, she sold 75 at a stamp show. How many stamps does Pam have left?

3. The school auditorium has 550 seats. The cost of a ticket to a concert to raise money for team uniforms is $8.00. Twenty seats were empty during the concert. How much money was taken in through the concert?

Cooperative Learning

4. Explain to a partner how you solve number **2** in **Practice**.

5. Write a problem that needs addition and multiplication to solve. Ask a partner to solve it. Check the work.

On Monday, you are taking orders for school T-shirts at the school bookstore. You must keep a **tally** of how many of each size needs to be ordered.

A **frequency table** is a tool you can use to show how many of each size is ordered.

▶ **EXAMPLE 1**

Make a frequency table to show Monday's orders.

Remember
Count or tally by 5.

Size	Tally	Frequency
	The count of each size	Total of each size
S	ЛНТ	5
M	ЛНТ I	6
L	I I I	3
	Monday's total	14

On Monday, 14 T-shirts were ordered:
5 small, 6 medium, 3 large.

▶ **EXAMPLE 2**

Here is a frequency table to show Tuesday's orders.

Size	Tally	Frequency
	The count of each size	Total of each size
S	ЛНТ	5
M	I I I I	4
L	I	1
	Tuesday's total	10

On Tuesday, 10 T-shirts were ordered:
5 small, 4 medium, 1 large.

Try These

1. Complete the frequency table.

Size	Tally	Frequency
	The count of each size	Total of each size
S	ЈΗΤ III	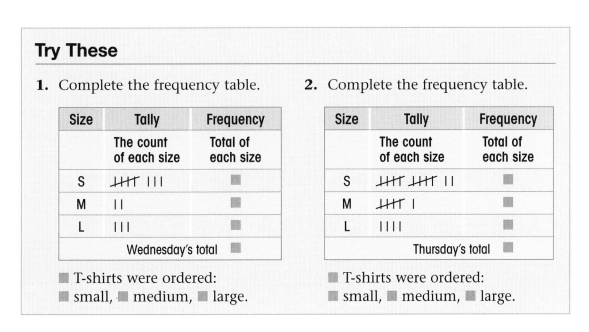
M	II	
L	III	
	Wednesday's total	

 T-shirts were ordered:
 small, medium, large.

2. Complete the frequency table.

Size	Tally	Frequency
	The count of each size	Total of each size
S	ЈΗΤ ЈΗΤ II	
M	ЈΗΤ I	
L	IIII	
	Thursday's total	

T-shirts were ordered:
small, medium, large.

Practice

Look at the frequency table below. It shows the number of cars, buses, and trucks that passed by the school during the day. Use it to answer the questions.

Car, Truck, or Bus	Tally	Frequency
Cars	ЈΗΤ ЈΗΤ ЈΗΤ	?
Buses	ЈΗΤ III	?
Trucks	IIII	?
	total	?

1. How many cars passed by the school?

2. How many trucks passed by the school?

3. How many buses passed by the school?

4. How many cars and buses passed by the school?

Cooperative Learning

5. Pick 3 colors. Work with a partner to make a frequency table showing how many students in your class are wearing each color.

6. Ask your classmates what their favorite sports are. Work with a partner to make a frequency table to show this.

Summary

Digits to the left of the decimal point have a value of 1 or greater.
Digits to the right of the decimal point have a value of less than 1.
There are the same number of places in the sum or difference as in the decimals you are adding or subtracting.
When you multiply, the number of decimal places in the product is equal to the sum of the decimal places in the factors.
To multiply by 10, 100, or 1,000, move the decimal point to the right.
To divide by 10, 100, or 1,000, move the decimal point to the left.
A number in scientific notation has two factors.
When coefficients are decimals, add or subtract them to simplify.
When you combine more than two like terms, combine them two at a time.
You may have to change the order of terms to simplify expressions with decimals.
When you solve equations with decimals, remember that addition and subtraction undo each other. Multiplication and division undo each other.
Working backward and making a plan is a good way to solve problems.
You can make a frequency table to show counts.

decimals
decimal point
scientific notation
tally
frequency table

Vocabulary Review

Complete the sentences with words from the box.

1. The dot that separates the part greater than 1 from the part less than 1 is called the _____.

2. A _____ is a way to keep a count.

3. A _____ shows counts of items in different groups.

4. Numbers written with a dot are called _____.

5. A large number written as the product of two factors is _____.

Chapter Quiz

Give the value of each digit.

1. 3.12   **2.** 25.603   **3.** 425.89

Compare the numbers.

4. 89.1 and 8.91   **5.** 177.5 and 1.775   **6.** 19.5 and 1.95

Round to the nearest hundredth.

7. 0.321   **8.** 2.564   **9.** 14.798

Round to the nearest tenth.

10. 2.311   **11.** 7.652   **12.** 20.215

Add or subtract.

13. 7.3 + 4   **14.** 8.35 − 6.693   **15.** 2 − 1.956

Multiply.

16. .7 × 1.35   **17.** .4 × 2.75   **18.** 11.5 × 2.5

Multiply or divide by moving the decimal point.

19. 25.85 × 10   **20.** 7.30 ÷ 100   **21.** 14 ÷ 10

Write each number in scientific notation.

22. 76   **23.** 240   **24.** 1,694

Simplify.

25. $32.2x^2 - 32.2x$ **26.** $1.5x + 4.2x^2 + x + .9x^2$

Evaluate the variable expression.

27. $(a + b) - 12$ when $a = 7.5$ and $b = 6.25$

Unit 2 **Review**

Choose the letter for the correct answer.

Here is a frequency table of a survey. Use the table to answer Questions 1 and 2.

Favorite Colors	
Color	**Tally**
Red	~~IIII~~ III
Blue	~~IIII~~
Green	~~IIII~~ ~~IIII~~ I

1. How many people like the color red?

   A. 3
   B. 4
   C. 8
   D. 12

2. How many people answered the survey about favorite colors?

   A. 8
   B. 12
   C. 15
   D. 24

3. Bill wants to fence in a garden that is 10 ft wide and 20 ft long. Which expression can be used to find how much fencing he needs?

   A. $l \times w$
   B. $2l + 2w$
   C. $l \times w \times h$
   D. $2(l \times w)$

4. Which is the volume of a box with height of 5 in., width of 3 in., and a length of 10 in.?

   A. 18 cubic inches
   B. 80 cubic inches
   C. 150 cubic inches
   D. 180 cubic inches

5. Which is the width of a rectangle with a length of 8 cm and an area of 48 cm²?

   A. 6 cm
   B. 12 cm
   C. 40 cm
   D. not given

6. Which are the next two numbers in this number pattern?

   8, 10, 9, 11, 10, _?_, _?_,

   A. 10, 11
   B. 12, 11
   C. 11, 12
   D. 10, 12

Critical Thinking

Al has 48 ft of fencing. He wants to enclose a rectangle with the greatest area. What is the length and width of this rectangle?

CHALLENGE Al can use the side of a barn for one side. Now what is the length and width of the rectangle with the greatest area?

Unit Three

A farmer plants crops in many rows. Using this simple pattern makes it easier to harvest. Can you think of some ways this plan makes the farmer's job easier?

Learning Objectives

- Find the factors of a number.
- Find the greatest common factor.
- Find the multiples of a number and the least common multiple of two numbers.
- Tell whether a number is prime or composite.
- Find the prime factorization of a number.
- Use a calculator to check the prime factorization of a number.
- Solve problems by finding a pattern.
- Apply concepts and skills to understand a bar graph.

Words to Know

factors	numbers multiplied to give a product; the product divided by the factor gives a 0 remainder.
divisible	able to be divided by a number giving a 0 remainder; one number is divisible by another.
common factor	a factor of two or more different numbers
greatest common factor (GCF)	the largest common factor of two or more numbers
multiple	the product of a number and a whole number
common multiple	a multiple of two or more different numbers
least common multiple	the smallest common multiple of two or more numbers that is not 0
prime number	a number that has only 1 and itself as factors
composite number	a number that has three or more factors
prime factorization	a number written as the product of its prime factors
bar graph	a way of showing information by using bars
horizontal axis	the line on a bar graph that goes in the left-and-right direction
vertical axis	the line on a bar graph that goes in the up-and-down direction

Numbers Project

Create your own multiplication chart on poster board. As you study the lessons, color code the chart. Use a different color for prime numbers, composite numbers, multiples, and common factors. Display your chart when it is completed.

6·1 Factors and Divisibility

Numbers you multiply are **factors** of the product.

$1 \times 6 = 6$ $2 \times 3 = 6$

$6 \times 1 = 6$ $3 \times 2 = 6$ Factors of 6: 1, 2, 3, 6

1 is a factor of every number. Every number is a factor of itself.

You can also find factors from division with a remainder of 0.

$$\begin{array}{cccc} 6 \text{ R0} & 1 \text{ R0} & 3 \text{ R0} & 2 \text{ R0} \\ 1\overline{)6} & 6\overline{)6} & 2\overline{)6} & 3\overline{)6} \\ \underline{-6} & \underline{-6} & \underline{-6} & \underline{-6} \\ 0 & 0 & 0 & 0 \end{array}$$

Look at 6 divided by 2. The remainder is 0. You can say 2 is a factor of 6. You can also say 6 is **divisible** by 2. Every number is divisible by 1. Every number is divisible by itself.

▶ **EXAMPLE 1**

Tell whether 4 is a factor of 24.

Divide 24 by 4.
Remainder is 0.

$$\begin{array}{r} 6 \text{ R0} \\ 4\overline{)24} \\ \underline{-24} \\ 0 \end{array}$$

4 is a factor of 24.

▶ **EXAMPLE 2**

Tell whether 96 is divisible by 5.

Divide 96 by 5.
Remainder is not 0.

$$\begin{array}{r} 19 \text{ R1} \\ 5\overline{)96} \\ \underline{-5} \\ 46 \\ \underline{-45} \\ 1 \end{array}$$

96 is not divisible by 5.

Try These

1. Tell whether 6 is a factor of 70.

Divide 70 by 6.　　　　　■■ R■
Remainder is ■.　　　6)‾7‾0‾

Is 6 a factor of 70? ■

2. Tell whether 165 is divisible by 15.

Divide 165 by 15.　　　　■■ R■
Remainder is ■.　　　15)‾1‾6‾5‾

Is 165 divisible by 15? ■

Practice

1. Tell whether 3 is a factor of 59.

2. Tell whether 7 is a factor of 84.

3. Tell whether 6 is a factor of 54.

4. Tell whether 4 is a factor of 46.

5. Tell whether 2 is a factor of 64.

6. Tell whether 5 is a factor of 75.

7. Tell whether 17 is a factor of 51.

8. Tell whether 25 is a factor of 130.

9. Tell whether 96 is divisible by 8.

10. Tell whether 67 is divisible by 7.

11. Tell whether 36 is divisible by 9.

12. Tell whether 78 is divisible by 2.

13. Tell whether 84 is divisible by 3.

14. Tell whether 83 is divisible by 2.

Cooperative Learning

15. Write two numbers. Ask a partner to tell whether one of the numbers is a factor of the other. Check the work.

16. Look at number **13** in **Practice**. Explain to a partner how you are able to tell whether or not 84 is divisible by 3.

You already can tell whether one number is a factor of another. Divide and look for a remainder of 0. Now you will see how to find all factors of a number. Use division. Start dividing by 2, then 3, and so on. Look for 0 remainders.

  EXAMPLE 1

Math Fact
1 and 15 divide into 15 with remainder 0.
1 and the number itself are always factors of a number.

Math Fact
Dividing by 5 or greater gives factors you already know.

Find all factors of 15.

1 and 15 are factors. Now, start dividing.

$$\begin{array}{r} 7 \text{ R1} \\ 2\overline{)15} \\ -14 \\ \hline 1 \end{array} \qquad \begin{array}{r} 5 \text{ R0} \\ 3\overline{)15} \\ -15 \\ \hline 0 \end{array} \qquad \begin{array}{r} 3 \text{ R3} \\ 4\overline{)15} \\ -12 \\ \hline 3 \end{array}$$

2 and 7 are not factors.   3 and 5 are factors.   4 is not a factor. Stop!

The factors of 15 are 1, 3, 5, and 15.

A number can be a factor of two different numbers. It is called a **common factor** of the two numbers. The largest common factor of two numbers is called the **greatest common factor** (GCF).

  EXAMPLE 2

Find all factors of 12. Then, find common factors of 12 and 15. Finally, find the greatest common factor of 12 and 15.

1 and 12 are factors of 12.

$$\begin{array}{r} 6 \text{ R0} \\ 2\overline{)12} \\ -12 \\ \hline 0 \end{array} \qquad \begin{array}{r} 4 \text{ R0} \\ 3\overline{)12} \\ -12 \\ \hline 0 \end{array} \qquad \begin{array}{r} 2 \text{ R2} \\ 5\overline{)12} \\ -10 \\ \hline 2 \end{array}$$

2 and 6 are factors.   3 and 4 are factors.   5 is not a factor. Stop!

The factors of 12 are 1, 2, 3, 4, 6, and 12.

From **Example 1,** the factors of 15 are 1, 3, 5, and 15. The factors of 12 are 1, 2, 3, 4, 6, and 12.
Common factors: 1 and 3. Greatest common factor: 3.

Try These

1. Find all factors of 20.

■ and 20 are factors of 20. Divide to find the others.

$$\begin{array}{r} 10 \text{ R}■ \\ 2\overline{)20} \\ -20 \\ \hline ■ \end{array} \qquad \begin{array}{r} ■ \text{ R}■ \\ 3\overline{)20} \\ -18 \\ \hline ■ \end{array} \qquad \begin{array}{r} ■ \text{ R}■ \\ 4\overline{)20} \\ -20 \\ \hline ■ \end{array}$$

Are 2 and 10 factors? ■

Are 3 and ■ factors? ■

Are 4 and ■ factors? ■

Stop!

The factors of 20 are ■, ■, ■, ■, ■, and 20.

2. Find the common factors of 12 and 20. Then, find the greatest common factor of 12 and 20.

From Example 2, the factors of 12 are 1, 2, 3, 4, 6, and 12.

From number 1 of Try These, the factors of 20 are ■, ■, ■, ■, ■, and 20.

The common factors of 12 and 20 are ■, ■, and ■.

The greatest common factor of 12 and 20 is ■.

Practice

Find the factors of each number.

1. 28

2. 32

3. 36

4. 48

5. 64

6. 13

Find the common factors and greatest common factor for each two numbers.

7. 16 and 24

8. 22 and 33

9. 27 and 63

10. 7 and 35

11. 13 and 17

12. 60 and 72

Cooperative Learning

13. Work with a partner to find all the factors of 96. Take turns doing the division. Check each other's work.

14. Find the factors of 45. Ask a partner to find the factors of 65. Work together to find the common factors and greatest common factor of 45 and 65.

6·3　Multiples

A **multiple** of a number is the product of the number and a whole number. To find multiples of a number, multiply the number by 0, 1, 2, 3, and so on. The first four multiples of 2 are:

$$0 \times 2 = 0 \qquad 1 \times 2 = 2 \qquad 2 \times 2 = 4 \qquad 3 \times 2 = 6$$

The first four multiples of 2 are 0, 2, 4, and 6.

 **EXAMPLE 1**

Math Fact
The first two multiples of any number are 0 and the number itself.

Find the first five multiples of 3.

Multiply 3 by the first five whole numbers.

$$0 \times 3 = 0$$
$$1 \times 3 = 3$$
$$2 \times 3 = 6$$
$$3 \times 3 = 9$$
$$4 \times 3 = 12$$

The first five multiples of 3 are 0, 3, 6, 9, and 12.

A **common multiple** of two different numbers is a multiple of both. The **least common multiple** is the smallest common multiple of the two numbers that is not 0.

EXAMPLE 2

Find the first three common multiples of 4 and 6. Then, find the least common multiple of 4 and 6.

Multiples of 4:　　　　0, 4, 8, 12, 16, 20, 24
Multiples of 6:　　　　0, 6, 12, 18, 24, 30, 36

Math Fact
The least common multiple is the smallest multiple that is not 0.

The first three common multiples of 4 and 6 are 0, 12, and 24.

The least common multiple of 4 and 6 is 12.

Try These

1. Find the first five multiples of 7.

   $0 \times 7 = $ ▨

   $1 \times 7 = $ ▨

   $2 \times 7 = $ ▨

   ▨ $\times 7 = 21$

   ▨ $\times 7 = 28$

   The first 5 multiples of 7 are ▨, ▨, ▨, 21, and 28.

2. Find the least common multiple of 6 and 9.

   Multiples of 6:

   $0 \times 6 = $ ▨ $1 \times 6 = $ ▨

   ▨ $\times 6 = 12$ $3 \times 6 = $ ▨

   Multiples of 9:

   $0 \times 9 = $ ▨   ▨ $\times 9 = 9$ $2 \times$ ▨ $= $ ▨

   The common multiples of 6 and 9 are ▨ and ▨.

   The least common multiple is not 0. The least common multiple of 6 and 9 is ▨.

Practice

Find the first five multiples of each.

1. 2   2. 5   3. 10   4. 1

5. 8   6. 12   7. 11   8. 20

Find the least common multiple of each two numbers. Remember that the least common multiple is not 0.

9. 4 and 10   10. 5 and 6   11. 4 and 8   12. 9 and 12

13. 5 and 10   14. 8 and 10   15. 10 and 15   16. 15 and 45

Cooperative Learning

17. Ask a partner to find the first five multiples of 13. Check the work.

18. Work with a partner to find the least common multiple of 2 and 17. Check each other's work.

6·4 Prime and Composite Numbers

A **prime number** is a number that has only two factors. These two factors are 1 and the number. A prime number is divisible by only 1 and the number. Here are some prime numbers.

2, 3, 5, 7

A **composite number** is a number that has more than two factors. A composite number is divisible by more than two numbers. Here are some composite numbers.

4, 6, 8, 9

The numbers 0 and 1 are neither prime nor composite.

EXAMPLE 1

Tell whether 13 is a prime or composite number.

Divide. Look for 0 remainder.

Math Fact
There is no need to divide by 5 or more. These would give you a quotient of 2 or less. We know these numbers are not factors.

$$
\begin{array}{r} 6\ \text{R}1 \\ 2)\overline{13} \\ -12 \\ \hline 1 \end{array}
\qquad
\begin{array}{r} 3\ \text{R}4 \\ 3)\overline{13} \\ -\ 9 \\ \hline 4 \end{array}
\qquad
\begin{array}{r} 3\ \text{R}1 \\ 4)\overline{13} \\ -12 \\ \hline 1 \end{array}
$$

2 and 6 are not factors.   3 and 3 are not factors.   4 and 3 are not factors.   Stop!

Since there are no 0 remainders, 13 is a prime number.

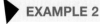
EXAMPLE 2

Tell whether 51 is a prime or composite number.

Divide. Look for 0 remainder.

$$
\begin{array}{r} 25\ \text{R}1 \\ 2)\overline{51} \\ -4 \\ \hline 11 \\ -10 \\ \hline 1 \end{array}
\qquad\qquad
\begin{array}{r} 17\ \text{R}0 \\ 3)\overline{51} \\ -3 \\ \hline 21 \\ -21 \\ \hline 0 \end{array}
$$

2 and 25 are not factors.   3 and 17 are factors.

$3 \times 17 = 51$ 51 is a composite number.

Try These

1. Tell whether 39 is a prime or composite number.

```
    19 R■           1■ R■
  2)39            ■)39
   -2              -3
   ──              ──
   19               9
  -18              -■
   ──              ──
    ■                ■
```

39 is a ■ number.

2. Tell whether 23 is a prime or composite number.

```
    11 R■          7 R■          ■ R■          4 R■
  2)23           ■)23          4)23          5)23
   -2             -21           -20           -20
   ──             ──            ──            ──
    3              ■             ■             ■         Stop!
   -2
   ──
    ■
```

23 is a ■ number.

Practice

Tell whether each of the following numbers is prime or composite.

1. 19	**2.** 21	**3.** 14	**4.** 25
5. 27	**6.** 31	**7.** 91	**8.** 53
9. 81	**10.** 85	**11.** 47	**12.** 120

Cooperative Learning

13. Explain to a partner how you can tell number **7** in **Practice** is a prime or composite number.

14. Work with a partner to tell whether 143 is prime or composite. Take turns doing the division. Check each other's work.

6·5 ▶ Prime Factorization

You can write any composite number as a product of prime numbers. This is called **prime factorization.**

$9 = \underbrace{3 \times 3}_{\text{prime factors}}$ $12 = \underbrace{2 \times 2 \times 3}_{\text{prime factors}}$ $18 = \underbrace{2 \times 3 \times 3}_{\text{prime factors}}$

You can use exponents to write a prime factorization.

$9 = 3^2$ $12 = 2^2 \times 3$ $18 = 2 \times 3^2$

To find the prime factorization of a composite number, you can start by dividing by prime numbers. You can also divide by any numbers you think are factors. Here are prime numbers you may want to use.

2, 3, 5, 7, 11, 13, 17, 19, 23, 29, 31, 37

▶ **EXAMPLE 1**

Find the prime factorization of 24.

Check

$\begin{array}{r} 12 \text{ R0} \\ 2\overline{)24} \\ -24 \\ \hline 0 \end{array}$

2 is a factor of 24.

$12 = 2 \times 6$

$6 = 2 \times 3$

Write using exponents.

$24 = 2 \times \underline{12}$

$24 = 2 \times 2 \times \underline{6}$

$24 = 2 \times 2 \times 2 \times 3$

$24 = 2^3 \times 3$

The prime factorization of 24 is $2^3 \times 3$.

▶ **EXAMPLE 2**

Find the prime factorization of 98.

Check

$\begin{array}{r} 14 \text{ R0} \\ 7\overline{)98} \\ -7 \\ \hline 28 \\ -28 \\ \hline 0 \end{array}$

7 is a factor of 98

$14 = 7 \times 2$

Write using exponents.

$98 = 7 \times \underline{14}$

$98 = 7 \times 7 \times 2$

$98 = 7^2 \times 2$

The prime factorization of 98 is $7^2 \times 2$.

Try These

1. Find the prime factorization of 54.

54

$54 = 3 \times 18$

$54 = 3 \times \blacksquare \times 2$

$54 = 3 \times \blacksquare \times \blacksquare \times 2$

$54 = 3^{\blacksquare} \times 2$

2. Find the prime factorization of 75.

75

$75 = 5 \times \blacksquare$

$75 = 5 \times \blacksquare \times 3$

$75 = 5^{\blacksquare} \times 3$

Practice

Find the prime factorization of each number. Write your answer using exponents whenever possible.

1. 26   **2.** 30   **3.** 45   **4.** 49

5. 27   **6.** 36   **7.** 72   **8.** 60

9. 25   **10.** 78   **11.** 48   **12.** 85

13. 50   **14.** 65   **15.** 90   **16.** 100

Cooperative Learning

17. Explain to a partner how you find the prime factorization of number **14** in **Practice.**

18. Work with a partner to find the prime factorization of 620. Check each other's work.

Calculator: Check the Prime Factorization

You can tell whether a product of prime numbers is a prime factorization of a composite number by using a calculator. Use the calculator to multiply. If the product is equal to the composite number, then the product is the prime factorization.

Here are some prime numbers that you might see in your work.

2, 3, 5, 7, 11, 13, 17, 19, 23, 29, 31, and 37

▶ **EXAMPLE**

Is $2^2 \cdot 3^3 \cdot 7$ the prime factorization of 756?

Write the prime factorization. $2^2 \cdot 3^3 \cdot 7$

Write the powers as products. $2 \cdot 2 \cdot 3 \cdot 3 \cdot 3 \cdot 7$

Use your calculator to multiply.

		Display
Enter 2.	2	2
Multiply by 2 by pressing:	× 2 =	4
Multiply by 3 three times:	× 3 =	12
	× 3 =	36
	× 3 =	108
Multiply by 7 by pressing:	× 7 =	756

$2^2 \cdot 3^3 \cdot 7$ is the prime factorization of 756.

Practice

Use your calculator to find the products.

1. $7^3 \cdot 13^2$

2. $3^4 \cdot 11^3$

3. $11^2 \cdot 13^2$

4. $3^2 \cdot 5^3 \cdot 7^2$

5. $2^2 \cdot 3^3 \cdot 7^2$

6. $5^3 \cdot 7^2 \cdot 11^2$

Use your calculator to check each prime factorization.

7. $5^2 \cdot 7^3$ is 8,575

8. $3^2 \cdot 11^2$ is 3,267

9. $7^2 \cdot 13^2$ is 8,281

10. $2^3 \cdot 3^2 \cdot 7$ is 504

11. $3^2 \cdot 5^3 \cdot 7^2$ is 18,375

12. $2^2 \cdot 3^4 \cdot 5^2$ is 8,100

Math Connection

A PERFECT NUMBER

To a bowler, the number 300 is perfect. It means that the person bowled a perfect game. On a test, the number 100 is perfect. It shows that every question was answered correctly. To a gymnast, 10 is a perfect score. It shows that the gymnastics were perfect.

In math, there are perfect numbers, too. About 2,000 years ago, a Greek named Euclid found that 6 is a perfect number. Why? Euclid found that when the factors of 6 are added, except 6, the sum is 6. The factors of 6 are 1, 2, and 3. The sum of these factors is 6—*perfect*.

Euclid was a third-century Greek mathematician.

Euclid was very interested in perfect numbers. He discovered four perfect numbers. They are 6, 28, 496, and 8,128. Since then, many more perfect numbers have been found. 33,550,336 and 8,589,869,056 are two. With today's computers, who knows how many more we will find.

6-7 ▶ Problem Solving: Find a Pattern

You can solve a problem by finding a pattern.

EXAMPLE

There are three square tables. Each table seats four people. How many people can be seated at the tables if the tables are lined up end to end?

READ   **What do you need to find out?**
You need to find the number of people that can sit at three tables lined up end to end.

PLAN   **What do you need to do?**
You need to draw a diagram to find a pattern.

DO   **Follow the plan.**

Start with 1 table.
One person is
at each side.

$2 + 2 = 4$
Seats 4 people.

Next, use two tables
placed end to end.

$4 + 2 = 6$
Seats 6 people.

Now use
three tables
placed end
to end.

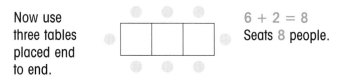

$6 + 2 = 8$
Seats 8 people.

CHECK   **Does your answer make sense?**
Each additional table seats two more people.
Six people can sit at two tables. $6 + 2 = 8$ ✓

Eight people can sit at three square tables lined up end to end.

Try These

Find a pattern to solve the problem.

1. There are four square tables. Each table seats four people. How many people can be seated at the tables if the tables are lined up end to end?

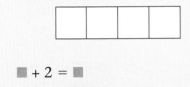

■ + 2 = ■

Four tables seat ■ people.

2. How many fence posts are needed to build a 20 ft fence? Each section of the fence is 5 ft wide. There is 1 post at each end.

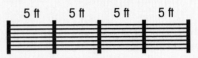

$20 \div 5 =$ ■ sections

4 sections with ■ posts

■ fence posts are needed to build a 20 ft fence.

Practice

Find a pattern to solve the problem.

1. There are six square tables. Each table seats four people. How many people can be seated at the tables if the tables are lined up end to end?

2. There are seven square tables. Each table seats four people. How many people can be seated at the tables if the tables are lined up end to end?

3. How many fence posts are needed to build a 35 ft fence? Each section of the fence is 5 ft wide. There is 1 post at each end.

Cooperative Learning

4. There are three rectangular tables. Each table seats six people, 2 people on each side and 1 person on each end. How many people can be seated at the tables if the tables are lined up end to end? Work with a partner to find out.

5. How many fence posts are needed to build a 48 ft fence? Each section of the fence is 8 ft wide. There is 1 post at each end. Work with a partner to find out.

Application: Bar Graphs

A **bar graph** is used to show amounts. This bar graph shows test scores. It also shows the number of students receiving each score. Bars are drawn on the **horizontal axis** over each test score. The horizontal axis goes in the left to right direction. The **vertical axis** goes in the up and down direction. It shows the number of students. The height of each bar graph tells how many students received that score.

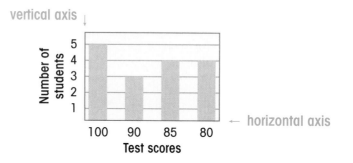

▶ **EXAMPLE 1**

How many students received a score of 85?

Find the bar for 85.   It is the third bar to the right.

Find the height by looking   The height of the 85 bar is 4.
across to the vertical axis.

4 students received a score of 85 each.

▶ **EXAMPLE 2**

What score was received by the most students? How many students received that score?

The highest bar stands
for the most students.   The bar for 100 is the highest.

Find the height by looking   The height of the 100 bar is 5.
across to the vertical axis.

A score of 100 was received by the most students.
5 students received a score of 100.

Try These

Use the bar graph on test scores to answer the questions.

1. What score was received by the fewest students?

The lowest bar stands for the fewest students.

The lowest bar is over ■.

Look at the vertical axis.

■ students received the lowest score.

2. How many more students received 100 than 90?

■ students received 100.

■ students received 90.

$5 - ■ = ■$

■ more students received 100 than 90.

Practice

Use the bar graph on letter grades to answer the questions.

1. What grade was received by the most students?

2. What grade was received by the fewest students?

3. How many more students received an A than a C?

4. How many more students received a D than a B?

5. How many students received a B or better?

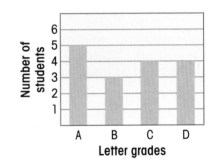

Cooperative Learning

6. Explain to a partner how you find the difference in number **4** in **Practice**.

7. Write a new question about the bar graph on letter grades. Ask a partner to answer it.

Summary

Every number is divisible by 1. Every number is divisible by itself.
You can find all the factors of a number.
1 and the number itself are always factors of a number.
You can find a multiple of a number by multiplying it by a whole number.
You can tell whether a number is prime or composite by dividing.
You can write any composite number as a product of prime factors.
An exponent can be used to write a prime factorization.
You can solve a problem by looking for a pattern.
A bar graph can be used to find amounts.

factor

divisible

common factor

greatest common factor

multiple

common multiple

least common multiple

prime number

composite number

Vocabulary Review

Complete the sentences with words from the box.

1. A number divided by a second number giving a 0 remainder is ____ by that number.

2. The ____ is the largest common factor of two or more numbers.

3. The smallest multiple of two or more numbers that is not 0 is called the ____.

4. A ____ is a number multiplied to give a product.

5. A factor of two different numbers is called a ____.

6. A multiple of two different numbers is a ____.

7. A ____ is the product of a number and a whole number.

8. A number that has only one and itself as factors is called a ____.

9. A number that has three or more factors is a ____.

Chapter Quiz

1. Tell whether 168 is divisible by 12.   **2.** Tell whether 230 is divisible by 10.

Find the factors of each number.

  3. 44   **4.** 52   **5.** 72

Find the common factors and greatest common factor for each two numbers.

  6. 24 and 32   **7.** 62 and 41   **8.** 35 and 71

Find the first five multiples of each number.

  9. 12   **10.** 14   **11.** 24

Find the least common multiple of each two numbers.

12. 15 and 20   **13.** 12 and 114   **14.** 20 and 45

Tell whether each of the following numbers is prime or composite.

15. 23   **16.** 36   **17.** 49

Find the prime factorization of each number. Write your answer using exponents.

18. 12   **19.** 64   **20.** 88

Use the bar graph on page 161 to answer the questions.

21. How many more students received an A than a B?

22. How many students received a C or better?

Chapter 7 ▷ Fractions and Mixed Numbers

Musicians must understand fractions in order to read music. Do you know what the term "three-quarters" time means? What is a "quarter note"?

Learning Objectives

- Explain the meaning of a fraction.
- Write fractions and mixed numbers.
- Find equivalent fractions.
- Reduce fractions to lowest terms.
- Compare like and unlike fractions.
- Write a fraction as a decimal.
- Write a decimal as a fraction.
- Use a calculator to write a fraction as a decimal.
- Use counting to solve a problem.
- Apply concepts and skills to find average.

Words to Know

fraction	a number that names part of a whole or part of an object
numerator	the top number of a fraction
denominator	the bottom number of a fraction
proper fraction	a fraction in which the numerator is less than the denominator
improper fraction	a fraction in which the numerator is larger than or equal to the denominator
mixed number	a number with a whole number part and a fraction part
equivalent fractions	fractions with different numerators and denominators that name the same amount
lowest terms fraction	when the greatest common factor of the numerator and denominator is 1
like fractions	fractions with the same denominators
unlike fractions	fractions with different denominators
average	a number that tells you something about a group of numbers

Recipe Project

Find a recipe with ingredients that are measured in fractions and whole numbers. Then, suppose you have only the following supplies: a $\frac{1}{4}$ cup measuring cup, a $\frac{1}{3}$ cup measuring cup, a $\frac{1}{2}$ teaspoon measuring spoon, and a tablespoon. Rewrite the recipe using only the supplies you have.

You can write a **fraction** for part of an object.

▶ **EXAMPLE 1**

Write a fraction for the shaded part.

One part is shaded. → The fraction is $\frac{1}{2}$.
Two equal parts in all.   Read: one-half

▶ **EXAMPLE 2**

Write a fraction for the shaded parts.

Two parts are shaded. → The fraction is $\frac{2}{3}$.
Three equal parts in all.   Read: two-thirds

You can also write a fraction for part of a group.

▶ **EXAMPLE 3**

Write a fraction for the shaded parts.

Three parts are shaded. → The fraction is $\frac{3}{4}$.
Four equal parts in all.   Read: three-fourths

The top number in a fraction is called the **numerator.**
The bottom number is called the **denominator.**

numerator   → 4
denominator → 5

When the numerator is less than the denominator, the fraction is a **proper fraction.** When the numerator is greater than or equal to the denominator, the fraction is an **improper fraction.**

proper fraction: $\frac{2}{3}$

improper fraction: $\frac{6}{5}$

Math Fact
2 is less than 3.
6 is greater than 5.

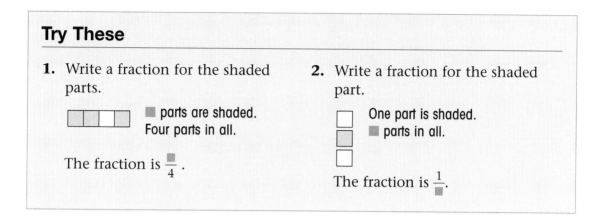

1. Write a fraction for the shaded parts.

   ■ parts are shaded.
   Four parts in all.

   The fraction is $\frac{■}{4}$.

2. Write a fraction for the shaded part.

   One part is shaded.
   ■ parts in all.

   The fraction is $\frac{1}{■}$.

Practice

Write a fraction for the shaded part.

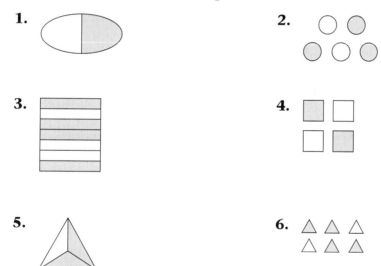

1.

2.

3.

4.

5.

6.

Cooperative Learning

7. Draw a group of six equal boxes. Shade in some of them. Have a partner write a fraction for the shaded part. Check the work.

8. Write a fraction. Have a partner name the numerator and the denominator of the fraction. Then ask if the fraction is proper or improper.

You can write a whole number as a fraction.

$\frac{2}{2}$ or 1 strip is shaded. $\frac{4}{2}$ or 2 strips are shaded.

$$\frac{2}{2} = 1$$ $$\frac{4}{2} = 2$$

▶ **EXAMPLE 1**

Write a fraction and a whole number for the shaded strips.

Each strip has three equal parts. Nine parts are shaded.

The fraction is $\frac{9}{3}$. The whole number is 3.

$$\frac{9}{3} = 3$$

You can also write a **mixed number** for a fraction. A mixed number has a whole number part and a fraction part.

Remember
Read $1\frac{3}{4}$ as one and three-fourths.

Each of the strips has four equal parts. Seven parts are shaded.

$\frac{7}{4}$ or $1\frac{3}{4}$

$$\frac{7}{4} = 1\frac{3}{4} \qquad 1\frac{3}{4} \text{ is a mixed number.}$$

▶ **EXAMPLE 2**

Remember
Read $1\frac{4}{5}$ as one and four-fifths.

Write a fraction and a mixed number for the shaded strips.

Each strip has five equal parts. Nine parts are shaded.

The fraction is $\frac{9}{5}$.   The mixed number is $1\frac{4}{5}$.

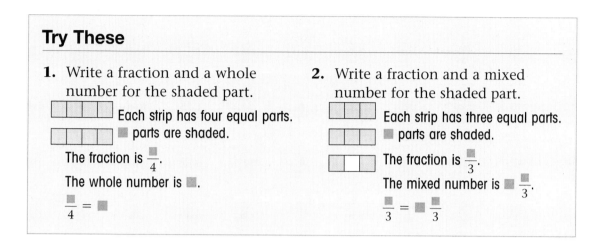

1. Write a fraction and a whole number for the shaded part.

   Each strip has four equal parts.
   ■ parts are shaded.

   The fraction is $\dfrac{■}{4}$.

   The whole number is ■.

   $\dfrac{■}{4} = ■$

2. Write a fraction and a mixed number for the shaded part.

   Each strip has three equal parts.
   ■ parts are shaded.

   The fraction is $\dfrac{■}{3}$.

   The mixed number is ■ $\dfrac{■}{3}$.

   $\dfrac{■}{3} = ■ \dfrac{■}{3}$

Practice

Write a fraction and a whole number or a mixed number for the shaded parts.

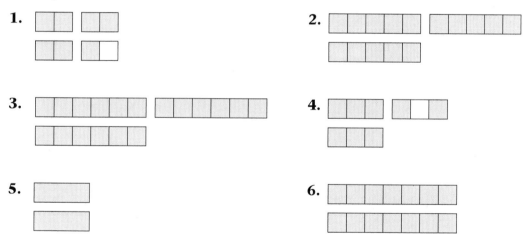

1.
2.
3.
4.
5.
6.

Cooperative Learning

7. Look at number 4 in **Practice**. On a separate sheet of paper draw the same three strips but shade in different parts. Have a partner write a fraction for the parts that are shaded. Then, have a partner write a whole number or a mixed number for the fraction.

You have seen how strips can be used to help you write a whole number or a mixed number as a fraction. You can also use division to do the same thing. Just divide the numerator of the fraction by the denominator.

▶ **EXAMPLE 1**

Find a whole number for $\frac{20}{5}$.

The numerator is 20.
The denominator is 5.
Divide 20 by 5.

$$5\overline{)20} \atop \underline{-20} \atop 0$$

with quotient 4.

$$\frac{20}{5} = 4$$

▶ **EXAMPLE 2**

Find a mixed number for $\frac{17}{3}$.

The numerator is 17.
The denominator is 3.
Divide 17 by 3.

$$3\overline{)17} \atop \underline{-15} \atop 2$$

with quotient $5\frac{2}{3}$.

$$\frac{17}{3} = 5\frac{2}{3}$$

Here is a shortcut you can use to write an improper fraction for a mixed number.

▶ **EXAMPLE 3**

Write an improper fraction for $3\frac{4}{5}$.

Multiply the whole number by the denominator of the fraction.

$3 \times 5 = 15$

Add the numerator to this product.
Use this sum as the numerator.
The denominator stays the same.

$4 + 15 = 19$

$$\frac{19}{5}$$

$$3\frac{4}{5} = \frac{19}{5}$$

Try These

Write a whole number or a mixed number for each fraction.

1. $\frac{15}{5}$

The numerator is 15.
The denominator is ▨.

Divide 15 by ▨. $\overset{\blacksquare}{\blacksquare\overline{)\blacksquare}}$

$\frac{15}{\blacksquare} = \blacksquare$

2. $\frac{19}{2}$

The numerator is 19.
The denominator is 2.

Divide ▨ by 2. $\overset{\blacksquare}{2\overline{)\blacksquare}}$

$\frac{\blacksquare}{2} = \blacksquare$

Write an improper fraction for each mixed number.

3. $4\frac{1}{5}$

$4 \times 5 = \blacksquare.$

$\blacksquare + \blacksquare = \blacksquare.$

$4\frac{1}{5} = \frac{\blacksquare}{5}$

4. $2\frac{3}{4}$

$\blacksquare \times 4 = \blacksquare.$

$3 + \blacksquare = \blacksquare.$

$2\frac{3}{4} = \frac{\blacksquare}{4}$

Practice

Write a whole number or a mixed number for each.

1. $\frac{8}{3}$ **2.** $\frac{12}{2}$ **3.** $\frac{5}{5}$ **4.** $\frac{17}{6}$

5. $\frac{9}{8}$ **6.** $\frac{4}{1}$ **7.** $\frac{24}{7}$ **8.** $\frac{23}{10}$

Write an improper fraction for each.

9. $5\frac{2}{3}$ **10.** $8\frac{3}{5}$ **11.** $2\frac{3}{8}$ **12.** $4\frac{1}{2}$

Cooperative Learning

13. Write three improper fractions. Have a partner write a whole number or mixed number for each. Check the work.

14. Write three mixed numbers. Have a partner write an improper fraction for each.

7·4 Equivalent Fractions

Equivalent fractions name the same amount. They have different numerators and denominators.

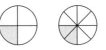

Math Fact
Read as one-fourth equals two-eighths.

$\frac{1}{4}$ and $\frac{2}{8}$ are equivalent fractions.

$$\frac{1}{4} = \frac{2}{8}$$

► **EXAMPLE 1**

Write a pair of equivalent fractions for the shaded parts.

One part is shaded.
Two equal parts in all. $\rightarrow$ $\frac{1}{2}$

Math Fact
Read as one-half equals two-fourths.

Two parts are shaded.
Four equal parts in all. $\rightarrow$ $\frac{2}{4}$

Write the equivalent fractions as $\frac{1}{2} = \frac{2}{4}$.

► **EXAMPLE 2**

Write a pair of equivalent fractions for the shaded parts.

Two parts are shaded.
Five equal parts in all. $\rightarrow$ $\frac{2}{5}$

Four parts are shaded.
Ten equal parts in all. $\rightarrow$ $\frac{4}{10}$

Write the equivalent fractions as $\frac{2}{5} = \frac{4}{10}$.

Try These

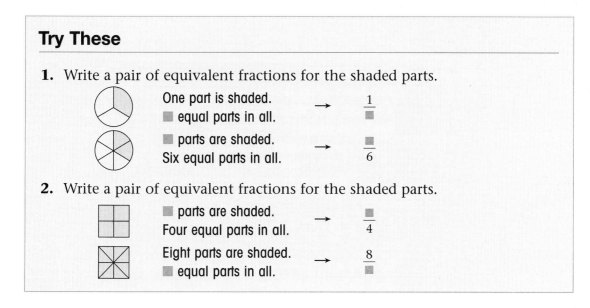

1. Write a pair of equivalent fractions for the shaded parts.

   One part is shaded.
   ▨ equal parts in all. → $\dfrac{1}{▨}$

   ▨ parts are shaded.
   Six equal parts in all. → $\dfrac{▨}{6}$

2. Write a pair of equivalent fractions for the shaded parts.

   ▨ parts are shaded.
   Four equal parts in all. → $\dfrac{▨}{4}$

   Eight parts are shaded.
   ▨ equal parts in all. → $\dfrac{8}{▨}$

Practice

Write a pair of equivalent fractions for the shaded parts.

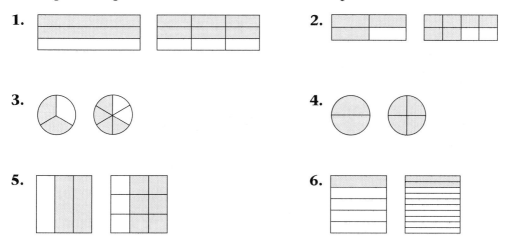

1.

2.

3.

4.

5.

6.

Cooperative Learning

7. Tell a partner how you found the equivalent fractions in number **3** in **Practice**.

8. Tell a partner how you found the equivalent fractions in number **6** in **Practice**.

You have used drawings to find equivalent fractions.
You can also find equivalent fractions by using
multiplication.

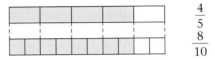

$$\frac{4}{5}$$
$$\frac{8}{10}$$

Check

$8 = 4 \times 2$

$10 = 5 \times 2$

$$\frac{4}{5} = \frac{8}{10} \leftarrow \frac{4 \times 2}{5 \times 2}$$

To find an equivalent fraction, multiply the numerator
and denominator by the same number.

▶ **EXAMPLE 1**

Multiply numerator and denominator by 3 to find a
fraction equivalent to $\frac{2}{3}$.

$$\frac{2}{3}$$

Multiply numerator and denominator by 3. $\quad \frac{2 \times 3}{3 \times 3} = \frac{6}{9}$

Write the equivalent fractions. $\qquad\qquad \frac{2}{3} = \frac{6}{9}$

You can write multiple fractions that are equivalent to
the same fraction.

▶ **EXAMPLE 2**

Multiply the numerator and denominator of $\frac{1}{2}$ by 4 and
then by 5 to find two equivalent fractions.

Using 4: $\qquad\qquad\qquad\qquad\qquad\qquad \frac{1}{2}$

Multiply numerator and denominator by 4. $\quad \frac{1 \times 4}{2 \times 4} = \frac{4}{8}$

Write the equivalent fractions. $\qquad\qquad \frac{1}{2} = \frac{4}{8}$

Using 5: $\qquad\qquad\qquad\qquad\qquad\qquad \frac{1}{2}$

Multiply numerator and denominator by 5. $\quad \frac{1 \times 5}{2 \times 5} = \frac{5}{10}$

Math Fact

$\frac{1}{2}, \frac{4}{8}$ and $\frac{5}{10}$ are all equivalent.

Write the equivalent fractions. $\qquad\qquad \frac{1}{2} = \frac{5}{10}$

$$\frac{1}{2} = \frac{4}{8} = \frac{5}{10}$$

Try These

Multiply the numerator and denominator by 2 to find an equivalent fraction.

1. $\frac{4}{5}$

$$\frac{4}{5} = \frac{4 \times 2}{5 \times 2} = \frac{\blacksquare}{\blacksquare}$$

$$\frac{4}{5} = \frac{\blacksquare}{\blacksquare}$$

2. $\frac{5}{8}$

$$\frac{5}{8} = \frac{5 \times 2}{8 \times \blacksquare} = \frac{\blacksquare}{\blacksquare}$$

$$\frac{5}{8} = \frac{\blacksquare}{\blacksquare}$$

Multiply the numerator and denominator of $\frac{3}{4}$ by 3 and then by 4 to find two equivalent fractions.

3. $\frac{3}{4}$ using 3

$$\frac{3}{4} = \frac{3 \times \blacksquare}{4 \times 3} = \frac{\blacksquare}{\blacksquare}$$

$$\frac{3}{4} = \frac{\blacksquare}{\blacksquare}$$

4. $\frac{3}{4}$ using 4

$$\frac{3}{4} = \frac{3 \times 4}{4 \times \blacksquare} = \frac{\blacksquare}{\blacksquare}$$

$$\frac{3}{4} = \frac{\blacksquare}{\blacksquare}$$

$$\frac{3}{4} = \frac{\blacksquare}{\blacksquare} = \frac{\blacksquare}{\blacksquare}$$

Practice

Multiply each numerator and denominator by 2 to find an equivalent fraction.

1. $\frac{1}{6}$ **2.** $\frac{2}{9}$ **3.** $\frac{3}{8}$ **4.** $\frac{3}{7}$

Multiply the numerator and denominator of each fraction by 4 and then 5 to find two equivalent fractions.

5. $\frac{2}{5}$ **6.** $\frac{1}{3}$ **7.** $\frac{5}{6}$ **8.** $\frac{3}{10}$

9. $\frac{1}{8}$ **10.** $\frac{2}{2}$ **11.** $\frac{4}{3}$ **12.** $\frac{4}{1}$

Cooperative Learning

13. Write a fraction. Ask a partner to write two fractions equivalent to it. Check the work.

14. Write two fractions equivalent to $\frac{4}{5}$. Explain your work to a partner.

You have used multiplication to find equivalent fractions. You can also use division to find equivalent fractions.

Check
$4 = 8 \div 2$
$5 = 10 \div 2$

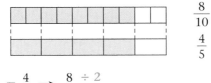

$\dfrac{8}{10}$

$\dfrac{4}{5}$

$$\dfrac{8}{10} = \dfrac{4}{5} \longrightarrow \dfrac{8 \div 2}{10 \div 2}$$

To find an equivalent fraction, divide the numerator and the denominator by the same number.

▶ **EXAMPLE 1**

Find a fraction equivalent to $\frac{6}{12}$.

$$\dfrac{6}{12}$$

Math Fact
3 is a common factor of 6 and 12.

Divide the numerator and denominator by 3.　$\dfrac{6 \div 3}{12 \div 3} = \dfrac{2}{4}$

Write the equivalent fractions.　$\dfrac{6}{12} = \dfrac{2}{4}$

You can use equivalent fractions to find the **lowest terms fraction**. A fraction is in lowest terms if the greatest common factor of the numerator and denominator is 1.

▶ **EXAMPLE 2**

Write $\frac{12}{18}$ as a lowest terms fraction.

$$\dfrac{12}{18}$$

Math Fact
You can also start by dividing 12 and 18 by 6.

Divide 12 and 18 by 2.　$\dfrac{12 \div 2}{18 \div 2} = \dfrac{6}{9}$

Divide 6 and 9 by 3.　$\dfrac{6 \div 3}{9 \div 3} = \dfrac{2}{3}$

Write the lowest terms fraction.　$\dfrac{2}{3}$

$$\dfrac{12}{18} = \dfrac{2}{3}$$

Try These

Write each fraction in lowest terms.

1. $\frac{4}{10}$

$$\frac{4 \div \blacksquare}{10 \div 2} = \frac{\blacksquare}{\blacksquare}$$

$$\frac{4}{10} = \frac{\blacksquare}{\blacksquare}$$

2. $\frac{9}{15}$

$$\frac{9 \div 3}{15 \div \blacksquare} = \frac{\blacksquare}{\blacksquare}$$

$$\frac{9}{15} = \frac{\blacksquare}{\blacksquare}$$

3. $\frac{18}{24}$

$$\frac{18 \div 2}{24 \div \blacksquare} = \frac{9}{\blacksquare} \rightarrow \frac{9 \div \blacksquare}{\blacksquare \div 3} = \frac{\blacksquare}{\blacksquare}$$

$$\frac{18}{24} = \frac{\blacksquare}{\blacksquare}$$

4. $\frac{8}{16}$

$$\frac{8 \div \blacksquare}{16 \div 8} = \frac{\blacksquare}{\blacksquare}$$

$$\frac{8}{16} = \frac{\blacksquare}{\blacksquare}$$

Practice

Write each fraction in lowest terms.

1. $\frac{8}{12}$ **2.** $\frac{10}{20}$ **3.** $\frac{9}{12}$ **4.** $\frac{5}{15}$

5. $\frac{3}{9}$ **6.** $\frac{8}{24}$ **7.** $\frac{16}{20}$ **8.** $\frac{7}{14}$

9. $\frac{4}{24}$ **10.** $\frac{18}{27}$ **11.** $\frac{14}{24}$ **12.** $\frac{25}{100}$

13. $\frac{9}{36}$ **14.** $\frac{16}{18}$ **15.** $\frac{6}{8}$ **16.** $\frac{8}{64}$

Cooperative Learning

17. Ask a partner to write $\frac{20}{32}$ in lowest terms. Check the work.

18. Explain to a partner how you would write $\frac{10}{100}$ in lowest terms.

Comparing Fractions

Fractions with the same denominator are called **like fractions.**

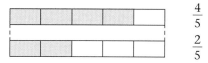

$\frac{4}{5}$

$\frac{2}{5}$

$\frac{4}{5}$ and $\frac{2}{5}$ are like fractions. To compare like fractions, compare their numerators. The larger numerator makes the larger fraction.

► EXAMPLE 1

Compare. Use $>$, $<$, or $=$ for ▬. $\frac{4}{5}$ ▬ $\frac{2}{5}$

$\frac{4}{5}$ ▬ $\frac{2}{5}$

Compare the numerators.   4 is greater than 2.

Compare the fractions. $\frac{4}{5}$ is greater than $\frac{2}{5}$.

$\frac{4}{5} > \frac{2}{5}$

Unlike fractions have different denominators. To compare unlike fractions, write them as like fractions using equivalent fractions. Then compare the like fractions.

► EXAMPLE 2

Compare. Use $>$, $<$, or $=$ for ▬ $\frac{1}{2}$ ▬ $\frac{2}{3}$

$\frac{1}{2}$ ▬ $\frac{2}{3}$

Write $\frac{1}{2}$ and $\frac{2}{3}$ as like fractions. $\frac{1 \times 3}{2 \times 3} = \frac{3}{6}$

$\frac{2 \times 2}{3 \times 2} = \frac{4}{6}$

Compare the like fractions. $\frac{3}{6}$ ▬ $\frac{4}{6}$

Compare the numerator.   3 is less than 4.

Compare the fractions. $\frac{3}{6}$ is less than $\frac{4}{6}$.

$\frac{1}{2} < \frac{2}{3}$ So, $\frac{1}{2}$ is less than $\frac{2}{3}$.

Try These

1. Compare. Use >, <, or = for ■.

   $\frac{2}{3}$ ■ $\frac{1}{3}$

   $2 > 1$

   $\frac{2}{3}$ ■ $\frac{1}{3}$

2. Compare. Use >, <, or = for ■.

   $\frac{3}{4}$ ■ $\frac{4}{8}$

   $\frac{3 \times ■}{4 \times 2} = \frac{■}{8}$

   ■ > 4

   $\frac{3}{4}$ ■ $\frac{4}{8}$

Practice

Compare. Use >, <, or = for ■.

1. $\frac{6}{7}$ ■ $\frac{1}{7}$

2. $\frac{5}{6}$ ■ $\frac{5}{6}$

3. $\frac{7}{8}$ ■ $\frac{3}{4}$

4. $\frac{1}{2}$ ■ $\frac{4}{8}$

5. $\frac{1}{5}$ ■ $\frac{1}{10}$

6. $\frac{4}{9}$ ■ $\frac{2}{2}$

7. $\frac{1}{3}$ ■ $\frac{2}{5}$

8. $\frac{2}{3}$ ■ $\frac{1}{4}$

9. $\frac{3}{4}$ ■ $\frac{4}{8}$

10. $\frac{1}{5}$ ■ $\frac{1}{6}$

11. $\frac{2}{5}$ ■ $\frac{1}{4}$

12. $\frac{1}{20}$ ■ $\frac{1}{10}$

13. $\frac{5}{6}$ ■ $\frac{7}{8}$

14. $\frac{4}{5}$ ■ $\frac{1}{3}$

15. $\frac{3}{7}$ ■ $\frac{8}{9}$

16. $\frac{1}{10}$ ■ $\frac{7}{8}$

Cooperative Learning

17. Write two like fractions. Have a partner compare them. Check the work.

18. Use 3 and 4 as denominators and write two unlike fractions. Have a partner compare them. Check the work.

7·8 Fractions and Decimals

You can use what you know about decimals and place value to write a fraction for a decimal and a decimal for some fractions.

Math Fact
.3 means 3 tenths.
.41 means 41 hundredths.

.3 ← one place

$\frac{3}{10}$ ← one zero

.41 ← two places

$\frac{41}{100}$ ← two zeros

▶ **EXAMPLE 1**

Write a fraction for .09.

.09

Two decimal places
means hundredths.

$\frac{9}{100}$

$.09 = \frac{9}{100}$

▶ **EXAMPLE 2**

Write $\frac{25}{100}$ as a decimal.

$\frac{25}{100}$

Hundredths means
two decimal places.

.25

$\frac{25}{100} = .25$

▶ **EXAMPLE 3**

Write 2.7 as a mixed number.

2.7

Look at the decimal part.

2.7

One place means tenths.

$2\frac{7}{10}$

$2.7 = 2\frac{7}{10}$

Try These

Write a decimal for each.

1. $\dfrac{7}{100}$

Hundredths means ■ decimal places.

$\dfrac{7}{100}$ = ■

2. $3\dfrac{9}{10}$

Tenths means ■ decimal place.

$3\dfrac{9}{10}$ = ■

Write a fraction or mixed number for each.

3. .21

■ decimal places means hundredths.

$.21 = \dfrac{21}{■}$

4. 1.7

■ decimal place means tenths.

$1.7 = 1\dfrac{7}{■}$

Practice

Write a decimal for each.

1. $\dfrac{8}{100}$ **2.** $\dfrac{3}{100}$ **3.** $\dfrac{5}{10}$ **4.** $\dfrac{15}{100}$

5. $5\dfrac{6}{10}$ **6.** $\dfrac{91}{100}$ **7.** $5\dfrac{8}{10}$ **8.** $\dfrac{12}{100}$

Write a fraction or mixed number for each.

9. .01   **10.** 3.5   **11.** .75   **12.** .9

13. 2.04   **14.** 4.1   **15.** .45   **16.** .8

Cooperative Learning

17. Write a decimal with two places. Have a partner write a fraction for it. Check the work.

18. Write three fractions with 10 or 100 as a denominator. Have a partner write a decimal for each fraction. Check the work.

Use your calculator to write decimals for fractions or mixed numbers.

EXAMPLE 1

Write $\frac{2}{5}$ as a decimal.

$\frac{2}{5}$ → divide 2 by 5.   Display

Press: [2] [÷] [5] [=] | 0.4 |

                                    $\frac{2}{5}$ = | 0.4 |

EXAMPLE 2

Write $\frac{19}{25}$ as a decimal.

$\frac{19}{25}$ → divide 19 by 25.   Display

Press: [1] [9] [÷] [2] [5] [=] | 0.76 |

                                    $\frac{19}{25}$ = | 0.76 |

Sometimes, the calculator will display many decimal places. Round the display to the nearest hundredth.

EXAMPLE 3

Write $\frac{200}{300}$ as a decimal.

$\frac{200}{300}$ → divide 200 by 300.   Display

Press: [2] [0] [0] [÷] [3] [0] [0] [=] | 0.6666666 |

                            Rounds to | 0.67 |

                    $\frac{200}{300}$ is about | 0.67 |

EXAMPLE 4

Write $5\frac{17}{50}$ as a decimal.

Work with the fraction part. $5\frac{17}{50}$

$\frac{17}{50}$ → divide 17 by 50.   Display

Press: [1] [7] [÷] [5] [0] [=] | 0.34 |

Write the whole number part. $5\frac{17}{50}$ = | 5.34 |

Practice

Use your calculator. Write a decimal for each fraction or mixed number. Round the answer to the nearest hundredth.

1. $5\frac{1}{5}$

2. $\frac{6}{20}$

3. $27\frac{1}{2}$

4. $\frac{2}{3}$

5. $17\frac{1}{4}$

6. $7\frac{1}{6}$

7. $2\frac{6}{24}$

8. $10\frac{1}{4}$

9. $1\frac{1}{16}$

10. $2\frac{20}{64}$

Math Connection

OLYMPIC TIME

The Olympic games are held every four years. The world's greatest athletes come together for the games. They compete in many different events.

Most of these events are timed. People who work at the Olympics record how long it takes each athlete to complete an event. The records they keep must be exact. A second or two may not mean a lot to you, but it does at the Olympics. A second or two can mean the difference between first and second place for a runner or swimmer.

For the winner, sometimes even less than one-thousandth of a second can make a difference. A mistake as small as a fraction of a second can cost an athlete the gold medal.

7·10 Problem Solving: Counting

You can use a picture to help you count and
solve problems.

▶ **EXAMPLE**

Freddie can take two friends to a movie. He has
5 friends: Jose, Luis, Monica, Cheryl, and Diane. He
wants to take 1 boy and 1 girl. How many pairs of
friends can he choose from?

READ   **What do you need to find out?**
You need to find out how many different pairs
of friends Freddie can take to the movie.

PLAN   **What do you need to do?**
You need to draw a diagram. First, list the boys.
Then, list the girls. Make pairs and count them.

DO   **Follow the plan.**

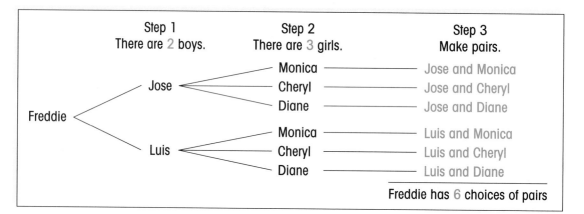

We could have used multiplication. There are
2 choices for boys and 3 choices for girls.

$2 \times 3 = 6$

CHECK   **Does your answer make sense?**
All possible pairs are listed in the Do step. ✓

Freddie can choose from 6 different pairs of friends.

Try These

1. A new car comes in 5 inside colors and 8 outside colors. How many choices of colors are there?

   Step 1.   5 choices

   Step 2.   ■ choices

   Multiply.   5 × ■ = ■

   There are ■ combinations of colors.

2. Armando has 3 shirts, 2 suits, and 5 ties. How many outfits can he make?

   Step 1.   ■ choices

   Step 2.   2 choices

   Step 3.   5 choices

   Multiply.   ■ × 2 × ■ = ■

   He can make ■ outfits.

Practice

Find the number of choices.

1. A menu has 3 soups and 2 meats. How many different meals can you have with 1 soup and 1 meat?

2. A store owner has 6 flavors of frozen yogurt and 3 toppings. How many cones can the owner make using 1 flavor and 1 topping?

3. Kim has 5 sweatshirts, 4 sweatpants, and 3 headbands. How many outfits could she make to wear jogging?

4. You can have a sandwich with your choice of 2 different kinds of cheeses and 2 different breads. How many choices do you have?

Cooperative Learning

5. A store offers 20 different T-shirts and 8 different backpacks. Ask a partner to explain how to find the number of choices for the T-shirts and backpacks.

6. Look at number **2** in **Practice**. Ask your partner how the answer would change if there were 4 flavors of frozen yogurt and 2 toppings.

Application: Average

The **average** is a number that tells you something about a group of numbers. To find the average of a group of numbers, add first. Then, divide.

 **EXAMPLE 1**

Here are scores for 3 tests.

87, 75, 90

To find the average, first add the scores.

Remember
The total of the scores is the sum of the scores.

Then, divide this total by the number of scores.

Add the scores. $87 + 75 + 90 = 252$

↑
total of the scores

Divide the total by
the number of tests.

There are 3 tests,
so divide by 3. $252 \div 3 = 84$

↑
number of tests

The average score is 84.

 **EXAMPLE 2**

The amount of snow that falls is measured in inches. Here are the amounts that fell in a city during five months.

.36, .71, .95, 2.88, and 3.85.

Find the average amount of snow that fell during the five months.

Add the number of $.36 + .71 + .95 + 2.88 + 3.85 = 8.75$
inches that fell.

Divide the total by
the number of months $8.75 \div 5 = 1.75$

The average amount is 1.75 inches.

Try These

1. Last week, Carla ran 2.5 miles, 1.75 miles, 2 miles, 2.25 miles, and .75 miles. What was the average number of miles she ran in each day?

   Add the number of miles. $2.5 + 1.75 + 2 + 2.25 + .75 = \blacksquare$

   Divide the total by
   the number of days. $\blacksquare \div \blacksquare = \blacksquare$

   The average number of miles she ran each day was $\blacksquare$.

2. Marco spent $2.65, $3.30, and $3.95 on lunches in three days. What was the average Marco spent on lunch each day?

   Add the amounts. $\blacksquare + \blacksquare + \blacksquare = \$9.90$

   Divide the total by
   the number of days. $\$9.90 \div \blacksquare = \blacksquare$

   The average Marco spent on lunch each day was $\blacksquare$.

Practice

Find the average.

1. 10, 12, 17

2. 8, 7, 11, 6, 18

3. 120, 132, 145, 163

4. .25, .5, .60

5. 2.2, 8.6, 10.2, 7

6. .75, 1.22, 1.35, 3

7. $1.10, $1.29, $1.99

8. $3.50, $3.50, $5.30

9. $1.50, $2, $3, $4, $5

Cooperative Learning

10. Ask each member of your group how many hours a day they spend doing homework. Together, find the average for five days.

11. Look at number **8** in **Practice.** Work with a partner to find the average if the amounts were $3.50, $3.50, $5.30, and $5.30.

Summary

A fraction can be written to show part of an object.
You can write a whole number as a fraction.
A mixed number has a whole number part and a fraction part.
Equivalent fractions name the same amount.
To find an equivalent fraction, multiply or divide the numerator and denominator by the same number.
You can use equivalent fractions to find the lowest terms fraction.
To compare like fractions, compare the numerators.
To compare unlike fractions, find equivalent fractions with the same denominator.
You can write a fraction as a decimal and a decimal as a fraction.
To find an average of a group of numbers, add the numbers, then divide.

numerator

proper fraction

mixed number

equivalent fractions

like fractions

unlike fractions

lowest terms

average

Vocabulary Review

Complete the sentences with words from the box.

1. The _____ is the top number of a fraction.

2. Fractions with the same denominators are _____.

3. When the numerator is less than the denominator, it is called a _____.

4. A fraction is in _____ when the greatest common factor of the numerator and denominator is 1.

5. A number that tells you something about a group of numbers is called the _____.

6. A _____ is a number with a whole part and a fraction part.

7. _____ are fractions with different numerators and denominators that name the same amount.

8. Fractions with different denominators are _____.

Chapter Quiz

Write a fraction for the shaded part.

1. 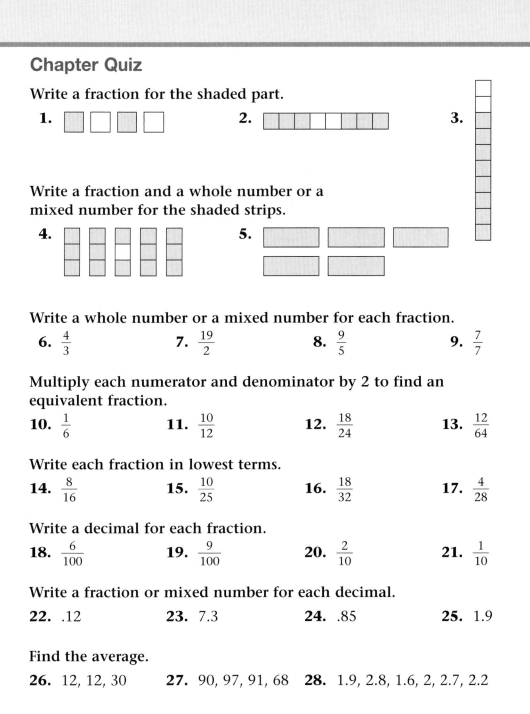   **2.**   **3.**

Write a fraction and a whole number or a
mixed number for the shaded strips.

4.   **5.**

Write a whole number or a mixed number for each fraction.

6. $\frac{4}{3}$ **7.** $\frac{19}{2}$ **8.** $\frac{9}{5}$ **9.** $\frac{7}{7}$

Multiply each numerator and denominator by 2 to find an
equivalent fraction.

10. $\frac{1}{6}$ **11.** $\frac{10}{12}$ **12.** $\frac{18}{24}$ **13.** $\frac{12}{64}$

Write each fraction in lowest terms.

14. $\frac{8}{16}$ **15.** $\frac{10}{25}$ **16.** $\frac{18}{32}$ **17.** $\frac{4}{28}$

Write a decimal for each fraction.

18. $\frac{6}{100}$ **19.** $\frac{9}{100}$ **20.** $\frac{2}{10}$ **21.** $\frac{1}{10}$

Write a fraction or mixed number for each decimal.

22. .12   **23.** 7.3   **24.** .85   **25.** 1.9

Find the average.

26. 12, 12, 30   **27.** 90, 97, 91, 68   **28.** 1.9, 2.8, 1.6, 2, 2.7, 2.2

Unit 3 **Review**

Use the bar graph to answer Questions 1 and 2.

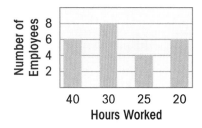

1. What is the number of employees that work 25 hours?

   A. 2

   B. 4

   C. 6

   D. 8

2. What is the number of hours worked by most employees?

   A. 8

   B. 25

   C. 30

   D. 40

3. The rainfall for four months is 2.7 in., 4.6 in., 1.8 in., and 0.9 in. What is the average rainfall?

   A. 2.25 in.

   B. 4.0 in.

   C. 2.5 in.

   D. not given

4. A restaurant has 3 sizes of pizza and 9 toppings. How many pizzas can you order with 1 topping?

   A. 11

   B. 5

   C. 3

   D. 27

5. What is the factorization of 54?

   A. 2×3^3

   B. 2×3^2

   C. $2^3 \times 3$

   D. $2^2 \times 3^2$

6. A company makes a shirt in 4 sizes, 9 colors, and either long or short sleeves. How many shirts does the company make?

   A. 54

   B. 72

   C. 15

   D. 38

Critical Thinking

The team went to a restaurant after a game. There are 10 players and 2 coaches. They need to rearrange the square tables end to end so they can sit together. Each table seats 4 people. How many tables will they need?

CHALLENGE The 12 people can choose chicken or steak and French fries or baked potato. How many different orders are possible?

Unit Four

Construction workers need to understand fractions because they cannot always measure things in whole numbers. What are some tools construction workers use to help them build things?

Learning Objectives

- Add and subtract fractions.

- Add and subtract mixed numbers.

- Evaluate variable expressions with fractions and mixed numbers.

- Solve equations by adding or subtracting fractions and mixed numbers.

- Use a calculator to add and subtract fractions.

- Solve problems with too much or too little information.

- Apply concepts and skills to find the median and mode of a set of numbers.

Words to Know

common denominator	a common multiple of the denominators
least common denominator	the smallest common denominator
mode	the number that appears the most often in a group of numbers
median	the middle number in a group of numbers when the numbers are in order from smallest to largest.

Salad Project

You are making a salad for dinner. You will need $2\frac{1}{4}$ lbs. of lettuce, $\frac{1}{3}$ lb. of carrots, $\frac{1}{8}$ lb. of red peppers, $\frac{1}{2}$ lb. of mushrooms, and $\frac{2}{3}$ lb. of tomatoes. Find out how much the salad will weigh when it is finished. In your math journal, write the steps you need to follow in order to complete this project.

Adding and Subtracting Like Fractions

Like fractions have the same denominators. These fraction strips show how to add or subtract like fractions.

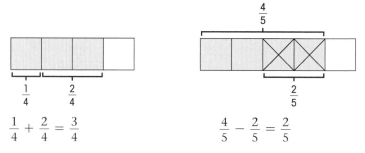

$$\frac{1}{4} + \frac{2}{4} = \frac{3}{4}$$

$$\frac{4}{5} - \frac{2}{5} = \frac{2}{5}$$

To add or subtract like fractions, add or subtract the numerators. Use the common denominator as the denominator of your answer.

► EXAMPLE 1

Add. $\frac{3}{8} + \frac{7}{8}$

Add the numerators.
Keep the denominator.

$$\frac{3}{8} + \frac{7}{8} = \frac{3+7}{8} = \frac{10}{8}$$

Math Fact
Your answer may be an improper fraction. Write it as a mixed number.

Reduce the answer to lowest terms.

$$\frac{10}{8} = \frac{10 \div 2}{8 \div 2} = \frac{5}{4} = 1\frac{1}{4}$$

$$\frac{3}{8} + \frac{7}{8} = 1\frac{1}{4}$$

► EXAMPLE 2

Subtract.
$$\begin{array}{r} \frac{11}{12} \\ -\frac{4}{12} \end{array}$$

Subtract the numerators.

Keep the denominator.

The answer is in lowest terms.

$$\begin{array}{r} \frac{11}{12} \\ -\frac{4}{12} \\ \hline \frac{11-4}{12} = \frac{7}{12} \end{array}$$

$$\frac{11}{12} - \frac{4}{12} = \frac{7}{12}$$

Try These

Add or subtract.

1. $\frac{3}{8} - \frac{1}{8}$

Subtract the numerators.

Keep the denominator.

$\frac{\blacksquare - \blacksquare}{8}$

$= \frac{\blacksquare}{8}$

Write the answer in lowest terms.

$= \frac{\blacksquare}{\blacksquare}$

$\frac{3}{8} - \frac{1}{8} = \frac{\blacksquare}{\blacksquare}$

2. $\frac{9}{16} + \frac{13}{16}$

Add the numerators.
Keep the denominator.

$\frac{9 + \blacksquare}{\blacksquare}$

$= \frac{\blacksquare}{\blacksquare}$

Write the improper fraction as a mixed number.

$= 1 \frac{\blacksquare}{\blacksquare}$

Write the fraction part in lowest terms $= 1 \frac{\blacksquare \div 2}{\blacksquare \div 2} = 1 \frac{\blacksquare}{\blacksquare}$

$\frac{9}{16} + \frac{13}{16} = 1 \frac{\blacksquare}{\blacksquare}$

Practice

Add or subtract.

1. $\frac{1}{4}$
$+ \frac{2}{4}$

2. $\frac{5}{8}$
$+ \frac{2}{8}$

3. $\frac{2}{5}$
$+ \frac{3}{5}$

4. $\frac{9}{10}$
$+ \frac{7}{10}$

5. $\frac{5}{6} - \frac{4}{6}$

6. $\frac{5}{6} + \frac{2}{6}$

7. $\frac{3}{12} + \frac{7}{12}$

8. $\frac{7}{4} + \frac{2}{4}$

9. $\frac{7}{8} + \frac{7}{8}$

10. $\frac{7}{9} - \frac{5}{9}$

11. $\frac{3}{7} + \frac{4}{7}$

12. $\frac{19}{20} - \frac{4}{20}$

Cooperative Learning

13. Explain to a partner how to add in number **4** in **Practice**.

14. Write two like fractions. Ask a partner to add them. Then ask a partner to subtract the smaller fraction from the larger fraction. Check the work.

8·2 ▶ Least Common Denominators

Math Fact
Unlike fractions have different denominators.

You can replace unlike fractions with equivalent fractions that have the same denominator. This is called finding a **common denominator.** A common denominator of two or more fractions is a common multiple of the denominators.

▶ **EXAMPLE 1**

Find fractions with a common denominator equivalent to $\frac{1}{3}$ and $\frac{7}{18}$.

Look at the smaller denominator 3. $3 \times 6 = 18$

Write a fraction equivalent to $\frac{1}{3}$. $\dfrac{1 \times 6}{3 \times 6} = \dfrac{6}{18}$

$\frac{6}{18}$ and $\frac{7}{18}$ are equivalent to $\frac{1}{3}$ and $\frac{7}{18}$.

You can always find a common denominator by multiplying the denominators.

▶ **EXAMPLE 2**

Find fractions with a common denominator equivalent to $\frac{1}{6}$ and $\frac{1}{4}$.

Multiply the denominators. $6 \times 4 = 24$

Write fractions equivalent to

$\frac{1}{6}$ and $\frac{1}{4}$ with denominator of 24. $\dfrac{1 \times 4}{6 \times 4} = \dfrac{4}{24}$ and $\dfrac{1 \times 6}{4 \times 6} = \dfrac{6}{24}$

$\frac{4}{24}$ and $\frac{6}{24}$ are equivalent to $\frac{1}{6}$ and $\frac{1}{4}$.

Remember
Least means smallest.

The **least common denominator** is the least common multiple of the denominators.

$$\frac{5}{6} \text{ and } \frac{3}{4}$$

Common denominator: $\dfrac{5 \times 4}{6 \times 4} = \dfrac{20}{24}$ and $\dfrac{3 \times 6}{4 \times 6} = \dfrac{18}{24}$

Least common denominator: $\dfrac{5 \times 2}{6 \times 2} = \dfrac{10}{12}$ and $\dfrac{3 \times 3}{4 \times 3} = \dfrac{9}{12}$

Try These

Find equivalent fractions with the least common denominator.

1. $\frac{1}{2}$ and $\frac{2}{3}$

$2 \times \blacksquare = 6$

$3 \times \blacksquare = \blacksquare$

$\frac{1 \times \blacksquare}{2 \times \blacksquare} = \frac{\blacksquare}{6}$

$\frac{2 \times \blacksquare}{3 \times \blacksquare} = \frac{\blacksquare}{\blacksquare}$

$\frac{\blacksquare}{6}$ and $\frac{\blacksquare}{\blacksquare}$ are equivalent

to $\frac{1}{2}$ and $\frac{2}{3}$.

2. $\frac{1}{6}$ and $\frac{2}{9}$

$6 \times \blacksquare = 18$

$9 \times \blacksquare = \blacksquare$

$\frac{1 \times \blacksquare}{6 \times \blacksquare} = \frac{\blacksquare}{18}$

$\frac{2 \times \blacksquare}{9 \times \blacksquare} = \frac{\blacksquare}{\blacksquare}$

$\frac{\blacksquare}{18}$ and $\frac{\blacksquare}{\blacksquare}$ are equivalent

to $\frac{1}{6}$ and $\frac{2}{9}$.

Practice

Find equivalent fractions with the least common denominator.

1. $\frac{3}{10}$ and $\frac{4}{5}$

2. $\frac{2}{3}$ and $\frac{3}{8}$

3. $\frac{4}{9}$ and $\frac{5}{12}$

4. $\frac{7}{9}$ and $\frac{5}{18}$

5. $\frac{5}{6}$ and $\frac{7}{8}$

6. $\frac{3}{16}$ and $\frac{1}{4}$

7. $\frac{3}{10}$ and $\frac{9}{20}$

8. $\frac{5}{6}$ and $\frac{1}{2}$

9. $\frac{1}{6}$ and $\frac{3}{10}$

10. $\frac{2}{5}$ and $\frac{5}{6}$

11. $\frac{1}{3}$ and $\frac{1}{12}$

12. $\frac{1}{2}$ and $\frac{5}{9}$

Cooperative Learning

13. Explain to a partner how you find equivalent fractions with the least common denominator for number **10** in **Practice**.

14. Write two unlike fractions. Ask a partner to find fractions with the least common denominator equivalent to your fractions. Check the work.

Adding Unlike Fractions

When adding fractions with different denominators, replace them with equivalent fractions with the least common denominator. Then, add. Be sure your answer is in lowest terms.

► **EXAMPLE 1**

Check

$$\frac{2 \times 4}{3 \times 4} = \frac{8}{12}$$

Add. $\qquad$ $\frac{2}{3} + \frac{7}{12}$

12 is the least common multiple of 3 and 12.

$$\frac{2}{3} \longrightarrow \frac{8}{12}$$

Use 12 as the least common denominator.

$$+ \frac{7}{12} \longrightarrow + \frac{7}{12}$$

$$\frac{8 + 7}{12} = \frac{15}{12} = 1\frac{3}{12} = 1\frac{1}{4}$$

$$\frac{2}{3} + \frac{7}{12} = 1\frac{1}{4}$$

► **EXAMPLE 2**

Check

$$\frac{1 \times 4}{6 \times 4} = \frac{4}{24}$$

$$\frac{5 \times 3}{8 \times 3} = \frac{15}{24}$$

Add. $\qquad$ $\frac{1}{6} + \frac{5}{8}$

24 is the least common multiple of 6 and 8.

$$\frac{1}{6} \longrightarrow \frac{4}{24}$$

Use 24 as the least common denominator.

$$+ \frac{5}{8} \longrightarrow + \frac{15}{24}$$

$$\frac{4 + 15}{24} = \frac{19}{24}$$

$$\frac{1}{6} + \frac{5}{8} = \frac{19}{24}$$

Adding whole numbers and fractions is easy.

► **EXAMPLE 3**

Check

$$\frac{2 \times 5}{1 \times 5} = \frac{10}{5}$$

Remember
A proper fraction is a fraction with the numerator less than the denominator.

Add. $\qquad$ $2 + \frac{4}{5}$

5 is the least common multiple of 1 and 5.

$$2 \longrightarrow \frac{2}{1} \longrightarrow \frac{10}{5}$$

Use 5 as the least common denominator.

$$+ \frac{4}{5} \longrightarrow \frac{4}{5} \longrightarrow + \frac{4}{5}$$

$$\frac{10 + 4}{5} = \frac{14}{5} = 2\frac{4}{5}$$

$$2 + \frac{4}{5} = 2\frac{4}{5}$$

To add a whole number and a proper fraction, write a mixed number.

Try These

Add.

1. $\frac{2}{3} + \frac{3}{5}$

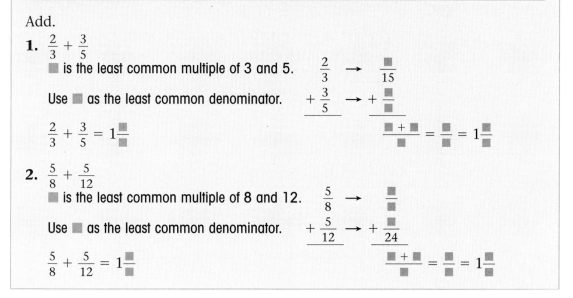

■ is the least common multiple of 3 and 5.

Use ■ as the least common denominator.

$\frac{2}{3} + \frac{3}{5} = 1\frac{■}{■}$

2. $\frac{5}{8} + \frac{5}{12}$

■ is the least common multiple of 8 and 12.

Use ■ as the least common denominator.

$\frac{5}{8} + \frac{5}{12} = 1\frac{■}{■}$

Practice

Add.

1.
$$\begin{array}{r} \frac{2}{5} \\ \frac{11}{15} \\ \hline + \end{array}$$

2.
$$\begin{array}{r} \frac{7}{10} \\ \frac{3}{4} \\ \hline + \end{array}$$

3.
$$\begin{array}{r} \frac{3}{5} \\ \frac{17}{25} \\ \hline + \end{array}$$

4.
$$\begin{array}{r} 5 \\ \frac{3}{4} \\ \hline + \end{array}$$

5. $\frac{11}{14} + \frac{5}{7}$

6. $\frac{2}{15} + \frac{3}{10}$

7. $\frac{1}{3} + \frac{7}{18}$

8. $\frac{5}{6} + \frac{9}{30}$

9. $\frac{5}{12} + \frac{1}{5}$

10. $\frac{7}{20} + \frac{2}{25}$

11. $\frac{3}{4} + 8$

12. $\frac{7}{10} + \frac{17}{100}$

Cooperative Learning

13. Explain to a partner how you add the fractions in number **9** in **Practice**.

14. Write any two unlike fractions. Ask a partner to add them. Check the work.

8·4 Subtracting Unlike Fractions

When subtracting fractions with different denominators, replace them with equivalent fractions with the least common denominator. Then subtract. Write your answer in lowest terms.

▶ **EXAMPLE 1**

Check

$$\frac{5 \times 3}{8 \times 3} = \frac{15}{24}$$

Subtract. $\frac{19}{24} - \frac{5}{8}$

24 is the least common multiple of 24 and 8.

$$\frac{19}{24} \quad \longrightarrow \quad \frac{19}{24}$$

Use 24 as the least common denominator.

$$-\frac{5}{8} \quad \longrightarrow \quad -\frac{15}{24}$$

$$\frac{19 - 15}{24} = \frac{4}{24} = \frac{1}{6}$$

▶ **EXAMPLE 2**

Check

$$\frac{8 \times 2}{9 \times 2} = \frac{16}{18}$$

$$\frac{5 \times 3}{6 \times 3} = \frac{15}{18}$$

Subtract. $\frac{8}{9} - \frac{5}{6}$

18 is the least common multiple of 9 and 6.

$$\frac{8}{9} \quad \longrightarrow \quad \frac{16}{18}$$

Use 18 as the least common denominator.

$$-\frac{5}{6} \quad \longrightarrow \quad -\frac{15}{18}$$

$$\frac{16 - 15}{18} = \frac{1}{18}$$

When you subtract a fraction from a whole number, replace the whole number with an equivalent fraction.

▶ **EXAMPLE 3**

Check

$$\frac{3 \times 5}{1 \times 5} = \frac{15}{5}$$

Subtract. $3 - \frac{4}{5}$

5 is the least common multiple of 1 and 5.

$$3 \quad \longrightarrow \quad \frac{3}{1} \quad \longrightarrow \quad \frac{15}{5}$$

Use 5 as the least common denominator.

$$-\frac{4}{5} \quad \longrightarrow \quad -\frac{4}{5} \quad \longrightarrow \quad -\frac{4}{5}$$

$$\frac{11}{5} = 2\frac{1}{5}$$

Try These

Subtract.

1. $\dfrac{11}{20} - \dfrac{2}{5}$

■ is the least common multiple of 20 and 5.

Use ■ as the least common denominator.

$\dfrac{11}{20} - \dfrac{2}{5} = \dfrac{\blacksquare}{\blacksquare}$

$\begin{aligned}\dfrac{11}{20} &\rightarrow \dfrac{11}{20}\\ -\dfrac{2}{5} &\rightarrow -\dfrac{\blacksquare}{\blacksquare}\\ \hline\end{aligned}$ $\dfrac{\blacksquare - \blacksquare}{\blacksquare} = \dfrac{\blacksquare}{\blacksquare}$

2. $\dfrac{3}{4} - \dfrac{1}{3}$

■ is the least common multiple of 4 and 3.

Use ■ as the least common denominator.

$\dfrac{3}{4} - \dfrac{1}{3} = \dfrac{\blacksquare}{\blacksquare}$

$\begin{aligned}\dfrac{3}{4} &\rightarrow \dfrac{\blacksquare}{12}\\ -\dfrac{1}{3} &\rightarrow -\dfrac{\blacksquare}{\blacksquare}\\ \hline\end{aligned}$ $\dfrac{\blacksquare - \blacksquare}{\blacksquare} = \dfrac{\blacksquare}{\blacksquare}$

Practice

Subtract.

1. $\begin{aligned}\dfrac{4}{5}\\ -\dfrac{3}{10}\\ \hline\end{aligned}$ **2.** $\begin{aligned}1\\ -\dfrac{3}{8}\\ \hline\end{aligned}$ **3.** $\begin{aligned}\dfrac{2}{3}\\ -\dfrac{1}{8}\\ \hline\end{aligned}$ **4.** $\begin{aligned}\dfrac{3}{4}\\ -\dfrac{3}{4}\\ \hline\end{aligned}$

5. $\dfrac{7}{8} - \dfrac{5}{12}$ **6.** $\dfrac{11}{12} - \dfrac{1}{6}$ **7.** $\dfrac{14}{15} - \dfrac{1}{6}$ **8.** $\dfrac{5}{6} - \dfrac{9}{30}$

9. $\dfrac{18}{25} - \dfrac{3}{5}$ **10.** $\dfrac{1}{2} - \dfrac{3}{25}$ **11.** $\dfrac{3}{10} - \dfrac{7}{30}$ **12.** $\dfrac{7}{10} - \dfrac{17}{100}$

Cooperative Learning

13. Explain to a partner how to subtract the fraction in number **1** in **Practice**.

14. Write any two unlike fractions. Ask a partner to subtract the smaller fraction from the larger fraction. Check the work.

Add mixed numbers by adding the fraction parts. Then, add the whole number parts. Write your answer in lowest terms.

 EXAMPLE 1

Add. $3\frac{5}{8} + 4\frac{1}{8}$

Add the fraction parts. Add the whole number parts.

Math Fact
$\frac{6}{8}$ in lowest terms is $\frac{3}{4}$.

$$\begin{array}{r} 3\frac{5}{8} \\ + 4\frac{1}{8} \\ \hline \frac{6}{8} \end{array} \qquad \longrightarrow \qquad \begin{array}{r} 3\frac{5}{8} \\ + 4\frac{1}{8} \\ \hline 7\frac{6}{8} = 7\frac{3}{4} \end{array}$$

The sum of $3\frac{5}{8} + 4\frac{1}{8}$ is $7\frac{3}{4}$.

Sometimes, you will need to find the least common denominator for the fraction parts.

▶ **EXAMPLE 2**

Add. $5\frac{1}{4} + 4\frac{2}{3}$

Add the fraction parts. Add the whole number parts.

Math Fact
12 is the least common multiple of 4 and 3. Use 12 as the least common denominator.

$$\begin{array}{r} 5\frac{1}{4} \\ + 4\frac{2}{3} \end{array} \longrightarrow \begin{array}{r} 5\frac{3}{12} \\ + 4\frac{8}{12} \\ \hline \frac{11}{12} \end{array} \longrightarrow \begin{array}{r} 5\frac{3}{12} \\ + 4\frac{8}{12} \\ \hline 9\frac{11}{12} \end{array}$$

The sum of $5\frac{1}{4} + 4\frac{2}{3}$ is $9\frac{11}{12}$.

The fraction part of the answer may be an improper fraction. Write a mixed number for this improper fraction.

▶ **EXAMPLE 3**

Add. $8\frac{7}{10} + 9\frac{9}{10}$

Add the fraction parts. Add the whole number parts.

Math Fact
$\frac{16}{10}$ in lowest terms is $\frac{8}{5}$.

$$\begin{array}{r} 8\frac{7}{10} \\ + 9\frac{9}{10} \\ \hline \frac{16}{10} \end{array} \longrightarrow \begin{array}{r} 8\frac{7}{10} \\ + 9\frac{9}{10} \\ \hline 17\frac{16}{10} = 17\frac{8}{5} = 17 + \frac{8}{5} = 17 + 1\frac{3}{5} \end{array}$$

The sum of $8\frac{7}{10} + 9\frac{9}{10}$ is $18\frac{3}{5}$.

Try These

Add.

1. $2\frac{5}{9} + 4\frac{2}{9}$

$$2\frac{5}{9} \quad \rightarrow \quad 2\frac{5}{9}$$
$$+ 4\frac{2}{9} \qquad + 4\frac{2}{9}$$
$$\overline{\frac{\blacksquare}{9}} \qquad \blacksquare\frac{\blacksquare}{9} = \blacksquare\frac{\blacksquare}{\blacksquare}$$

$$2\frac{5}{9} + 4\frac{2}{9} = \blacksquare\frac{\blacksquare}{\blacksquare}$$

2. $2\frac{3}{4} + 6\frac{1}{2}$

$$2\frac{3}{4} \quad \rightarrow \quad 2\frac{3}{4} \quad \rightarrow \quad 2\frac{3}{4}$$
$$+ 6\frac{1}{2} \qquad + 6\frac{\blacksquare}{\blacksquare} \qquad + 6\frac{\blacksquare}{4}$$
$$\overline{\frac{\blacksquare}{4}} \qquad \blacksquare\frac{\blacksquare}{4} = \blacksquare + 1\frac{\blacksquare}{4} = \blacksquare\frac{\blacksquare}{4}$$

$$2\frac{3}{4} + 6\frac{1}{2} = \blacksquare\frac{\blacksquare}{4}$$

Practice

Add.

1. $1\frac{3}{4}$
$+ 4\frac{4}{5}$

2. $7\frac{1}{3}$
$+ 2\frac{5}{6}$

3. $4\frac{3}{4}$
$+ 8$

4. $3\frac{2}{5}$
$+ 2\frac{9}{20}$

5. $6\frac{3}{4}$
$+ 9\frac{5}{6}$

6. $5\frac{1}{3}$
$+ 2\frac{5}{18}$

7. $3\frac{1}{12}$
$+ 2\frac{5}{8}$

8. $7\frac{5}{6}$
$+ 3\frac{1}{6}$

9. $8\frac{1}{2} + 4\frac{1}{2}$

10. $9\frac{1}{3} + 4$

11. $5\frac{11}{16} + 1\frac{5}{8}$

12. $2\frac{7}{10} + 6\frac{3}{5}$

13. $8\frac{1}{2} + 4\frac{1}{6}$

14. $5\frac{7}{10} + 4\frac{9}{10}$

15. $2\frac{5}{6} + 7\frac{1}{12}$

16. $10\frac{3}{4} + 9\frac{3}{4}$

Cooperative Learning

17. Explain to a partner how to add the mixed numbers in number **6** in **Practice**.

18. Write a pair of mixed numbers. Ask a partner to add them. Check the work.

Subtracting Mixed Numbers

Subtract mixed numbers by subtracting the fraction parts. Then, subtract the whole number parts. You may have to find the least common denominator for the fraction parts.

▶ **EXAMPLE 1**

Subtract. $5\frac{11}{15} - 2\frac{1}{3}$

Subtract the fraction parts.   Subtract the whole number parts.

$$5\frac{11}{15} \rightarrow 5\frac{11}{15}$$
$$-\ 2\frac{1}{3} \rightarrow -\ 2\frac{5}{15}$$
$$\overline{\hphantom{-\ 2}\frac{6}{15}}$$

$\rightarrow$

$$5\frac{11}{15}$$
$$-\ 2\frac{5}{15}$$
$$\overline{3\frac{6}{15} = 3\frac{2}{5}}$$

$$5\frac{11}{15} - 2\frac{1}{3} = 3\frac{2}{5}$$

Sometimes, you have to regroup a mixed number so you can subtract.

▶ **EXAMPLE 2**

Math Fact

$\frac{1}{4}$ is less than $\frac{3}{4}$.

Subtract. $6\frac{1}{4} - 3\frac{3}{4}$

$$6\frac{1}{4} \rightarrow 6\frac{1}{4} = 5 + 1\frac{1}{4} = 5 + \frac{5}{4} = 5\frac{5}{4} \rightarrow 5\frac{5}{4}$$
$$-\ 3\frac{3}{4} \qquad\qquad\qquad\qquad\qquad\qquad\qquad\qquad -\ 3\frac{3}{4}$$
$$\overline{\hphantom{-\ 3\frac{3}{4}} \qquad\qquad\qquad\qquad\qquad\qquad\qquad 2\frac{2}{4} = 2\frac{1}{2}}$$

$$6\frac{1}{4} - 3\frac{3}{4} = 2\frac{1}{2}$$

▶ **EXAMPLE 3**

Subtract. $8 - 2\frac{4}{5}$

$$8 \rightarrow 7 + 1 = 7 + \frac{5}{5} = 7\frac{5}{5} \rightarrow 7\frac{5}{5}$$
$$-\ 2\frac{4}{5} \qquad\qquad\qquad\qquad\qquad\qquad -\ 2\frac{4}{5}$$
$$\overline{\hphantom{-\ 2\frac{4}{5}} \qquad\qquad\qquad\qquad\qquad\quad 5\frac{1}{5}}$$

$$8 - 2\frac{4}{5} = 5\frac{1}{5}$$

Practice

Subtract.

1. $\begin{array}{r} 7\frac{3}{4} \\ -5\frac{1}{4} \\ \hline \end{array}$

2. $\begin{array}{r} 5\frac{4}{5} \\ -3\frac{2}{5} \\ \hline \end{array}$

3. $\begin{array}{r} 4\frac{4}{5} \\ -2\frac{3}{10} \\ \hline \end{array}$

4. $\begin{array}{r} 4\frac{5}{6} \\ -1\frac{1}{3} \\ \hline \end{array}$

5. $\begin{array}{r} 4\frac{2}{5} \\ -4\frac{1}{3} \\ \hline \end{array}$

6. $\begin{array}{r} 10\frac{1}{3} \\ -5\frac{1}{6} \\ \hline \end{array}$

7. $\begin{array}{r} 11\frac{1}{2} \\ -8\frac{3}{4} \\ \hline \end{array}$

8. $\begin{array}{r} 10 \\ -4\frac{1}{2} \\ \hline \end{array}$

9. $7\frac{1}{8} - 4\frac{3}{8}$

10. $4\frac{3}{8} - 1\frac{1}{2}$

11. $9\frac{9}{12} - 4\frac{1}{6}$

12. $4\frac{1}{4} - 2\frac{1}{2}$

13. $5 - 2\frac{1}{4}$

14. $4\frac{3}{4} - 1\frac{5}{12}$

15. $10\frac{1}{16} - 2\frac{5}{8}$

16. $8\frac{3}{8} - 4\frac{3}{4}$

Cooperative Learning

17. Explain to a partner how to subtract the mixed number in number **12** in **Practice**.

18. Write two mixed numbers. Ask a partner to subtract the smaller from the larger. Check the work.

Evaluating Variable Expressions

To evaluate a variable expression, replace the variables with numbers. You have already done this with whole numbers and decimals. You can also evaluate variable expressions by replacing the variables with fractions or mixed numbers.

▶ EXAMPLE 1

Find the value of $x + \frac{3}{5}$ when $x = \frac{4}{5}$.

Replace x with $\frac{4}{5}$. $x + \frac{3}{5}$

Add. $\frac{4}{5} + \frac{3}{5}$

$$\frac{7}{5} = 1\frac{2}{5}$$

The value of $x + \frac{3}{5}$ is $1\frac{2}{5}$ when $x = \frac{4}{5}$.

▶ EXAMPLE 2

Remember
Subtract the fraction parts.
Then, subtract the whole
number parts.

Find the value of $r - s$ when $r = 5\frac{5}{6}$ and $s = 3\frac{1}{6}$.

Replace r with $5\frac{5}{6}$ and s with $3\frac{1}{6}$. $r - s$

Subtract. $5\frac{5}{6} - 3\frac{1}{6}$

$$2\frac{4}{6} = 2\frac{2}{3}$$

The value of $r - s$ is $2\frac{2}{3}$ when $r = 5\frac{5}{6}$ and $s = 3\frac{1}{6}$.

You may have to find the least common denominator of the fractions.

▶ EXAMPLE 3

Math Fact
4 is the least common
denominator of 2 and 4.

Find the value of $a + b$ when $a = 2\frac{1}{2}$ and $b = \frac{3}{4}$.

Replace a with $2\frac{1}{2}$ $a + b$

and b with $\frac{3}{4}$. $2\frac{1}{2} + \frac{3}{4}$

Use 4 as the least $2\frac{2}{4} + \frac{3}{4}$
common denominator.

Add. $2\frac{5}{4} = 2 + \frac{5}{4} = 2 + 1\frac{1}{4} = 3\frac{1}{4}$.

The value of $a + b$ is $3\frac{1}{4}$ when $a = 2\frac{1}{2}$ and $b = \frac{3}{4}$.

Try These

Evaluate these expressions.

1. $3\frac{1}{3} + z$ when $z = 1\frac{1}{3}$.

Replace z with ▓. $\qquad 3\frac{1}{3} + z$

Add. $\qquad\qquad\qquad 3\frac{1}{3} + $ ▓

$\qquad\qquad\qquad\qquad$ ▓

The value of $3\frac{1}{3} + z$ is ▓ when $z = 1\frac{1}{3}$.

2. $c - d$ when $c = 4$ and $d = \frac{3}{4}$.

Replace c with 4. $\qquad c - d$

and d with ▓ $\qquad\qquad 4 - $ ▓

Regroup 4. $\qquad\qquad 3\frac{4}{4} - $ ▓

Subtract. $\qquad\qquad\qquad$ ▓

The value of $c - d$ is ▓ when $c = 4$ and $d = \frac{3}{4}$.

Practice

Evaluate each expression.

1. $n + 2$ when $n = \frac{3}{4}$

2. $a + b$ when $a = 5\frac{1}{3}$ and $b = \frac{2}{3}$

3. $x - y$ when $x = \frac{3}{4}$ and $y = \frac{1}{4}$

4. $6 - x$ when $x = \frac{1}{2}$

5. $\frac{4}{5} - r$ when $r = \frac{2}{3}$

6. $t + \frac{3}{8}$ when $t = 4\frac{1}{4}$

7. $b + c$ when $b = 2\frac{1}{3}$ and $c = 4\frac{1}{6}$

8. $c - 3\frac{1}{2}$ when $c = 7\frac{3}{4}$

9. $m - n$ when $m = 5\frac{1}{3}$ and $n = 2\frac{1}{2}$

10. $x + y$ when $x = 1\frac{4}{5}$ and $y = 2\frac{1}{2}$

Cooperative Learning

11. Explain to a partner how to evaluate the expression in number 6 in **Practice.**

12. Write a variable expression using addition. Use fractions or mixed numbers for the values of the variables. Ask a partner to find the value of your variable expression. Check the work.

8-8   Solving Equations

You have already solved equations containing addition or subtraction of whole numbers and decimals. You solve equations with fractions and mixed numbers the same way. Remember, addition and subtraction undo each other.

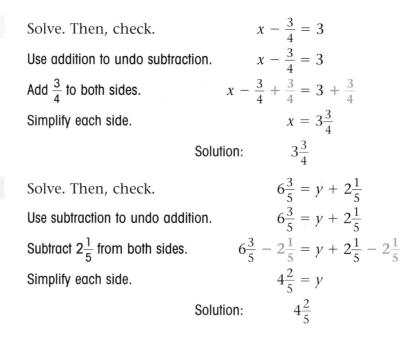

▶ **EXAMPLE 1**

Check
Replace x with $3\frac{3}{4}$.

$$x - \frac{3}{4} = 3$$

$$3\frac{3}{4} - \frac{3}{4} = 3$$

$$3 = 3 \quad \text{True}$$

Solve. Then, check. $x - \frac{3}{4} = 3$

Use addition to undo subtraction. $x - \frac{3}{4} = 3$

Add $\frac{3}{4}$ to both sides. $x - \frac{3}{4} + \frac{3}{4} = 3 + \frac{3}{4}$

Simplify each side. $x = 3\frac{3}{4}$

Solution: $3\frac{3}{4}$

▶ **EXAMPLE 2**

Check
Replace y with $4\frac{2}{5}$.

$$6\frac{3}{5} = y + 2\frac{1}{5}$$

$$6\frac{3}{5} = 4\frac{2}{5} + 2\frac{1}{5}$$

$$6\frac{3}{5} = 6\frac{3}{5} \quad \text{True}$$

Solve. Then, check. $6\frac{3}{5} = y + 2\frac{1}{5}$

Use subtraction to undo addition. $6\frac{3}{5} = y + 2\frac{1}{5}$

Subtract $2\frac{1}{5}$ from both sides. $6\frac{3}{5} - 2\frac{1}{5} = y + 2\frac{1}{5} - 2\frac{1}{5}$

Simplify each side. $4\frac{2}{5} = y$

Solution: $4\frac{2}{5}$

Sometimes, you will have to find the least common denominator.

▶ **EXAMPLE 3**

Check
Replace x with $\frac{1}{10}$.

$$x + \frac{1}{5} = \frac{3}{10}$$

$$\frac{1}{10} + \frac{2}{10} = \frac{3}{10}$$

$$\frac{3}{10} = \frac{3}{10} \quad \text{True}$$

Solve. Then, check. $x + \frac{1}{5} = \frac{3}{10}$

Use subtraction to undo addition. $x + \frac{1}{5} = \frac{3}{10}$

Subtract $\frac{1}{5}$ from both sides. $x + \frac{1}{5} - \frac{1}{5} = \frac{3}{10} - \frac{1}{5}$

Simplify each side. $x = \frac{3}{10} - \frac{2}{10}$

$$x = \frac{1}{10}$$

Solution: $\frac{1}{10}$

Try These

Solve. Then, check.

1. $y - 3\frac{2}{7} = 1\frac{1}{7}$

Add ■ to both sides. $\quad y - 3\frac{2}{7} + ■ = 1\frac{1}{7} + ■$

Simplify each side. $\qquad\qquad y = ■$

Solution: $\qquad\qquad\qquad ■$

Check. Replace y with ■.

$y - 3\frac{2}{7} = 1\frac{1}{7}$

$■ - 3\frac{2}{7} = 1\frac{1}{7}$

$■ = 1\frac{1}{7}$ True

2. $\frac{2}{3} = x + \frac{3}{5}$

Subtract ■ from both sides. $\quad \frac{2}{3} - \frac{3}{5} = x + \frac{3}{5} - ■$

Simplify each side. $\qquad\qquad \frac{10}{15} - ■ = x$

$\qquad\qquad\qquad\qquad ■ = x$

Solution: $\qquad\qquad\qquad ■$

Check. Replace x with ■.

$\frac{2}{3} = x + \frac{3}{5}$

$\frac{2}{3} = ■ + \frac{3}{5}$

$\frac{2}{3} = ■ + \frac{9}{15}$

$\frac{2}{3} = ■$ True

Practice

Solve. Then, check.

1. $x + \frac{1}{5} = \frac{4}{5}$

2. $\frac{1}{3} = n - \frac{2}{3}$

3. $y - 3\frac{1}{2} = 4$

4. $4\frac{5}{6} = a + 1\frac{1}{6}$

5. $b + 1\frac{5}{8} = 2\frac{7}{8}$

6. $3\frac{4}{5} = c - 5\frac{3}{5}$

7. $\frac{1}{9} = x - \frac{2}{3}$

8. $y - 2\frac{1}{2} = 5$

9. $a + 2\frac{2}{3} = 4\frac{5}{6}$

10. $c - 1\frac{3}{4} = 2\frac{5}{8}$

Cooperative Learning

11. Explain to a partner how to solve the equation in number **10** in **Practice**.

12. Write a variable equation that uses subtraction and mixed numbers. Ask a partner to solve your equation. Check the solution.

8-9 Calculator: Adding and Subtracting Fractions

Use your calculator to add and subtract fractions.

Add. $\dfrac{8}{15} + \dfrac{11}{25}$

► **EXAMPLE**

First, find a common denominator

Display

Multiply 15 and 25
by pressing: [1] [5] [×] [2] [5] [=] $3\,75$

Replace each fraction with an equivalent fraction.
The denominator is 375.

Write: $\dfrac{8}{15} = \dfrac{8 \times 25}{15 \times 25}$ → Use a calculator to find 8×25.
  → You already know $15 \times 25 = 375$.

Multiply 8 and 25
by pressing: [8] [×] [2] [5] [=] 200

So, $\dfrac{8}{15} = \dfrac{8 \times 25}{15 \times 25} = \dfrac{200}{375}$.

Write: $\dfrac{11}{25} = \dfrac{11 \times 15}{25 \times 15}$

Multiply 11 and 15
by pressing: [1] [1] [×] [1] [5] [=] 165

So, $\dfrac{11}{25} = \dfrac{11 \times 15}{25 \times 15} = \dfrac{165}{375}$.

$\dfrac{8}{15} + \dfrac{11}{25}$ → $\dfrac{200 + 165}{375}$

Just add the numerators. Use the same denominator.

Add 200 and 165
by pressing: [2] [0] [0] [+] 200

[1] [6] [5] 165

[=] 365

So, $\dfrac{8}{15} + \dfrac{11}{25} = \dfrac{365}{375}$.

To subtract fractions, follow the same steps. Find a common denominator. Replace each fraction with an equivalent fraction with the common denominator. Then, subtract the numerators. Keep the denominator.

Practice

Use your calculator to add or subtract.

1. $\frac{3}{16} + \frac{3}{7}$

2. $\frac{2}{7} + \frac{1}{6}$

3. $\frac{3}{8} + \frac{2}{9}$

4. $\frac{7}{13} - \frac{3}{15}$

5. $\frac{7}{8} - \frac{3}{10}$

6. $\frac{9}{25} + \frac{3}{4}$

On-the-Job Math

CARPENTRY

Have you ever wanted to build something out of wood? That is what carpenters do. In order to be a carpenter, you need to understand fractions. Carpenters use fractions to take exact measurements.

Carpenters work with wood. They build, finish, and repair wooden objects and structures. Rough carpenters assemble the framework of a building. Finish carpenters work on the inside of a building. Some carpenters even have specialties, such as cabinetmaking.

You can learn carpentry in many ways. You can attend a technical or vocational school. You can get on-the-job-training. Or you can join an apprentice program. No matter how you learn the skill, you need to learn how to work with fractions.

Some problems have more information than you need to solve them. Other problems do not have enough information.

EXAMPLE

Paula has 100 stamps in her collection. Jim has 20 stamps. Paula sells 50 stamps. How many stamps does Paula has left?

Tell whether there is too much information or too little information.

READ **What do you need to find out?**
You need to find out how many stamps Paula has left. Is there too much or too little information?

PLAN **What do you need to do?**
You need to try to solve the problem. If you are not able to, there may be too little information. If you are able to solve it, there may be too much information.

DO **Follow the plan.**

Stamps had − Stamps traded = Stamps left

100 stamps − 50 stamps = 50 stamps

Paula has 50 stamps left.

You do not need to know that Jim has 20 stamps.

CHECK **Does your answer make sense?**
50 stamps is less than 100 stamps. ✓

There was too much information.

Try These

1. Rosa did homework for 1 hour after school. Later, she did homework again. How many hours in all did Rosa do homework that day?

   1 hour + ■ hour = ■ hours in all

   Stop!

   You need to know ■.

   Too ■ information.

2. Eric rented two movies from the video store. Each movie cost $3.50 to rent. He watched the movies for $2\frac{1}{2}$ hours. How much did it cost for Eric to rent two movies?

   2 movies × $3.50 each = ■

   You do not need to know ■.

   Too ■ information.

Practice

Solve the problem if you can. Tell whether there is too much information or too little information to do the problem.

1. Lee rented a bicycle for $5.00 an hour. He rode the bike for 3 miles. How much did Lee pay in all to rent the bike?

2. Della and Marco baked bread for the bake sale. Marco baked 3 loaves. He sold each loaf for $1.50. Della sold her loaf for $2.00. How much did Marco make in all selling bread?

3. It takes Mario 10 minutes to walk to school each day. He walks to school 4 days a week. On Friday, he always gets a ride. How many minutes a week in all does Mario walk to school?

4. Anna is 16 years old. Carlos is three years older than Anna. Luisa is the youngest. How old is Luisa?

Cooperative Learning

5. Explain to a partner how you solved number **3** in **Practice**. Tell your partner what information you did not need.

6. Make up a problem that is missing information. Then, have your partner make up what is missing. Together, solve the problem.

Application: Mode and Median

An item that appears most often in a group is called the **mode.**

► **EXAMPLE 1**

The grades on a recent math quiz were B, A, B, C, C, B, A, A, B, and C. Find the mode.

Remember
When you reorder a list, count the items to make sure you did not forget any.

Write the letters in order.   A, A, A, B, B, B, B, C, C, C

Count the number of times   A appears 3 times,
each letter appears.   B appears 4 times, and
                                 C appears 3 times.

B appears most often. B is the mode.

When you order a group of numbers from smallest to largest, the middle number is the **median.**

► **EXAMPLE 2**

Find the median for 8, 7, 6, 9, 11, 5, 6.

Write the numbers in order   5, 6, 6, 7, 8, 9, 11
from smallest to largest.

Find the middle number.   5, 6, 6, 7, 8, 9, 11
                                             ↑

The median is 7.

When there are two middle numbers, the median is the average of the two middle numbers.

► **EXAMPLE 3**

Find the median for 10, 14, 13, 10, 11, 17.

Write the numbers in order   10, 10, 11, 13, 14, 17
from smallest to largest.

Find the middle numbers.   10, 10, 11, 13, 14, 17

Find the average of 11 and 13. $\frac{11 + 13}{2} = \frac{24}{2} = 12$

The median is 12.

Try These

1. Find the mode of 4, 5, 3, 4, 5, 5, 4, 4.

   Write the numbers in order from smallest to largest.

   Count the number of times each number appears.

   3, 4, 4, 4, 4, 5, 5, 5

   3 appears ■ time.

   4 appears ■ times.

   5 appears ■ times.

   The mode is ■.

2. Find the median for 9, 6, 4, 21, 2, 11, 18, 11.

   Write the numbers in order from smallest to largest.

   ■, ■, ■, ■, ■, ■, ■, ■

   Find the middle numbers.

   2, 4, 6, ■, ■, 11, 18, 21

   Find the average of ■ and ■.

   $\dfrac{■ + ■}{2} = \dfrac{■}{2} = ■$

   The median is ■.

Practice

Find the mode.

1. 2, 3, 2, 4, 4, 2, 4, 2, 3

2. 6, 8, 8, 9, 8, 9, 6, 7, 10

3. 5, 6, 8, 4, 7, 8, 5, 5

4. 3, 5, 7, 9, 6, 6

Find the median.

5. 2, 3, 2, 4, 4, 2, 4

6. 6, 10, 8, 9, 8, 9, 6, 7

7. 5, 6, 8, 4, 7, 8, 5

8. 3, 5, 7, 9, 6, 6

Cooperative Learning

9. Write a group of ten numbers. Have a partner find the mode.

10. Write a group of nine numbers. Have a partner find the median.

Summary

Like fractions have the same denominators.

To add or subtract like fractions, add or subtract the numerators. Use the denominator as the denominator of your answer.

A common denominator for two or more fractions is a common multiple of the denominators.

One way to find a common denominator is by multiplying the denominators.

When adding fractions with different denominators, replace them with equivalent fractions with the least common denominator.

A proper fraction is a fraction with the numerator less than the denominator.

To add a whole number and a proper fraction, write a mixed number.

When subtracting fractions with different denominators, replace them with equivalent fractions with the least common denominator.

Add mixed numbers by adding the fraction parts. Then, add the whole number parts.

Subtract mixed numbers by subtracting the fraction parts. Then, subtract the whole number parts.

To evaluate a variable expression, replace the variables with numbers. You can evaluate variable expressions by replacing the variables with fractions or mixed numbers.

You solve equations with fractions and mixed numbers the same way you solve equations with whole numbers.

A problem may have too much or too little information.

common denominator

least common denominator

median

mode

Vocabulary Review

Complete the sentences with words from the box.

1. The middle number in a group of numbers is the _____.

2. The number that appears most often in a group of numbers is the _____.

3. The _____ is the smallest common denominator.

4. A common multiple of the denominators is a _____.

Chapter Quiz

Add or subtract.

1. $\dfrac{15}{20} - \dfrac{5}{20}$

2. $\dfrac{11}{15} + \dfrac{13}{15}$

3. $\dfrac{18}{25} - \dfrac{13}{25}$

4. $\dfrac{17}{18} + \dfrac{9}{18}$

Find equivalent fractions with the least common denominator.

5. $\dfrac{7}{10}$ and $\dfrac{9}{30}$

6. $\dfrac{3}{4}$ and $\dfrac{1}{10}$

7. $\dfrac{9}{25}$ and $\dfrac{3}{100}$

8. $\dfrac{5}{16}$ and $\dfrac{3}{4}$

Add.

9. $\dfrac{4}{25} + \dfrac{1}{20}$

10. $\dfrac{5}{6} + \dfrac{3}{10}$

11. $\dfrac{7}{12} + \dfrac{9}{16}$

12. $\dfrac{2}{15} + \dfrac{1}{6}$

Subtract.

13. $\dfrac{3}{4} - \dfrac{7}{10}$

14. $\dfrac{15}{16} - \dfrac{7}{12}$

15. $\dfrac{19}{15} - \dfrac{3}{10}$

16. $\dfrac{21}{25} - \dfrac{11}{20}$

Add or subtract.

17. $9\dfrac{1}{2} - 4\dfrac{1}{6}$

18. $7\dfrac{7}{10} - 4\dfrac{9}{10}$

19. $11\dfrac{1}{16} + 4\dfrac{5}{8}$

20. $6 + 4\dfrac{1}{4}$

Evaluate each expression.

21. $c + d$ when $c = 2\dfrac{2}{3}$ and $d = 2$

22. $10 - y$ when $y = 2\dfrac{5}{16}$

Solve. Then, check.

23. $b + 1\dfrac{1}{4} = 5\dfrac{2}{3}$

24. $10 = 2\dfrac{1}{2} + x$

Solve the problem if you can. Tell whether there is too much or too little information.

25. Kyle rented a car for $50.00 a day. He also had to pay $15.00 for gas. He drove 200 miles and used the car for 3 days. How much did Kyle pay in all to use the car he rented?

Chapter 9

Multiplying and Dividing Fractions

Architects use math to draw plans and to calculate how much material is needed in buildings. What measurements do architects need to know?

Learning Objectives

- Multiply and divide fractions and mixed numbers.
- Simplify variable expressions with fractions and mixed numbers.
- Evaluate equations with fractions and mixed numbers.
- Solve equations with fractions and mixed numbers.
- Use a calculator to multiply and divide fractions.
- Solve problems by reading information from a table.
- Apply concepts and skills to find the minimum, maximum, and range.

Words to Know

reciprocal of a fraction	the fraction you get when you exchange the numerator and denominator
minimum	the smallest number in a group of numbers
maximum	the largest number in a group of numbers
range	the difference between the largest and the smallest number in a group of numbers

Stock Market Project

Choose two stocks listed on the stock market. Follow them daily for a week, keeping a log of their progress. Suppose you were to buy 100 shares. Note your losses and gains. By the end of the chapter, be prepared to give a report on your success. Tell about the stocks you chose and how well they did. Note the daily ups and downs on a line graph that you will use to present your report.

This picture shows a way to multiply fractions.

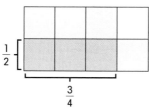

From the picture, the product of $\frac{1}{2}$ and $\frac{3}{4}$ is shown by the parts where the shading for $\frac{1}{2}$ and the shading for $\frac{3}{4}$ overlap.

From the picture: $\frac{1}{2} \times \frac{3}{4} = \frac{3}{8}$

You can also use multiplication: $\frac{1}{2} \times \frac{3}{4} = \frac{1 \times 3}{2 \times 4} = \frac{3}{8}$

To multiply fractions, multiply numerators and multiply denominators. Write the product in lowest terms.

▶ **EXAMPLE 1**

Multiply.　　$\frac{4}{5} \times \frac{1}{4}$

Multiply numerators and denominators.

$$\frac{4 \times 1}{5 \times 4} = \frac{4}{20} = \frac{1}{5}$$

$$\frac{4}{5} \times \frac{1}{4} = \frac{1}{5}$$

▶ **EXAMPLE 2**

Multiply.　　$\frac{3}{4} \times 5$

Remember
When multiplying whole numbers and fractions, replace whole numbers with fractions.

Replace 5 with a fraction.

$$\frac{3}{4} \times \frac{5}{1}$$

Multiply numerators and denominators.

$$\frac{3 \times 5}{4 \times 1} = \frac{15}{4} = 3\frac{3}{4}$$

$$\frac{3}{4} \times 5 = 3\frac{3}{4}$$

Sometimes the product of two fractions is 1. These fractions are reciprocals of each other.

$$\frac{2}{3} \times \frac{3}{2} = \frac{2 \times 3}{3 \times 2} = \frac{6}{6} = 1$$

$\frac{3}{2}$ and $\frac{2}{3}$ are **reciprocals** of each other. To find the reciprocal of a fraction, exchange the numerator and denominator.

Check
$7 = \frac{7}{1}$

The reciprocal of $\frac{4}{5}$ is $\frac{5}{4}$.

The reciprocal of 7 is $\frac{1}{7}$.

Try These

Multiply.

1. $\frac{1}{6} \times \frac{3}{5}$

Multiply the numerators and denominators.

$$\frac{\blacksquare \times \blacksquare}{6 \times \blacksquare}$$

$$= \frac{\blacksquare}{30}$$

$$= \frac{\blacksquare}{\blacksquare}$$

$$\frac{1}{6} \times \frac{3}{5} = \frac{\blacksquare}{\blacksquare}$$

2. $7 \times \frac{3}{4}$

Write 7 as a fraction.

$$\frac{7}{\blacksquare} \times \frac{3}{4}$$

Multiply the numerators and denominators.

$$\frac{7}{\blacksquare} \times \frac{\blacksquare}{4}$$

$$= \frac{\blacksquare}{4}$$

$$5\frac{\blacksquare}{4}$$

$$7 \times \frac{3}{4} = 5\frac{\blacksquare}{4}$$

Find the reciprocal.

3. $\frac{3}{8}$ **4.** $\frac{7}{8}$ **5.** 12 **6.** $\frac{1}{3}$

Practice

Multiply.

1. $\frac{2}{3} \times \frac{5}{8}$ **2.** $\frac{5}{7} \times 8$ **3.** $\frac{2}{5} \times \frac{3}{5}$ **4.** $1 \times \frac{4}{7}$

5. $\frac{2}{3} \times \frac{4}{5}$ **6.** $\frac{8}{9} \times \frac{9}{8}$ **7.** $\frac{1}{5} \times \frac{3}{4}$ **8.** $\frac{7}{8} \times \frac{2}{7}$

Find the reciprocal.

9. $\frac{9}{10}$ **10.** 1 **11.** $\frac{5}{16}$ **12.** $\frac{9}{6}$

13. 10 **14.** $\frac{12}{11}$ **15.** $\frac{1}{20}$ **16.** $\frac{6}{7}$

Cooperative Learning

17. Explain to a partner how you find the product in number 8 in **Practice**.

18. Write two fractions. Ask a partner to find their product. Check the work.

Multiplication Shortcut

You may want to use this shortcut for multiplying fractions. Divide numerators and denominators by their greatest common factors. Then, multiply.

▶ **EXAMPLE 1**

Multiply. $\dfrac{5}{8} \times \dfrac{3}{10}$

$$\dfrac{5}{8} \times \dfrac{3}{10}$$

Check

$5 \div 5 = 1$
$10 \div 5 = 2$

5 is the greatest common factor of 5 and 10.

$\dfrac{5}{8} \times \dfrac{3}{10} = \dfrac{3}{16}$

$$\dfrac{^1\cancel{5} \times 3}{8 \times \cancel{10}_2} = \dfrac{3}{16}$$

▶ **EXAMPLE 2**

Multiply. $\dfrac{9}{10} \times \dfrac{25}{36}$

$$\dfrac{9}{10} \times \dfrac{25}{36}$$

9 is the greatest common factor of 9 and 36.
5 is the greatest common factor of 10 and 25.

$\dfrac{9}{10} \times \dfrac{25}{36} = \dfrac{5}{8}$

$$\dfrac{^1\cancel{9} \times \cancel{25}^5}{_2\cancel{10} \times \cancel{36}_4} = \dfrac{5}{8}$$

▶ **EXAMPLE 3**

Multiply. $\dfrac{7}{9} \times \dfrac{9}{7}$

$$\dfrac{7}{9} \times \dfrac{9}{7}$$

Math Fact

$\dfrac{7}{9}$ and $\dfrac{9}{7}$ are reciprocals of each other.

7 is the greatest common factor of 7 and 7.
9 is the greatest common factor of 9 and 9.

$\dfrac{7}{9} \times \dfrac{9}{7} = 1$

$$\dfrac{^1\cancel{7} \times \cancel{9}^1}{_1\cancel{9} \times \cancel{7}_1} = \dfrac{1}{1} = 1$$

Try These

Multiply.

1. $\frac{5}{12} \times \frac{18}{25}$

■ is the greatest common factor of 5 and 25. ■ is the greatest common factor of 12 and 18.

$\frac{5}{12} \times \frac{18}{25} = \frac{■}{■}$

$$\frac{^1\cancel{5} \times \cancel{18}^■}{_2\cancel{12} \times \cancel{25}_■}$$

$$= \frac{■}{■}$$

2. $\frac{3}{4} \times 20$

Write 20 as a fraction.

■ is the greatest common factor of 4 and 20.

$\frac{3}{4} \times 20 = ■$

$$\frac{3 \times 20}{4 \times 1}$$

$$\frac{3 \times \cancel{20}^■}{_■\cancel{4} \times 1}$$

$$= \frac{■}{1} = ■$$

Practice

Multiply.

1. $\frac{2}{3} \times \frac{3}{5}$

2. $\frac{3}{4} \times \frac{5}{18}$

3. $\frac{5}{7} \times \frac{7}{6}$

4. $7 \times \frac{1}{7}$

5. $\frac{2}{9} \times \frac{3}{4}$

6. $16 \times \frac{5}{8}$

7. $\frac{5}{8} \times 80$

8. $\frac{1}{2} \times \frac{8}{25}$

9. $\frac{20}{30} \times \frac{3}{10}$

10. $\frac{9}{16} \times \frac{2}{3}$

11. $\frac{1}{9} \times 9$

12. $\frac{2}{3} \times \frac{9}{10}$

13. $30 \times \frac{1}{3}$

14. $\frac{4}{7} \times \frac{7}{4}$

15. $\frac{1}{10} \times \frac{25}{40}$

Cooperative Learning

16. Explain to a partner how you find the product in number **10** in **Practice.**

17. Write any two fractions. Ask a partner to find their product. Check the work.

Dividing Fractions

This picture shows a way to divide fractions. The strip is 3 units long. Look for pieces $\frac{3}{4}$ of a unit in length.

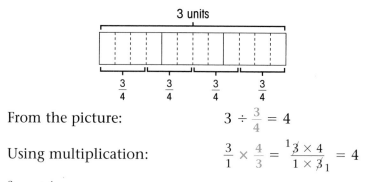

3 units

$\frac{3}{4}$ $\frac{3}{4}$ $\frac{3}{4}$ $\frac{3}{4}$

From the picture: $3 \div \frac{3}{4} = 4$

Using multiplication: $\frac{3}{1} \times \frac{4}{3} = \frac{{}^1\cancel{3} \times 4}{1 \times \cancel{3}_1} = 4$

$\frac{3}{4}$ and $\frac{4}{3}$ are reciprocals of each other.

To divide by a fraction, multiply by the reciprocal of the fraction.

▶ **EXAMPLE 1**

Divide. $\frac{4}{5} \div \frac{2}{3}$

$$\frac{4}{5} \div \frac{2}{3}$$

Math Fact

$\frac{2}{3}$ and $\frac{3}{2}$ are reciprocals of each other.

Multiply by the reciprocal of $\frac{2}{3}$.

$\frac{4}{5} \times \frac{3}{2} = \frac{{}^2\cancel{4} \times 3}{5 \times \cancel{2}_1} = \frac{6}{5} = 1\frac{1}{5}$

$\frac{4}{5} \div \frac{2}{3} = 1\frac{1}{5}$

Be sure to replace whole numbers with fractions.

▶ **EXAMPLE 2**

Divide. $\frac{8}{15} \div 4$

$$\frac{8}{15} \div 4$$

Math Fact

$\frac{4}{1}$ and $\frac{1}{4}$ are reciprocals of each other.

Replace 4 with $\frac{4}{1}$.

$\frac{8}{15} \div \frac{4}{1}$

Multiply by the reciprocal of $\frac{4}{1}$.

$\frac{8}{15} \times \frac{1}{4} = \frac{{}^2\cancel{8} \times 1}{15 \times \cancel{4}_1} = \frac{2}{15}$

$\frac{8}{15} \div 4 = \frac{2}{15}$

Try These

Divide.

1. $\frac{3}{5} \div \frac{4}{25}$

Multiply by the reciprocal of $\frac{4}{25}$.

$\frac{3}{5} \times \frac{25}{\blacksquare}$

$\frac{3}{1\cancel{5}} \times \frac{\cancel{25}^{\blacksquare}}{\blacksquare}$

$\frac{3}{5} \div \frac{4}{25} = \blacksquare \frac{3}{4}$

2. $9 \div \frac{3}{4}$

Replace 9 with $\frac{9}{1}$.

$\frac{9}{1} \div \frac{3}{4}$

Multiply by the reciprocal of $\frac{3}{4}$.

$\frac{\blacksquare 9}{1} \times \frac{\blacksquare}{3} {}_1$

$= \frac{\blacksquare}{1} = \blacksquare$

$9 \div \frac{3}{4} = \blacksquare$

Practice

Divide.

1. $\frac{3}{5} \div \frac{2}{3}$

2. $\frac{9}{10} \div \frac{3}{4}$

3. $\frac{7}{12} \div \frac{5}{6}$

4. $\frac{7}{8} \div \frac{1}{2}$

5. $\frac{9}{16} \div \frac{4}{9}$

6. $\frac{1}{4} \div \frac{1}{2}$

7. $\frac{1}{2} \div 4$

8. $\frac{7}{8} \div \frac{4}{7}$

9. $5 \div \frac{3}{5}$

10. $\frac{2}{5} \div \frac{2}{5}$

11. $\frac{3}{4} \div \frac{3}{4}$

12. $\frac{3}{8} \div \frac{8}{3}$

13. $\frac{5}{6} \div \frac{5}{24}$

14. $2 \div \frac{4}{7}$

15. $\frac{4}{5} \div \frac{8}{15}$

Cooperative Learning

16. Explain to a partner how you divide the fractions in number **13** in **Practice**.

17. Write two fractions. Ask a partner to divide one by the other. Check the work.

You know that a mixed number can be written as a fraction. To multiply or divide mixed numbers, first replace mixed numbers with fractions. Then, multiply or divide.

▶ **EXAMPLE 1**

Multiply. $2\frac{1}{2} \times 3\frac{3}{5}$

$$2\frac{1}{2} \times 3\frac{3}{5}$$

Replace $2\frac{1}{2}$ and $3\frac{3}{5}$ with fractions.

$$\frac{5}{2} \times \frac{18}{5}$$

Multiply the fractions.

$$\frac{{}^1\cancel{5} \times \cancel{18}^9}{{}_1\cancel{2} \times \cancel{5}_1} = \frac{9}{1} = 9$$

$$2\frac{1}{2} \times 3\frac{3}{5} = 9$$

▶ **EXAMPLE 2**

Divide. $3\frac{1}{8} \div 3\frac{3}{4}$

$$3\frac{1}{8} \div 3\frac{3}{4}$$

Replace $3\frac{1}{8}$ and $3\frac{3}{4}$ with fractions.

$$\frac{25}{8} \div \frac{15}{4}$$

Multiply by the reciprocal of $\frac{15}{4}$.

$$\frac{25}{8} \times \frac{4}{15}$$

$$\frac{{}^5\cancel{25} \times \cancel{4}^1}{{}_2\cancel{8} \times \cancel{15}_3} = \frac{5}{6}$$

$$3\frac{1}{8} \div 3\frac{3}{4} = \frac{5}{6}$$

▶ **EXAMPLE 3**

Divide. $2\frac{2}{3} \div 8$

$$2\frac{2}{3} \div 8$$

Remember
Remember to replace whole numbers with fractions.

Replace 8 with a fraction.

$$2\frac{2}{3} \div \frac{8}{1}$$

Replace $2\frac{2}{3}$ with a fraction.

$$\frac{8}{3} \div \frac{8}{1}$$

Multiply by the reciprocal of 8.

$$\frac{8}{3} \times \frac{1}{8} = \frac{{}^1\cancel{8} \times 1}{3 \times \cancel{8}_1} = \frac{1}{3}$$

$$2\frac{2}{3} \div 8 = \frac{1}{3}$$

Try These

Multiply or divide.

1. $1\frac{2}{3} \times 2\frac{2}{5}$

Replace $1\frac{2}{3}$ and $2\frac{2}{5}$ with fractions.

$\frac{5}{3} \times \frac{\blacksquare}{5}$

Multiply.

$\frac{1\cancel{5}}{\cancel{3}_1} \times \frac{4\cancel{4}}{\cancel{5}_1}$

$= \frac{\blacksquare}{1} = \blacksquare$

$1\frac{2}{3} \times 2\frac{2}{5} = \blacksquare$

2. $2\frac{3}{4} \div 1\frac{1}{2}$

Replace $2\frac{3}{4}$ and $1\frac{1}{2}$ with fractions.

$\frac{11}{\blacksquare} \div \frac{3}{2}$

Multiply by the reciprocal of $\frac{3}{2}$.

$\frac{11}{\blacksquare} \times \frac{\blacksquare}{3}$

$= \frac{11}{2\cancel{\blacksquare}} \times \frac{\cancel{\blacksquare}^1}{3}$

$= \frac{11}{\blacksquare} \times \frac{1}{\blacksquare}$

$2\frac{3}{4} \div 1\frac{1}{2} = 1\frac{\blacksquare}{\blacksquare}$

Practice

Multiply or divide.

1. $3\frac{1}{10} \div \frac{3}{5}$

2. $2\frac{5}{8} \times 1\frac{5}{7}$

3. $4\frac{1}{2} \times 3\frac{1}{5}$

4. $3\frac{1}{8} \div 3\frac{1}{3}$

5. $5\frac{2}{3} \times 6$

6. $9 \times 5\frac{1}{6}$

7. $3\frac{3}{4} \times 5\frac{1}{3}$

8. $8\frac{4}{5} \div 2$

9. $6\frac{8}{9} \div 2$

10. $2\frac{1}{8} \times 4$

11. $4\frac{1}{4} \div 2\frac{1}{8}$

12. $2\frac{1}{6} \times 2\frac{2}{3}$

13. $2\frac{1}{5} \div \frac{4}{5}$

14. $3\frac{3}{4} \times 2\frac{7}{8}$

15. $9\frac{1}{2} \div 9\frac{1}{2}$

Cooperative Learning

16. Explain to a partner how to multiply the mixed numbers in number **7** in **Practice**.

17. Write two mixed numbers. Ask a partner to divide one by the other.

Simplifying Expressions with Fractions for Coefficients

From your work with whole numbers you know that a coefficient of a variable is a number that multiplies a variable. A fraction can be a coefficient of a variable.

$\frac{4x^2}{5}$ or $\frac{4}{5}x^2$ means $\frac{4}{5} \bullet x^2$. $\frac{4}{5}$ is the coefficient of x^2.

$y \div 3$ means $\frac{y}{3}$ or $\frac{1}{3} \bullet y$. $\frac{1}{3}$ is the coefficient of y.

To simplify expressions with fractions for coefficients, do the same thing you did with whole numbers. Combine like terms by adding their coefficients.

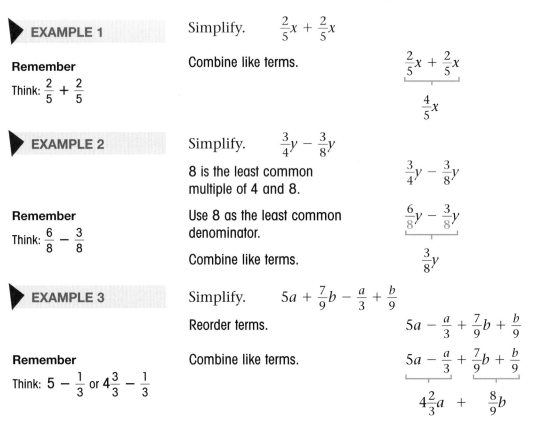

▶ **EXAMPLE 1**

Simplify. $\frac{2}{5}x + \frac{2}{5}x$

Remember

Think: $\frac{2}{5} + \frac{2}{5}$

Combine like terms.

$$\frac{2}{5}x + \frac{2}{5}x$$

$$\frac{4}{5}x$$

▶ **EXAMPLE 2**

Simplify. $\frac{3}{4}y - \frac{3}{8}y$

8 is the least common multiple of 4 and 8.

$$\frac{3}{4}y - \frac{3}{8}y$$

Remember

Think: $\frac{6}{8} - \frac{3}{8}$

Use 8 as the least common denominator.

$$\frac{6}{8}y - \frac{3}{8}y$$

Combine like terms.

$$\frac{3}{8}y$$

▶ **EXAMPLE 3**

Simplify. $5a + \frac{7}{9}b - \frac{a}{3} + \frac{b}{9}$

Reorder terms.

$$5a - \frac{a}{3} + \frac{7}{9}b + \frac{b}{9}$$

Remember

Think: $5 - \frac{1}{3}$ or $4\frac{3}{3} - \frac{1}{3}$

Combine like terms.

$$5a - \frac{a}{3} + \frac{7}{9}b + \frac{b}{9}$$

$$4\frac{2}{3}a + \frac{8}{9}b$$

Practice

Simplify.

1. $\frac{a}{7} + \frac{2a}{7}$

2. $\frac{t}{3} + \frac{5t}{6}$

3. $\frac{x}{7} + \frac{x}{7}$

4. $\frac{5}{9}y - \frac{4}{9}y$

5. $\frac{5}{12}s + \frac{5}{12}s$

6. $\frac{x}{3} + \frac{x}{6}$

7. $a^2 + b^2 - \frac{a^2}{3}$

8. $c^2 - d^2 + \frac{3}{4}c^2$

9. $\frac{2x}{7} + \frac{3x}{7}$

10. $\frac{3}{8}z^2 + \frac{2}{3}z + \frac{3}{8}z^2$

11. $a^2 + \frac{2}{3}b^2 + a^2$

12. $4x^2 - \frac{2}{3}y - 2x^2$

13. $\frac{s}{3} + \frac{s}{9}$

14. $g + \frac{h}{2} + \frac{h}{2}$

15. $4x + 7y - \frac{x}{2}$

16. $a + b + \frac{a}{2}$

17. $2d + \frac{3}{2}d$

18. $\frac{3}{4}c + \frac{c}{4} + c$

Cooperative Learning

19. Explain to a partner how to simplify the expression in number **13** in **Practice**.

20. Write an expression with fractions for coefficients. Use only the operation of addition in your expression. Ask a partner to simplify it. Check the work.

Evaluating Expressions

You can evaluate a variable expression by replacing the variables with fractions or mixed numbers. Then, perform the operations.

▶ **EXAMPLE 1**

Find the value of lw when $l = 10$ and $w = 4\frac{1}{2}$.

$$lw$$

Replace l with 10 and w with $4\frac{1}{2}$. $\quad l \cdot w$

$$10 \times 4\frac{1}{2}$$

Multiply. $\quad \dfrac{10}{1} \times 4\frac{1}{2} = \dfrac{^{5}\cancel{10} \times 9}{1 \times \cancel{2}_1} = \dfrac{45}{1} = 45$

The value of lw is 45 when $l = 10$ and $w = 4\frac{1}{2}$.

▶ **EXAMPLE 2**

Find the value of $A \div w$ when $A = 48$ and $w = 3\frac{1}{5}$.

$$A \div w$$

Replace A with 48 and w with $3\frac{1}{5}$.
Divide.

$$48 \div 3\frac{1}{5}$$

$$\dfrac{48}{1} \div \dfrac{16}{5}$$

$$\dfrac{48}{1} \times \dfrac{5}{16} = \dfrac{^{3}\cancel{48} \times 5}{1 \times \cancel{16}_1} = \dfrac{15}{1} = 15$$

The value of $A \div w$ is 15 when $A = 48$ and $w = 3\frac{1}{5}$.

When there is more than one operation, be sure to follow the order of operations.

▶ **EXAMPLE 3**

Find the value of $2l + 2w$ when $l = 5$ and $w = 2\frac{1}{2}$.

$$2l + 2w$$

Check

$\dfrac{2}{1} \cdot \dfrac{5}{2} = \dfrac{^{1}\cancel{2} \times 5}{1 \times \cancel{2}_1} = 5$

Replace l with 5 and w with $2\frac{1}{2}$.

$$2 \cdot 5 + 2 \cdot 2\frac{1}{2}$$

$$2 \cdot 5 + 2 \cdot \dfrac{5}{2}$$

$$\underbrace{10}\ +\ \underbrace{5}$$

$$15$$

The value of $2l + 2w$ is 15 when $l = 5$ and $w = 2\frac{1}{2}$.

Try These

Evaluate.

1. s^2 when $s = \frac{1}{4}$

Replace s with $\frac{1}{4}$.

$$s^2$$
$$s \cdot \blacksquare$$
$$\blacksquare \cdot \blacksquare$$
$$\blacksquare$$

The value of s^2 is ■ when $s = \frac{1}{4}$.

2. $\frac{3}{4}a - b$ when $a = 4$ and $b = 1$

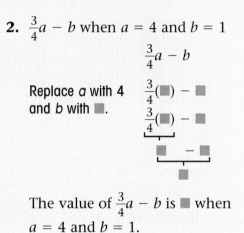

Replace a with 4 and b with ■.

$$\frac{3}{4}a - b$$
$$\frac{3}{4}(\blacksquare) - \blacksquare$$
$$\frac{3}{4}(\blacksquare) - \blacksquare$$
$$\blacksquare - \blacksquare$$
$$\blacksquare$$

The value of $\frac{3}{4}a - b$ is ■ when $a = 4$ and $b = 1$.

Practice

Evaluate.

1. $4s$ when $s = 2\frac{1}{2}$

2. $a \div b$ when $a = 2$ and $b = \frac{1}{2}$

3. ab when $a = \frac{3}{4}$ and $b = 1\frac{1}{3}$

4. $2c \div 1$ when $c = \frac{1}{2}$

5. $\frac{1}{2}x$ when $x = 2$

6. $3\frac{1}{2} \div y$ when $y = 3$

7. rt when $r = 40$ and $t = \frac{3}{4}$

8. $d \div t$ when $d = 5$ and $t = \frac{1}{2}$

9. $2x + 1$ when $x = 4\frac{3}{8}$

10. $3y - \frac{1}{2}$ when $y = 2$

11. $a + 2b$ when $a = 1$ and $b = 5\frac{1}{2}$

12. $2c - d$ when $c = 5$ and $d = 3\frac{2}{5}$

13. $3x - y$ when $x = \frac{7}{9}$ and $y = 1$

14. $4a \div b$ when $a = 4$ and $b = 4$

Cooperative Learning

15. Explain to a partner how to evaluate the expression in number **10** in **Practice**.

16. Write a variable expression using multiplication or division. Give fractions or mixed numbers as values for the variables. Ask a partner to evaluate the expression. Check the work.

9-7 Solving Equations

You have already solved equations using multiplication and division in your work with whole numbers and decimals. You solve the equations the same way when you work with fractions and mixed numbers. Remember, multiplication and division undo each other.

▶ **EXAMPLE 1**

Solve. $1\frac{3}{4}x = \frac{7}{10}$

Check

$1\frac{3}{4}x = \frac{7}{10}$

$\frac{7}{4} \times \frac{2}{5} = \frac{7}{10}$

$\frac{7 \times 2^1}{{}_2 4 \times 5} = \frac{7}{10}$

$\frac{7}{10} = \frac{7}{10}$

True.

Undo multiplication with division.

Divide both sides by $1\frac{3}{4}$.

Simplify each side.

$1\frac{3}{4}x = \frac{7}{10}$

$1\frac{3}{4}x \div 1\frac{3}{4} = \frac{7}{10} \div 1\frac{3}{4}$

$x = \frac{7}{10} \div \frac{7}{4}$

$x = \frac{{}^1 7 \times 4^2}{{}_5 10 \times 7_1}$

$x = \frac{2}{5}$

Solution: $\frac{2}{5}$

▶ **EXAMPLE 2**

Solve. $\frac{y}{6} + 1 = 1\frac{2}{3}$

$\frac{y}{6} + 1 = 1\frac{2}{3}$

First undo addition with subtraction. Subtract 1 from both sides.

$\frac{y}{6} + 1 - 1 = 1\frac{2}{3} - 1$

Simplify each side.

$\frac{y}{6} = \frac{2}{3}$

Check

$\frac{y}{6} + 1 = \frac{12}{3}$

$\frac{4}{6} + 1 = 1\frac{2}{3}$

$\frac{2}{3} + 1 = 1\frac{2}{3}$

$1\frac{2}{3} = 1\frac{2}{3}$

True.

Next undo division with multiplication. Multiply both sides by 6.

Simplify each side.

$\frac{y}{6} \times 6 = \frac{2}{3} \times 6$

$y = \frac{2 \times 6}{3 \times 1}$

$y = \frac{2 \times 6^2}{{}_1 3 \times 1}$

$y = \frac{4}{1}$

Solution: 4

Try These

Solve. Then, check.

1. $3\frac{1}{2} = \frac{2}{3}x + 3$

Subtract ■ from each side.

$3\frac{1}{2} - ■ = \frac{2}{3}x + 3 - ■$

$\frac{1}{2} = \frac{2}{3}x$

Check: Replace x with ■.

$3\frac{1}{2} = \frac{2}{3}x + 3$

Divide each side by ■.

$\frac{1}{2} \div ■ = \frac{2}{3}x \div ■$

$3\frac{1}{2} = \frac{\overset{1}{2}}{1\overset{}{3}} \times \frac{■}{\overset{}{2}}^1 + 3$

$\frac{1 \times ■}{2 \times ■} = x$

$3\frac{1}{2} = 3\frac{1}{2}$ true

$■ = x$

Solution: ■

2. $\frac{1}{5} = \frac{y}{10}$

Multiply both sides by ■. $\frac{1}{5} \times ■ = \frac{y}{10} \times ■$

Check: Replace y with ■.

Simplify each side. $\frac{1}{1\overset{}{5}} \times \frac{\overset{2}{■}}{1} = y$

$\frac{1}{5} = \frac{y}{10}$

$■ = y$

$\frac{1}{5} = \frac{■}{10}$

Solution: ■

$\frac{1}{5} = \frac{1}{5}$ true

Practice

Solve. Then, check.

1. $4\frac{1}{2}m = 18$

2. $\frac{2}{8}a = 4$

3. $\frac{x}{12} = \frac{3}{8}$

4. $25 = 2\frac{1}{2}y$

5. $\frac{x}{9} = \frac{2}{3}$

6. $\frac{3}{5}y = 16$

7. $\frac{1}{3} = 4m$

8. $2\frac{2}{3} = 10x$

9. $\frac{5}{6}x - 8 = 2$

Cooperative Learning

10. Explain to a partner how to solve number **9** in **Practice**.

11. Write the equation $x = 2$. Multiply the left side by any fraction or mixed number. Ask a partner to solve your equation. Check the solution.

9-8 Calculator: Multiplying and Dividing Fractions

You can use your calculator to multiply and divide fractions.

EXAMPLE 1

Multiply. $\frac{7}{16} \times \frac{3}{8}$

First multiply the numerators.   **Display**

Multiply 7 and 3
by pressing: $\boxed{7}\ \boxed{\times}\ \boxed{3}\ \boxed{=}$ $\boxed{21}$

Then, multiply the
denominators.

Multiply 16 and 8
by pressing: $\boxed{1}\ \boxed{6}\ \boxed{\times}\ \boxed{8}\ \boxed{=}$ $\boxed{128}$

So: $\frac{7}{16} \times \frac{3}{8} = \frac{21}{128}$

EXAMPLE 2

Divide. $\frac{5}{24} \div \frac{2}{5}$

$\frac{5}{24} \div \frac{2}{5} = \frac{5}{24} \times \frac{5}{2}$

First multiply the numerators.   **Display**

Multiply 5 and 5
by pressing: $\boxed{5}\ \boxed{\times}\ \boxed{5}\ \boxed{=}$ $\boxed{25}$

Then, multiply the
denominators.

Multiply 24 and 2
by pressing: $\boxed{2}\ \boxed{4}\ \boxed{\times}\ \boxed{2}\ \boxed{=}$ $\boxed{48}$

$\frac{5}{24} \times \frac{5}{2} = \frac{25}{48}$

So: $\frac{5}{24} \div \frac{2}{5} = \frac{25}{48}$

Practice

Use your calculator to multiply or divide.

1. $\dfrac{4}{5} \times \dfrac{8}{9}$

2. $\dfrac{7}{8} \times \dfrac{9}{10}$

3. $\dfrac{5}{9} \times \dfrac{7}{16}$

4. $\dfrac{9}{16} \div \dfrac{2}{3}$

5. $\dfrac{2}{5} \div \dfrac{8}{9}$

6. $\dfrac{13}{17} \div \dfrac{7}{8}$

On-the-Job Math

AUTOMOBILE TECHNICIAN

Automobile technicians work on cars. They repair broken parts. They do tune-ups to keep a car's engine running properly. They also check the emissions system so that the exhaust fumes from the car do not pollute the air we breathe. Some automobile technicians even help design new kinds of engines.

To be successful, an automobile technician must understand how a car works. The technician must have a good understanding of math and science. Studying math, especially algebra and geometry, helps the technician become a good problem solver. An automobile technician uses math skills when trying to figure out just what is wrong with a car.

There are many opportunities for automobile technicians. There are many jobs. Millions of cars are used every day. Each one of these cars needs to be kept in good working condition. Thanks to automobile technicians, cars and their riders are kept safe.

Problem Solving: Using a Table

A table can provide information needed to solve problems.

The following table provides the calorie count and grams of protein for some foods.

Food	Calories	Grams Protein
1 apple	117	0.4
1 piece of bread	45	3.8
1 turkey burger	215	21.8
1 cup of yogurt	195	2.3
1 orange	65	1.1
1 portion of pasta	400	3.0

▶ EXAMPLE

Find the number of calories in 3 pieces of bread.

READ **What do you need to find out?**
You need to find how many calories are in 3 pieces of bread.

PLAN **What do you need to do?**
You need to use the table to find the number of calories in 1 piece of bread. Then mutiply to find the calories in 3 pieces.

DO **Follow the plan.**

1 piece of bread has 45 calories.
Multiply 3 and 45. $\qquad$ $3 \times 45 = 135$

CHECK **Does your answer make sense?**
1 piece of bread has 45 calories.
$3 \times 45 = 135$ ✓

3 pieces of bread have 135 calories.

Try These

1. Find the number of calories in 2 cups of yogurt.

   1 cup of yogurt has ■ calories.

   Multiply 2 and ■.   2 × ■

   The product is ■.   ■

   2 cups of yogurt have ■ calories.

2. How many grams of protein are in 6 oranges?

   1 orange has ■ grams of protein.

   Multiply 6 and ■.   6 × ■

   The product is ■.   ■

   6 oranges have ■ grams of protein.

Practice

Solve the problem by using the table.

1. Find the number of calories in 4 apples.

2. How many grams of protein are in 3 turkey burgers?

3. Find the number of calories in 2 turkey burgers.

4. How many grams of protein are in 3 portions of pasta?

5. Find the number of calories in 3 oranges.

6. How many grams of protein are in 4 cups of yogurt?

Cooperative Learning

7. Explain to a partner how you use the table to answer number 5 in **Practice**.

8. Plan a lunch. Use some of the items shown on the table. Ask a partner to find the total number of calories in the lunch. Check the work.

Application: Minimum, Maximum, and Range

The **minimum** is the smallest value in a group of numbers. The **maximum** is the largest value.

EXAMPLE 1

Find the minimum.

2, 3, 7, 8, 5, 4, 1, 3, 2

Order the numbers from the
smallest to the largest.   1, 2, 2, 3, 3, 4, 5, 7, 8

1 is the smallest value in the group of numbers.

The minimum is 1.

EXAMPLE 2

Find the maximum.

8, 1, 4, 3, 9, 7, 6

Order the numbers from the
smallest to the largest.   1, 3, 4, 6, 7, 8, 9

9 is the largest value in the group of numbers.

The maximum is 9.

The **range** tells you how far apart the maximum and minimum values are. To find the range, subtract the minimum from the maximum.

EXAMPLE 3

Find the range.

7, 6, 8, 4, 2, 5, 6, 3

Order the numbers from the
smallest to the largest.   2, 3, 4, 5, 6, 6, 7, 8

The minimum is 2. The maximum is 8.

Subtract 2 from 8. The difference is 6. $8 - 2 = 6$

The range is 6.

1. Find the minimum.

   4, 5, 6, 8, 4, 9, 4, 5, 3, 7

   Order the numbers from the smallest to the largest.

   3, 4, 4, 4, 5, 5, 6, 7, ■ , ■

   ■ is the smallest value in the group of numbers.

   The minimum is ■.

2. Find the range.

   5, 6, 3, 8, 4, 5, 3, 7

   Order the numbers from the smallest to the largest.

   3, 3, 4, 5, 5, 6, ■ , ■

   The minimum is ■ .

   The maximum is ■ .

   Subtract ■ from ■ .   ■ − ■ = ■

   The range is ■ .

Practice

Find the minimum, the maximum, and the range.

1. 1, 3, 2, 4, 5, 2, 6, 7, 3

2. 6, 2, 8, 9, 5, 3, 6, 7, 10

3. 2, 8, 4, 5, 7, 8, 6, 5

4. 3, 1, 7, 9, 4, 6

5. 5, 3, 2, 1, 4, 7, 4

6. 6, 10, 8, 9, 3, 5, 6, 7

7. 2, 8, 4, 5, 7, 7, 5

8. 3, 5, 7, 9, 6, 6

Cooperative Learning

9. Explain to a partner how to find the minimum, the maximum, and the range in number **4** in **Practice**.

10. Write a group of numbers. Ask a partner to find the minimum, the maximum, and the range of the group of numbers. Check the work.

Summary

To multiply fractions, multiply the numerators, and multiply the denominators.
You can find the reciprocal of a fraction by exchanging the numerator and the denominator.
To multiply, you can divide numerators and denominators by their greatest common factors. Then, multiply.
To divide by a fraction, multiply by the reciprocal of the fraction.
When you multiply or divide mixed numbers, first replace mixed numbers with fractions. Then, multiply or divide.
A fraction can be a coefficient of a variable.
To simplify expressions with fractions for coefficients, combine like terms by adding their coefficients.
You can evaluate a variable expression by replacing the variables with fractions or mixed numbers. Then, perform the operations.
When solving equations with fractions, remember that multiplication and division undo each other.
A table can provide information needed to solve problems.
To find the range, subtract the minimum from the maximum.

reciprocal

maximum

minimum

range

Review Vocabulary

Complete the sentences with words from the box.

1. The _____ is the smallest number in a group of numbers.

2. The difference between the largest and the smallest number in a group of numbers is called the _____.

3. The _____ is the largest number in a group of numbers.

4. The _____ of a fraction is the fraction you get when you exchange the numerator and the denominator.

Chapter Quiz

Multiply.

1. $3 \times \frac{1}{3}$ **2.** $\frac{3}{4} \times \frac{3}{10}$ **3.** $\frac{3}{4} \times \frac{3}{4}$ **4.** $\frac{1}{2} \times \frac{1}{2}$

Find the reciprocal.

5. $\frac{8}{15}$ **6.** 20 **7.** $\frac{3}{2}$ **8.** $\frac{1}{10}$

Multiply.

9. $\frac{3}{10} \times \frac{25}{40}$ **10.** $\frac{7}{12} \times \frac{4}{7}$ **11.** $\frac{9}{20} \times \frac{4}{15}$ **12.** $\frac{70}{100} \times \frac{10}{70}$

Divide.

13. $\frac{2}{5} \div \frac{8}{13}$ **14.** $\frac{7}{12} \div \frac{4}{7}$ **15.** $\frac{9}{20} \div \frac{4}{14}$ **16.** $\frac{6}{25} \div \frac{3}{5}$

Multiply or divide.

17. $4\frac{3}{5} \div 4\frac{3}{5}$ **18.** $2\frac{5}{6} \times 1\frac{3}{8}$ **19.** $4\frac{1}{2} \div 2\frac{2}{3}$ **20.** $5\frac{1}{3} \times 2\frac{1}{4}$

Simplify.

21. $\frac{b}{4} + \frac{b}{8}$ **22.** $2c - \frac{c}{2} + \frac{c^2}{2}$ **23.** $1 + \frac{a}{4}$ **24.** $\frac{2}{3}t + \frac{2}{3}s + \frac{2}{3}t$

Evaluate.

25. $2x + 2y$ when $x = \frac{1}{2}$, $y = \frac{3}{4}$ **26.** $A \div l$ when $A = 20$, $l = 4\frac{1}{2}$

Solve. Then, check.

27. $12 = \frac{3}{8}y + 3$ **28.** $1 = \frac{t}{2} - 6$

Find the minimum, the maximum, and the range.

29. 9, 4, 7, 3, 10, 8, 5, 1   **30.** 7, 5, 4, 9, 8, 9, 7

31. 3, 4, 8, 5, 7, 6, 4, 7   **32.** 9, 6, 8, 4, 7, 9, 7, 8

Ratio, Proportion, and Percent

The nautilus shell is an example of a pattern in nature. Ratios and proportions also form a pattern. What other patterns appear in nature?

Learning Objectives

- Explain the meaning of ratio, proportion, and percent.
- Write ratios, proportions, and percents.
- Solve proportions and other equations.
- Write percents for decimals and fractions.
- Write fractions and decimals for percents.
- Find the percent of a number.
- Find what percent one number is of another.
- Find a number when a percent of it is known.
- Find percent increase or decrease.
- Use a calculator to write percents for fractions.
- Use proportions to solve problems.
- Apply concepts and skills to find discount.

Words to Know

ratio	a comparison of two numbers or quantities
proportion	a statement that two ratios are equal
cross product	the product of numbers across from each other in a proportion; In $\frac{3}{6} = \frac{4}{8}$ the cross products are 3×8 and 6×4.
solving a proportion	finding a number in a proportion when the other three numbers are known
percent	a ratio of a number to 100
percent increase	the percent change when a number increases
percent decrease	the percent change when a number decreases
discount	the amount or percent a price is reduced

Sale Project

Look at a newspaper or a store flier to find an advertisement for a sale. Pick three sale items and find the regular price and the percent off. Use this information to make a chart. Write an equation for each savings. Then, use the equation to find how much you save by buying each item on sale.

Item	Regular Price	Percent Discount	Equation	Savings
Shirt	$15	30% off	$d = .30 \times 15$	$4.50

10·1 ▶ Ratio

A **ratio** is a comparison of two numbers. There are many ways to write ratios. Here are 7 squares. 3 of the squares are shaded.

The ratio of shaded squares to all squares is 3 to 7 or 3 : 7 or $\frac{3}{7}$.

The order of numbers in a ratio matters.
The ratio of 3 to 7 is not the same ratio as 7 to 3.

▶ **EXAMPLE 1**

Write the ratio of all squares to shaded squares.

There are 7 squares.   ⟶   7 to 3 or

3 squares are shaded.   7 : 3 or $\frac{7}{3}$

▶ **EXAMPLE 2**

Write the ratio of shaded squares to squares that are not shaded.

There are 3 shaded squares.   ⟶   3 to 4 or

There are 4 squares not shaded.   3 : 4 or $\frac{3}{4}$

Ratios can compare different quantities.

▶ **EXAMPLE 3**

A box of 144 pencils costs $5.25.
Write the ratio of the number of pencils to cost.

Math Fact
Decimals or fractions can be numbers in a ratio.

144 pencils   ⟶   144 pencils to $5.25

cost $5.25.   or 144 pencils : $5.25

                        or $\dfrac{144 \text{ pencils}}{\$5.25}$

Try These

1.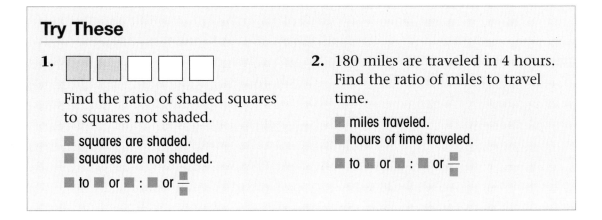

Find the ratio of shaded squares to squares not shaded.

■ squares are shaded.

■ squares are not shaded.

■ to ■ or ■ : ■ or $\frac{■}{■}$

2. 180 miles are traveled in 4 hours. Find the ratio of miles to travel time.

■ miles traveled.

■ hours of time traveled.

■ to ■ or ■ : ■ or $\frac{■}{■}$

Practice

1.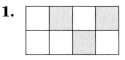

Write the ratio of shaded parts to all parts.

2.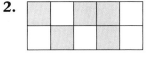

Write the ratio of shaded parts to parts not shaded.

3.

Write the ratio of parts not shaded to parts shaded.

4.

Write the ratio of all parts to shaded parts.

5. There are 91 people in 4 buses. Write the ratio of people to buses.

6. On a map, 2 inches means 15 miles. Write the ratio of inches to miles.

7. Four cans of juice cost $2.40. Write the ratio of cost to cans.

8. Two baseball games took $6\frac{1}{2}$ hours. Write the ratio of hours to games.

Cooperative Learning

9. Explain to a partner how you write the ratio for number 7 in **Practice**.

10. Write two quantities. Ask a partner to write a ratio of the quantities. Check the work.

A **proportion** shows that two ratios are equal.

$$\frac{1}{6} = \frac{2}{12}$$

One way to check if the ratios in a proportion are equal is to find **cross products.** They should be equal.

$$\frac{1}{6} \bowtie \frac{2}{12}$$

The cross products are 6×2 and 1×12.
$6 \times 2 = 12$ and $1 \times 12 = 12$.

You can find any number in a proportion if you know the other three numbers. This is called **solving a proportion.**

▶ **EXAMPLE 1**

Solve. $\frac{x}{3} = \frac{8}{12}$

$$\frac{x}{3} = \frac{8}{12}$$

Find the cross products.

$x \bullet 12 = 3 \bullet 8$

$x \bullet 12 = 24$

Divide both sides by 12.

$x \bullet 12 \div 12 = 24 \div 12$

$x = 2$

Solution: 2

$\frac{2}{3} = \frac{8}{12}$ Check. $2 \times 12 = 3 \times 8$

$24 = 24$ true

▶ **EXAMPLE 2**

Solve. $\frac{.5}{1.2} = \frac{4}{y}$

$$\frac{.5}{1.2} = \frac{4}{y}$$

Find the cross products.

$.5 \bullet y = 1.2 \times 4$

$.5 \bullet y = 4.8$

Divide both sides by .5.

$.5 \bullet y \div .5 = 4.8 \div .5$

$y = 9.6$

Solution: 9.6

$\frac{.5}{1.2} = \frac{4}{9.6}$ Check. $.5 \times 9.6 = 1.2 \times 4$

$4.8 = 4.8$ true

Solve the proportion.

1. $\dfrac{4}{y} = \dfrac{5}{10}$

    Find the cross   ■ • ■ = ■ • y
    products.   ■ = ■ • y

    Divide both $\dfrac{\blacksquare}{\blacksquare} = y$
    sides by ■.   ■ = y

    $\dfrac{4}{\blacksquare} = \dfrac{5}{10}$ Check. $4 \times 10 = 5 \times \blacksquare$

                           ■ = ■

                        true

2. $\dfrac{12}{9} = \dfrac{x}{3}$

    Find the cross 12 • ■ = ■ • x
    products.   ■ = ■ • x

    Divide both $\dfrac{\blacksquare}{\blacksquare} = x$
    sides by ■.   ■ = x

    $\dfrac{12}{9} = \dfrac{\blacksquare}{\blacksquare}$ Check. $9 \times \blacksquare = 12 \times \blacksquare$

                           ■ = ■

                        true

Practice

Solve the proportions.

1. $\dfrac{3}{x} = \dfrac{1}{3}$ **2.** $\dfrac{2}{3} = \dfrac{y}{9}$ **3.** $\dfrac{4}{x} = \dfrac{3}{9}$

4. $\dfrac{6}{10} = \dfrac{3}{n}$ **5.** $\dfrac{4}{a} = \dfrac{12}{15}$ **6.** $\dfrac{10}{x} = \dfrac{15}{3}$

7. $\dfrac{y}{5} = \dfrac{3}{15}$ **8.** $\dfrac{20}{x} = \dfrac{16}{20}$ **9.** $\dfrac{1}{1.5} = \dfrac{4}{x}$

10. $\dfrac{12}{x} = \dfrac{3}{1.2}$ **11.** $\dfrac{n}{3} = \dfrac{8}{12}$ **12.** $\dfrac{y}{4} = \dfrac{1.2}{5}$

Cooperative Learning

13. Explain to a partner how you solve the proportion in number **9** in **Practice**.

14. Write a proportion. Ask a partner to solve it. How do you know the solution is correct?

Look at the ratio of the shaded parts to all parts.

47 parts are shaded. 100 parts in all. Ratio of shaded parts to all parts: 47 to 100 or 47 : 100 or $\frac{47}{100}$

Math Fact
Percent means *for each hundred.*

A ratio of a number to 100 is a **percent**.

$$\frac{47}{100} = 47\% \quad \text{Read: 47 percent}$$

47% of the square is shaded. A % sign means "percent."

 EXAMPLE 1

Look at the square above. Write the percent of the square that is not shaded.

53 parts not shaded.
100 parts in all. $\longrightarrow$ $\frac{53}{100} = 53\%$

53% of the square is not shaded.

A percent can be equal to or greater than 100%.

EXAMPLE 2

Write a percent for the shaded part.

100 parts are shaded.
100 parts in all. $\longrightarrow$ $\frac{100}{100} = 100\%$

100% of the square is shaded.

You can use more than one whole shaded square to show more than 100%.

 EXAMPLE 3

Write a percent for the shaded part.

$\frac{100}{100}$ whole squares shaded $\longrightarrow$ 100%

$\frac{50}{100}$ of squares shaded $\longrightarrow$ $\dfrac{+50\%}{150\%}$

150% of the square is shaded.

Try These

Write a percent for each ratio.

1. 9 to 100
 9 to 100 or $\dfrac{9}{\blacksquare} = \blacksquare\%$

2. 148 : 100
 148 : 100 or $\dfrac{\blacksquare}{100} = \blacksquare\%$

Write a percent for the shaded part.

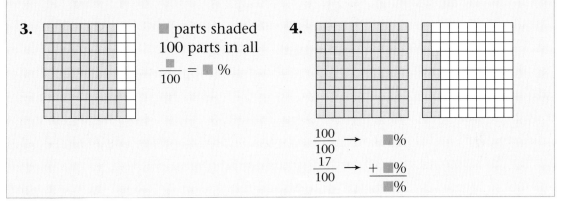

3. ■ parts shaded
 100 parts in all
 $\dfrac{\blacksquare}{100} = \blacksquare\%$

4.

$\dfrac{100}{100} \rightarrow \blacksquare\%$

$\dfrac{17}{100} \rightarrow \dfrac{+\ \blacksquare\%}{\blacksquare\%}$

Practice

Write a percent for each ratio.

1. 15 to 100 **2.** 253 to 100 **3.** 1 to 100 **4.** 200 to 100

5. 77 to 100 **6.** 3 to 100 **7.** 95 to 100 **8.** 89 to 100

Write a percent for the shaded parts.

9.

10.

Cooperative Learning

11. Explain to a partner how you write the percent in number **9** in **Practice**.

12. Write the ratio of any number to 100. Ask a partner to write a percent for your ratio. Check the work.

You can write a decimal for a percent.

$$7\% = \frac{7}{100} = .07 \qquad\qquad 29\% = \frac{29}{100} = .29$$

$$275\% = \frac{275}{100} = 2.75$$

There is a shortcut for writing a decimal for a percent.

$$7\% = .\,0\,7 = .07 \qquad\qquad 29\% = .\,2\,9 = .29$$

$$275\% = 2\,.\,75 = 2.75$$

Move the decimal point two places to the left.
Do not write the % sign.

▶ **EXAMPLE 1**

Write a decimal for 78%.

	78%
Move the decimal point two places to the left.	. 7 8
Do not write %.	.78

$$78\% = .78$$

You can also write a percent for a decimal.

$$.03 = \frac{3}{100} = 3\% \qquad\qquad .65 = \frac{65}{100} = 65\%$$

$$2.29 = 2\,\frac{29}{100} = \frac{229}{100} = 229\%$$

There is a shortcut for writing a percent for a decimal.

$$.03 = 0\,3\,.\% = 3\% \qquad\qquad .65 = 6\,5\,.\% = 65\%$$

$$2.29 = 2\,2\,9.\% = 229\%$$

Move the decimal point two places to the right.
Write the % sign.

▶ **EXAMPLE 2**

Math Fact
You may have to write zeros before you write the decimal point.

Write a percent for .7.

Move the decimal two places to the right.	.7
	7 0 .%
Write the percent sign.	70%

$$.7 = 70\%$$

Write a decimal for each percent.

1. 12%

Move the decimal point ■ places to the ■. Do not write %.	12% .12 ⌣⌣ ■

12% = ■

2. 175%

Move the decimal point ■ places to the ■. Do not write %.	175% 1.75 ⌣⌣ ■

175% = ■

Write a percent for each decimal.

3. .99

Move the decimal point ■ places to the ■. Write the % sign.	.99 99. ⌣ ■ %

.99 = ■ %

4. 1.25

Move the decimal point ■ places to the ■ Write the % sign.	1.25 125. ⌣ ■ %

1.25 = ■ %

Practice

Write a decimal for each percent.

1. 45%   **2.** 97%   **3.** 60%   **4.** 13%

5. 100%   **6.** 4%   **7.** 300%   **8.** 10%

Write a percent for each decimal.

9. .58   **10.** .32   **11.** 1   **12.** .8

13. .96   **14.** 1.5   **15.** .05   **16.** 2.06

Cooperative Learning

17. Explain to a partner how you write a decimal for number **10** in **Practice**.

18. Write a decimal. Ask a partner to write a percent for the decimal. Check the work.

Fractions and Percents

You can write a fraction for a percent from what you know about percents. Remember, a percent is a ratio of a number to 100.

▶ **EXAMPLE 1**

Write a fraction for 85%.

$$85\% = \frac{85}{100} = \frac{17}{20}$$

You can also write a percent for fractions with denominators of 100. Use the meaning of percent.

▶ **EXAMPLE 2**

Write a percent for $\frac{3}{100}$.

$$\frac{3}{100} = 3\%$$

Fractions that do not have denominators of 100 can be written as percents.

▶ **EXAMPLE 3**

Write a percent for $\frac{4}{5}$.

Remember

$\frac{4}{5}$ means 4 divided by 5.

Divide 4 by 5.

Write a percent for .8.

$$\frac{4}{5}$$

$$\begin{array}{r} .8 \\ 5\overline{)4.0} \end{array}$$

$$8\,0\,.\,\%$$

$$80\%$$

$$\frac{4}{5} = 80\%$$

▶ **EXAMPLE 4**

Write $1\frac{2}{25}$ as a percent.

Remember

$\frac{2}{25}$ means 2 divided by 25.

Divide by 25.

Replace $\frac{2}{25}$ with .08.

Write a percent for 1.08.

$$1\frac{2}{25}$$

$$\begin{array}{r} .08 \\ 25\overline{)2.00} \end{array}$$

$$1.08$$

$$1\,0\,8.\,\%$$

$$108\%$$

$$1\frac{2}{25} = 108\%$$

Try These

1. Write a fraction for 6%.

$$6\% = \frac{\blacksquare}{100} = \frac{3}{50}$$

2. Write a percent for $\frac{72}{100}$.

$$\frac{72}{100} = \blacksquare\%$$

Write a percent for each fraction.

3. $\frac{3}{10}$

    Divide ■ by ■.   ■$\overline{)\overline{\blacksquare}}$

    Write a percent for .3.   3 0. %

                               = ■ %

$$\frac{3}{10} = \blacksquare\%$$

4. $\frac{2}{50}$

    Divide ■ by ■.   ■$\overline{)\overline{\blacksquare}}$

    Write a percent for .04.   0 4. %

                               = ■ %

$$\frac{2}{50} = \blacksquare\%$$

Practice

Write a fraction for each percent.

1. 50%   **2.** 200%   **3.** 44%   **4.** 25%

5. 12%   **6.** 2%   **7.** 98%   **8.** 1.32%

Write a percent for each fraction or mixed number.

9. $\frac{10}{100}$ **10.** $\frac{38}{100}$ **11.** $\frac{120}{100}$ **12.** $\frac{7}{100}$

13. $\frac{1}{2}$ **14.** $\frac{1}{20}$ **15.** $\frac{3}{25}$ **16.** $\frac{17}{50}$

17. $\frac{9}{10}$ **18.** $2\frac{1}{4}$ **19.** $\frac{3}{5}$ **20.** $\frac{11}{20}$

Cooperative Learning

21. Explain to a partner how you write a percent for number **12** in **Practice**.

22. Write a fraction with a denominator of 25. Use any number as a numerator. Ask a partner to write a percent for your fraction.

There are many facts you know about percents. You can write number equations for these facts. Later you will use equations to solve problems about percents.

Facts	85 of 100 are shaded.
	85% of 100 is 85.
Number	
Equation	.85 × 100 = 85 true

To write a number equation, use the "×" sign for "of." Use the "=" sign for "is." Write the percent as a decimal or fraction.

▶ **EXAMPLE 1**

Write a number equation for this percent fact: 15 is 50% of 30.

Use = for "is."
Use × for "of."   15 is 50% of 30.

Write 50% as a decimal.   15 = .5 × 30   true

Remember
50% = .50 = .5

15 is 50% of 30.   →   15 = .5 × 30

▶ **EXAMPLE 2**

Write a number equation for this percent fact: 2 is 25% of 8.

Use = for "is."
Use × for "of."   2 is 25% of 8.

Write 25% as a decimal.   2 = .25 × 8   true

2 is 25% of 8.   →   2 = .25 × 8

▶ **EXAMPLE 3**

Write a number equation for this percent fact: 45% of 80 students is 36 students.

Use = for "is."
Use × for "of."   45% of 80 students is 36 students.

Write 45% as a decimal.   .45 × 80 = 36 true

45% of 80 students is 36 students.   →   .45 × 80 = 36

Write a number equation for each percent fact.

1. 3 is 60% of 5.

Use ■ for *is*.
Use ■ for *of*.

Write 60% as a decimal.   3 ■ .6 ■ 5   true

3 is 60% of 5.   →   3 ■ .6 ■ 5.

2. $150 is 75% of $200.

Use ■ for *is*. $150 is 75% of $200
Use ■ for *of*.

Write 75% as a decimal.   150 ■ .75 ■ 200   true

$150 is 75% of $200.   →   150 ■ .75 ■ 200

Practice

Write a number equation for each percent fact.

1. 60% of 100 is 60.

2. 30 is 75% of 40.

3. 4 is 2% of 200.

4. 2 ft is 50% of 4 ft.

5. 28 books is 70% of 40 books.

6. 10% of 150 cars is 15 cars.

7. 15% of $200 is $30.

8. 6 hours is 25% of 24 hours.

Cooperative Learning

9. Explain to a partner how you write a number equation for number **4** in **Practice**.

10. Write a percent fact. Ask a partner to write a number equation for your percent fact.

Find the Percent of a Number

If you need to solve a problem about percents, try to write an equation for the problem. Some numbers in your equation may be missing. Use a variable for a missing number.

$$\underbrace{What}_{} \quad \underset{\downarrow}{is \ 45\%} \ \underset{\downarrow}{of \ 200?}$$

$$don't \ know = .45 \times 200$$

Math Fact
Use any letter for the variable.

Use the variable y for what you don't know. Then, solve the equation to find y.

$$y = .45 \times 200$$
$$y = 90$$

Solution: 90

So, $90 = .45 \times 200$ true

90 is 45% of 200.

▶ **EXAMPLE 1**

75% of 32 students is what number?

$$75\% \ of \ 32 \ is \ \underbrace{what \ number?}_{}$$

Write an equation. $.75 \times 32 = don't \ know$
Use n for the variable. $.75 \times 32 = n$
Solve for n. $24 = n$

Solution: 24

So, $.75 \times 32 = 24$ true

75% of 32 is 24.

▶ **EXAMPLE 2**

What is 115% of 60 students?

$$\underbrace{What}_{} \quad is \ 115\% \ of \ 60 \ students?$$

Math Fact
115% = 1.15

Write an equation. $don't \ know = 1.15 \times 60$
Use x for the variable. $x = 1.15 \times 60$
Solve for x. $x = 69$

Solution: 69

So, $69 = 1.15 \times 60$ true

69 students is 115% of 60 students.

Practice

Solve the percent problems.

1. 25% of 64 is what number?

2. What is 10% of 40?

3. What is 30% of 30?

4. 50% of 40 is what number?

5. 90% of 200 is what number?

6. What is 9% of 300?

7. What is 70% of 50 people?

8. What is 5% of $36?

9. 150% of 20 is what number?

10. 2% of 50 is what number?

11. What is 10% of 920 cars?

12. 65% of 120 is what number?

13. 20% of 9 is what number?

14. What is 40% of 80?

15. What is 100% of 50?

16. 55% of 600 is what number?

Cooperative Learning

17. Explain to a partner how you solve number **10** in **Practice**.

18. Write any number. Ask a partner to find a percent of the number. Check the work.

Find What Percent One Number Is of Another

You can find what percent one number is of another. Start by writing an equation.

6 is what percent of 15?

$$6 = \text{don't know} \times 15$$

Use the variable y for what you don't know.

$$6 = y \times 15$$

Math Facts

$6 \div 15 = .4$

Solve for y. $\quad 6 \div 15 = y \times 15 \div 15$

$$.4 = y$$

Solution: $\quad .4$

$.4 = 40\%$

So, $6 = .4 \times 15$

6 is 40% of 15.

▶ **EXAMPLE 1**

What percent of 20 is 35?

What percent of 20 is 35?

Write an equation. $\quad$ don't know $\times 20 = 35$

Math Facts

Use n as a variable. $\quad n \quad \times 20 = 35$

$35 \div 20 = 1.75$

Solve for n. $\quad n \times 20 \div 20 = 35 \div 20$

$$n = 1.75$$

Solution: $\quad 1.75$

$1.75 = 175\%$

So, 1.75 of $20 = 35 \quad$ true

175% of 20 is 35.

▶ **EXAMPLE 2**

4 schools is what percent of 16 schools?

4 is what percent of 16?

$$4 = \text{don't know} \times 16$$

$$4 = p \times 16$$

Math Facts

$4 \div 16 = .25$

$$4 \div 16 = p \times 16 \div 16$$

$$.25 = p$$

Solution: $\quad .25$

$.25 = 25\%$

$$4 = .25 \times 16 \quad \text{true}$$

4 schools is 25% of 16 schools.

Try These

1. 18 people is what percent of 45 people?

Write an equation. $\blacksquare = \blacksquare \times 45$

Use x as the variable.

Solve for x. $\blacksquare \div 45 = \blacksquare \times 45 \div 45$

$$\blacksquare = \blacksquare$$

So, $\blacksquare = \blacksquare \times 45$

18 people is $\blacksquare$ of 45 people.

2. What percent of 50 is 20?

Write an equation. $\blacksquare \times 50 = \blacksquare$

Use n as a variable.

Solve for n. $\blacksquare \times 50 \div 50 = \blacksquare \div 50$

$$\blacksquare = \blacksquare$$

So, $\blacksquare \times 50 = \blacksquare$

$\blacksquare$ of 50 is 20.

Practice

Solve the percent problems.

1. 12 is what percent of 40?

2. 11 is what percent of 55?

3. What percent of 20 is 7?

4. $21 is what percent of $60?

5. 14 is what percent of 56?

6. What percent of 300 is 150?

7. 13 buses is what percent of 65 buses?

8. What percent of 52 points is 13 points?

9. What percent of 165 is 33?

10. 42 is what percent of 60?

11. What percent is 45 questions of 50 questions?

12. 15 lb is what percent of 30 lb?

13. 18 is what percent of 45?

14. What percent of 52 is 52?

Cooperative Learning

15. Explain to a partner how you find the percent in number **14** in **Practice**.

16. Write a number. Then write another number that is four times your first number. Ask a partner to find what percent one number is of another. Check the work.

10-9 Find a Number When a Percent of It Is Known

Sometimes, you know a percent of a number. You can find the number. Start by writing an equation.

10 is 25% of what number?

$10 = .25 \times$ don't know

Use the variable n for what you don't know.

$$10 = .25 \times n$$

Solve for n. $\quad 10 \div .25 = .25 \times n \div .25$

$$40 = n$$

Solution: $\qquad$ 40

So, $10 = .25 \times 40 \qquad$ true

10 is 25% of 40.

▶ EXAMPLE 1

35 is 50% of what number?

35 is 50% of what number?

Remember
50% = .50 = .5

Write an equation. $\quad 35 = .5 \times \quad$ don't know
Use y as a variable. $\quad 35 = .5 \times y$
Solve for y. $\quad 35 \div .5 = .5 \times y \div .5$

$$70 = y$$

Solution: $\qquad$ 70

So, $35 = .5 \times 70 \qquad$ true

35 is 50% of 70.

▶ EXAMPLE 2

$18 is 150% of how much money?

18 is 150% of what number?

Write an equation. $\quad 18 = 1.5 \times \quad$ don't know
Use t as a variable. $\quad 18 = 1.5 \times t$
Solve for t. $\quad 18 \div 1.5 = 1.5 \times t \div 1.5$

$$12 = t$$

Solution: $\qquad$ 12

So, $18 = 1.5 \times 12 \qquad$ true

$18 is 150% of $12.

Try These

1. 24 is 75% of what number?

Write an equation.

Use y as
a variable.   ■ = .75 × ■

Solve for y. ■ ÷ .75 = .75 × ■ ÷ .75

                                    ■ = ■

So,   ■ = .75 × ■ true

24 is 75% of ■.

2. 80 is 25% of what number?

Write an equation.

Use n as   80 = ■ × ■
a variable.

Solve for n. 80 ÷ ■ = ■ × ■ ÷ ■

                                ■ = ■

So,   80 = ■ × ■ true

80 is 25% of ■.

Practice

Solve the percent problems.

1. 16 is 40% of what number?

2. 22 is 11% of what number?

3. $20 is 80% of how much money?

4. 57 is 60% of what number?

5. 7 is 35% of what number?

6. 100 ft is 50% of how many ft?

7. 18 students is 15% of how many students?

8. 12 tickets is 60% of how many tickets?

9. 32 is 100% of what number?

10. 15 is 150% of what number?

11. 21 is 30% of what number?

12. 16 is 5% of what number?

13. 50 is 25% of what number?

14. 10 is 40% of what number?

15. 12 is 8% of what number?

16. 7 is 5% of what number?

Cooperative Learning

17. Explain to a partner how you solve number **10** in **Practice**.

18. Write the percent of a number. Ask your partner to find the number. Check the work.

10·10 Percent Increase or Decrease

You can describe the change in a number by using a percent. Write a fraction comparing the change to the original number. Then, write a percent for this fraction.

$$\frac{\text{Amount of Change}}{\text{Original Number}} = \text{Percent Change}$$

If the original number increased, the percent of change is a **percent increase.** If the original number decreased, the percent of change is a **percent decrease.**

▶ **EXAMPLE 1**

The population of a town went from 10,000 to 12,000. Find the percent increase or decrease.

Amount of change: $12{,}000 - 10{,}000 = 2{,}000$

Original population: 10,000

Remember

$\frac{\text{Amount of Change}}{\text{Original Number}} = \text{Percent Change}$

$$\frac{\text{Amount of Change}}{\text{Original Number}} = \frac{2{,}000}{10{,}000} = \frac{1}{5} = 20\%$$

The population went up. So, it is a 20% increase.

▶ **EXAMPLE 2**

The cost of gasoline for the Lopez family car last year was $1,000. This year, the family bought a new car and the cost is $950. Find the percent increase or decrease.

Amount of change: $\$1{,}000 - \$950 = \$50$

Original cost is: $1,000

$$\frac{\text{Amount of Change}}{\text{Original Number}} = \frac{50}{1{,}000} = \frac{1}{20} = 5\%$$

The cost of gasoline went down. So, it is a 5% decrease.

1. A number changed from 12 to 15. Find the percent increase or decrease.

   Amount of change: $15 - 12 = $ ■

   Original number: ■

   $\dfrac{\text{Amount of Change}}{\text{Original Number}} = \dfrac{■}{■} = 25\%$

   The number increased. So, it is a ■ % ■.

2. A number changed from 125 to 100. Find the percent increase or decrease.

   Amount of change: $125 - 100 = $ ■

   Original number: ■

   $\dfrac{\text{Amount of Change}}{\text{Original Number}} = \dfrac{■}{■} = 20\%$

   The number decreased. So, it is a ■ % ■.

Practice

Find the percent increase or decrease.

1. The population of a town went from 18,000 to 17,460.

2. The cost of a television went from $350 to $315.

3. The weight of a man went from 200 lb to 176 lb.

4. A number changes from 80 to 100.

5. A number changes from 28 to 35.

6. A cost changes from $120 to $132.

7. A number changes from 200 to 100.

8. A cost changes from $200 to $250.

Cooperative Learning

9. Explain to a partner how you find the percent increase or decrease in number 3 in **Practice**.

10. Write down a number. Then write a number that is two times the first number. Ask a partner to find the percent increase or decrease between the first number and the second number. Check the work.

10-11 ▸ Calculator: Percents for Fractions

You can use a calculator to write percents for fractions. First, write a decimal for the fraction. Then, move the decimal point two places to the right.

▸ **EXAMPLE 1**

Write $\frac{18}{45}$ as a percent.

Use your calculator to divide 18 by 45.

Display

Enter 18 by pressing:	[1] [8]	$|8$
Divide by 45 by pressing:	[÷] [4] [5]	45
	[=]	0.4

Write 0.4 as .40.	0.40
Move the decimal point 2 places to the right.	4 0 .
Write the percent symbol.	40%

$\frac{18}{45} = 40\%$

You may have to round the decimal before you move the decimal point.

▸ **EXAMPLE 2**

Write $\frac{17}{56}$ as a percent.

Use your calculator to divide 17 by 56.

Display

Enter 17 by pressing:	[1] [7]	17
Divide by 56 by pressing:	[÷] [5] [6]	56
	[=]	0.3035714

Round to the nearest hundredth.	0.30
Move the decimal point 2 places to the right.	0 3 0 .
Write the percent symbol.	30%

$\frac{17}{56}$ is about 30%

Practice

Write a percent for each fraction.

1. $\frac{3}{11}$ **2.** $\frac{2}{9}$ **3.** $\frac{5}{9}$

4. $\frac{5}{7}$ **5.** $\frac{48}{80}$ **6.** $\frac{16}{47}$

7. $\frac{101}{149}$ **8.** $\frac{84}{120}$ **9.** $\frac{1}{4}$

Math in Your Life

PICTURE PERFECT

Taking a good picture is not easy. It means thinking about many things. When you look through the lens, the camera has to be straight. You need to make sure the most important part of the picture is centered. If you are taking a picture of a friend and the person is over to one side, the picture will not look balanced. Part of your friend may even be cut off when the film is developed.

When you take a picture, you also have to know what kind of film to use. Films have different speeds. The speed of the film tells you how the film reacts to light. For example, a film with a fast speed reacts quickly to light. So, fast-speed films are good for pictures where the light is dim. It is also good to use when taking pictures indoors. Film with a slow speed reacts slowly to light. This kind of film is good for pictures in places where the light is bright. Slow-speed film is good to use when taking pictures outside.

After you take your pictures, you have to get the film developed. You can decide what the size of your pictures should be. You may want 4″ by 5″ prints. If one of your pictures turns out very well, you may want to give it to a friend or to a family member. You can use what you know about proportion to enlarge your 4″ × 5″ picture into an 8″ × 10″ print. What a great idea for a gift!

You can use proportions to solve many problems.

EXAMPLE

If 3 pounds of asparagus cost \$5, how many pounds can you buy for \$20?

READ **What do you need to find out?**
You need to find how many pounds of asparagus you can buy for \$20.

PLAN **What do you need to do?**
You need to set up a proportion to solve for the missing amount.

DO **Follow the plan.**

Set up a proportion.
$$\frac{\text{pounds}}{\text{dollars}} = \frac{\text{pounds}}{\text{dollars}}$$

3 pounds cost \$5.
$$\frac{3}{5} = \frac{\text{pounds}}{\text{dollars}}$$

Let x stand for pounds you can buy for \$20.
$$\frac{3}{5} = \frac{x}{20}$$

Cross multiply.
$$3 \cdot 20 = 5x$$

Simplify each side.
$$60 = 5x$$

Divide both sides by 5.
$$60 \div 5 = 5x \div 5$$

Simplify each side.
$$12 = x$$

Solution: 12

CHECK **Does your answer make sense?**
Cross multiply to check that the ratios are equal.
$$3 \cdot 20 = 5 \cdot 12$$
$$60 = 60 \checkmark$$

You can buy 12 pounds of asparagus for \$20.

Try These

Use a proportion to solve each problem.

1. Forty ounces of tomatoes cost $4. How much do 30 ounces cost?

Set up a proportion.

Let x stand for the cost of 30 ounces. $\dfrac{40}{\blacksquare} = \dfrac{\blacksquare}{x}$

Cross multiply. $40 \cdot x = \blacksquare \cdot \blacksquare$

Divide both sides by $\blacksquare$. $40x \div \blacksquare = \blacksquare \div \blacksquare$

$$x = \blacksquare$$

30 ounces cost $\blacksquare.

2. You walk 5 miles in 2 hours. How many miles can you walk in 6 hours?

Set up a proportion.

Let x stand for the number of miles you can walk in 6 hours. $\dfrac{\blacksquare}{2} = \dfrac{x}{\blacksquare}$

Cross multiply. $2 \cdot x = \blacksquare \cdot \blacksquare$

Divide both sides by $\blacksquare$. $2x \div \blacksquare = \blacksquare \div \blacksquare$

$$x = \blacksquare$$

You can walk $\blacksquare$ miles in 6 hours.

Practice

Use a proportion to solve each problem.

1. At Buywell's store, you can buy 3 pairs of socks on sale for $8. How many pairs of socks could you buy if you spent $24?

2. In 3 hours, Kramer can pack 48 cartons of books. How many cartons of books can he pack in 8 hours?

3. At a nursery, you can buy 5 plants for $18. How much would you spend if you bought 20 plants?

4. Kristen can run 15 miles in 2 hours. If she could run for 6 hours at the same rate, how many miles would she run?

Cooperative Learning

5. Explain to a partner how you solve number **3** in **Practice**.

6. Write a problem that is solved by using a proportion. Ask a partner to solve it. Check the work.

10-13 ▶ **Application: Discount Prices**

Discount is the amount by which a price is reduced. So it tells you how much you save when you buy something at a discount. You can find a discount by finding a percent of a number. A discount of 10% is easy to find. You can use 10% to find other discounts.

▶ **EXAMPLE 1**

A jacket costs $40.00. A store discounted it 20%. How much money would you save?

First, find 10% of $40.00.

Math Fact
To change 10% to a decimal, move the decimal point two places to the left.

Change 10% to a decimal. $10\% = 0\,.\,1\,0$

Then, multiply. $0.10 \times 40 = 4$

20% is two times 10%.
So, multiply 4 by 2. $2 \times 4 = 8$

You would save $8.00.

▶ **EXAMPLE 2**

A $30.00 shirt is discounted 25%. How much money would you save?

First, find 10% of $30.00.

Change 10% to a decimal. $10\% = 0\,.\,1\,0$

Then, multiply. $0.10 \times 30 = 3$

25% is two and one half times 10%.

So, multiply 3 by 2.5. $2.5 \times 3 = 7.50$

You would save $7.50.

Try These

1. Find the amount you would save on $10.00 jeans discounted 30%.

   Change 10% to a decimal. $10\% = 0.10$

   Then, multiply. $0.10 \times \blacksquare = \blacksquare$

   30% is ■ times 10%. $\blacksquare \times 1 = \blacksquare$

   You would save ■.

2. Find the amount you would save on a $25.00 sweatshirt discounted 35%.

   Change 10% to a decimal. $10\% = 0.10$

   Then, multiply. $0.10 \times \blacksquare = \blacksquare$

   35% is ■ times 2.5. $\blacksquare \times 2.5 = \blacksquare$

   You would save ■.

Practice

Solve the problems. Use what you know about finding 10% of a number to help you.

1. Find the amount you would save on a $50.00 sweater discounted 35%.

2. Find the amount you would save on a $60.00 outfit discounted 30%.

3. Find the amount you would save on a $20.00 basketball discounted 25%.

4. Find the amount you would save on an $80.00 video game discounted 40%.

5. Find the amount you would save on a $40.00 cassette player discounted 60%.

Cooperative Learning

6. Explain to a partner how you find the amount you would save in number **4** in **Practice**.

7. Work with a partner. An item costs $90.00. Think of a percent discount. Ask your partner to find how much would be saved with the discount. Check the work.

Summary

Ratios can compare different quantities.
One way to check if the ratios in a proportion are equal is to find cross products. They should be equal.
You can find any number in a proportion if you know the other three numbers. Use cross products.
A percent can be less than, equal to, or greater than 100%. A percent is a ratio of a number to 100.
To write a number equation, use the "×" sign for "of." Use the "=" sign for "equals." Write the percents as a decimal or fraction.
If you need to solve a problem about percents, write an equation.
You can use a proportion to solve word problems.
You can find a discount by finding a percent of a number.

ratio

proportion

cross product

solving a proportion

percent

percent increase

percent decrease

discount

Vocabulary Review

Complete the sentences with words from the box.

1. A statement that two ratios are equal is a _____.

2. The _____ is the product of numbers across from each other in a proportion.

3. Finding a number in a proportion when the other three are known is called _____.

4. The percent change when a number decreases is a _____.

5. The _____ is the amount a price is reduced.

6. A comparison of two quantities is called a _____.

7. A _____ is a ratio of a number to 100.

8. The percent change when a number increases is a _____.

Chapter Quiz

Write the ratio.

1. There are 14 people in 3 vans. Write the ratio of vans to people.

Solve the proportions.

2. $\frac{3}{1.2} = \frac{y}{4.8}$

3. $\frac{12}{9} = \frac{r}{3}$

4. $\frac{3}{6} = \frac{y}{16}$

Write a percent for each ratio.

5. 51 to 100

6. 99 to 100

7. 10 to 100

Write a decimal for each percent.

8. 1%

9. 115%

10. 20%

Write a percent for each decimal.

11. 3.75

12. .68

13. .33

Write a fraction for each percent.

14. 40%

15. 32%

16. 9%

Write a percent for each fraction or mixed number.

17. $\frac{16}{40}$

18. $3\frac{7}{10}$

19. $1\frac{3}{4}$

Write a number equation for each percent fact.

20. 15% of $15.00 is $2.25. **21.** 90% of 150 is 135. **22.** 10 is 1% of 1,000.

Solve the percent problems.

23. 1% of 100 is what number?

24. 120 is what percent of 160?

Find the percent increase or decrease.

25. A number changes from 25 to 20. **26.** A number changes from 9 to 10.

Unit 4 **Review**

Use the table to answer Questions 1 and 2.

Food	Calories	Grams Protein
1 cup milk	80	8
2 ounces of tuna	60	13
4 ounces of chicken breast	200	15
1 serving of raisin bran	190	4

1. Hannah ate 4 ounces of tuna for dinner. How many calories did she eat?
   A. 240
   B. 120
   C. 180
   D. 200

2. Noah drank 32 grams of protein by drinking milk with every meal. How many cups of milk did he drink?
   A. 4
   B. 24
   C. 6
   D. 8

3. A number changes from 8 to 12. What is the percent of increase?
   A. 40%
   B. 20%
   C. 15%
   D. 50%

4. What is the median for these numbers? 5, 3, 6, 8, 5, 9, 10, 13
   A. 6
   B. 7
   C. 8
   D. 9

5. What is the amount you would save on a pair of shoes that cost $75, discounted 20%?
   A. $60
   B. $15
   C. $30
   D. $20

6. What is the range of these numbers? 3, 2, 8, 11, 9, 15, 8
   A. 2
   B. 8
   C. 13
   D. 15

Critical Thinking

Brian wants to fence in his yard for his dog. The yard is 10 feet wide and 12 feet long. He can buy 4 feet of fence for $12. How much will it cost to fence in the yard?
CHALLENGE Brian buys five pieces of lumber that are each 4 feet wide and 5 feet long. The lumber costs $3 for 10 square feet. How much will Brian spend on the lumber?

Unit Five

Positive and negative numbers are used to tell the temperature. Temperatures above zero are positive. Temperatures below zero are negative. What words do we use to describe a temperature below zero?

Learning Objectives

- Identify positive and negative integers.
- Compare integers.
- Find the opposite of an integer.
- Find the absolute value of an integer.
- Add, subtract, multiply, and divide integers.
- Use a calculator to add, subtract, multiply, and divide integers.
- Solve problems by making groups.
- Apply concepts and skills to use number scales.

Words to Know

integers	numbers such as...⁻3, ⁻2, ⁻1, 0, 1, 2, 3,...
positive integers	integers to the right of 0 on the number line
negative integers	integers to the left of 0 on the number line
opposites	two numbers that are the same distance from 0 on the number line but are on opposite sides of 0
absolute value	the distance between 0 and an integer on the number line
number scale	shows numbers above and below 0
altitudes	heights above and below 0
Fahrenheit	a temperature scale that has the freezing point of water as 32°F and the boiling point as 212°F
Celsius	a temperature scale that has the freezing point of water as 0°C and the boiling point as 100°C

Weather Project

Choose two places on a world map or globe that are in different hemispheres. Use the Internet or a newspaper to follow the weather in each location. Record the temperature in each location every day for a week. Graph these temperatures on a line graph. Find the average high and the average low temperature during the week. Where was the temperature higher? Where was it lower? Report your findings to the class.

What Is an Integer?

The **integers** are the numbers, such as

...‾3, ‾2, ‾1, 0, 1, 2, 3,...

Positive integers are to the right of 0. **Negative integers** are to the left of 0. The whole number 0 is an integer that is not positive or negative. You can show integers on a number line.

Math Facts
+ is a positive sign.
− is a negative sign.

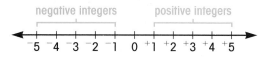

Read ⁺3 as "positive three" or "three." ⁺3 can also be written as 3. Read ‾4 as "negative four."

You can use a number line to compare integers.

On the number line, the integer to the left of another integer is less than that integer.

 EXAMPLE 1

Math Facts
> means *is greater than*.
< means *is less than*.
= means *is equal to*.

Compare. Use >, <, or = for ■.   ‾5 ■ 2

‾5 is to the left of 2 on the number line.   ‾5 ■ 2

‾5 is less than 2.   ‾5 < 2

‾5 < 2

On the number line, the integer to the right of another integer is greater.

 EXAMPLE 2

Compare. Use >, <, or = for ■.   ‾1 ■ ‾3

‾1 is to the right of ‾3 on the number line.   ‾1 ■ ‾3

‾1 is greater than ‾3.   ‾1 > ‾3

‾1 > ‾3

Try These

Complete.

1. ⁻5 is read as "■ five."

2. ⁺6 is read as "■ six" or "six."

3. ■ is read as "negative one."

4. ■ is read as "positive two" or "two."

Compare. Use >, <, or = for ■.

5. ⁻6 ■ ⁻3

⁻6 is to the left of ⁻3 on the number line.

⁻6 is less than ⁻3.

⁻6 ■ ⁻3

6. 4 ■ ⁻2

4 is to the right of ⁻2 on the number line.

4 is greater than ⁻2.

4 ■ ⁻2

Practice

Compare. Use >, <, or = for ■.

1. 5 ■ 0

2. ⁻1 ■ ⁻2

3. ⁻3 ■ 4

4. ⁻2 ■ ⁻3

5. 0 ■ ⁻1

6. ⁻6 ■ ⁻6

7. 0 ■ 7

8. ⁻5 ■ ⁻1

9. ⁻10 ■ 9

10. ⁻10 ■ ⁻20

11. 5 ■ 5

12. ⁻12 ■ 9

Cooperative Learning

13. Explain to a partner how you compare the integers in **9** in **Practice.**

14. Write two integers. Have a partner compare them. Check the work.

The integers 5 and ⁻5 are **opposites.** One is positive and one is negative.

▸ **EXAMPLE 1**

Find the opposite of ⁻4.

⁻4 is negative. The opposite is positive.

The opposite of ⁻4 is 4.

▸ **EXAMPLE 2**

Find the opposite of 3.

3 is positive. The opposite is negative.

The opposite of 3 is ⁻3.

Absolute value of an integer is its distance from 0.

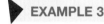

The absolute value of ⁻5 is 5 because ⁻5 is 5 units from 0. The absolute value of ⁻5 is written as $|^-5|$. So, we can write $|^-5| = 5$.

The absolute value of 5 is 5 because 5 is 5 units from 0. The absolute value of 5 is written as $|5|$. We can write $|5| = 5$.

▸ **EXAMPLE 3**

Find $|^-2|$.

⁻2 is 2 units from 0.

$|^-2| = 2$

▸ **EXAMPLE 4**

Find $|0|$.

0 is 0 units from 0.

$|0| = 0$

The absolute value of any positive or negative number is positive. The absolute value of 0 is 0.

Try These

Find the opposite of each integer.

1. ⁻7

    The opposite of a negative integer
is a ▪ integer.

    The opposite of ⁻7 is ▪.

2. 8

    The opposite of a positive integer is
a ▪ integer.

    The opposite of 8 is ▪.

Find each absolute value.

3. $|6|$

    6 is ▪ units from 0.

    $|6|$ = ▪.

4. $|{}^-1|$

    ⁻1 is ▪ unit from 0.

    $|{}^-1|$ = ▪.

Practice

Find the opposite of each integer.

1. 9   **2.** 1   **3.** 10   **4.** ⁻8

5. ⁻2   **6.** ⁻9   **7.** ⁻11   **8.** 7

9. 20   **10.** ⁻15   **11.** 25   **12.** ⁻14

Find the absolute value of each integer.

13. $|{}^-6|$ **14.** $|8|$ **15.** $|1|$ **16.** $|{}^-4|$

17. $|{}^-8|$ **18.** $|9|$ **19.** $|{}^-7|$ **20.** $|2|$

21. $|{}^-20|$ **22.** $|10|$ **23.** $|{}^-15|$ **24.** $|12|$

Cooperative Learning

25. Explain to a partner how you find the absolute value in number **19**
in **Practice**.

26. Write a positive integer and a negative integer. Ask a partner to
find the absolute value of each. Check the work.

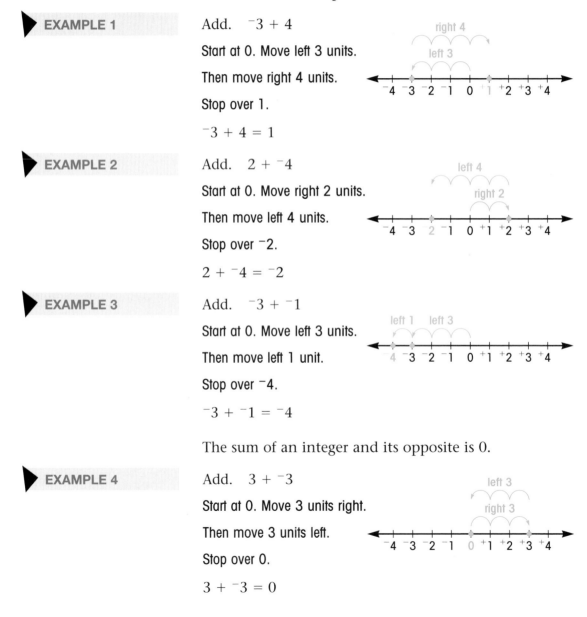

11·3 ▶ Adding on the Number Line

You can use a number line to add integers. Move right to add a positive integer. Move left to add a negative integer. You can make the number line any size you need to answer the problem.

▶ **EXAMPLE 1**

Add. $^-3 + 4$

Start at 0. Move left 3 units.

Then move right 4 units.

Stop over 1.

$^-3 + 4 = 1$

▶ **EXAMPLE 2**

Add. $2 + ^-4$

Start at 0. Move right 2 units.

Then move left 4 units.

Stop over $^-2$.

$2 + ^-4 = ^-2$

▶ **EXAMPLE 3**

Add. $^-3 + ^-1$

Start at 0. Move left 3 units.

Then move left 1 unit.

Stop over $^-4$.

$^-3 + ^-1 = ^-4$

The sum of an integer and its opposite is 0.

▶ **EXAMPLE 4**

Add. $3 + ^-3$

Start at 0. Move 3 units right.

Then move 3 units left.

Stop over 0.

$3 + ^-3 = 0$

Try These

Use this number line to add the integers.

$$\leftarrow \;|\; \overset{-}{8}\; \overset{-}{7}\; \overset{-}{6}\; \overset{-}{5}\; \overset{-}{4}\; \overset{-}{3}\; \overset{-}{2}\; \overset{-}{1}\; 0\; \overset{+}{1}\; \overset{+}{2}\; \overset{+}{3}\; \overset{+}{4}\; \overset{+}{5}\; \overset{+}{6}\; \overset{+}{7}\; \overset{+}{8}\; \rightarrow$$

1. Add. $^-2 + 3$

Start at 0.

Go left ■ units.

Then go right ■ units.

Stop over ■.

$^-2 + 3 = $ ■.

2. Add. $0 + 4$

Start at 0.

Then move ■ units to the ■.

$0 + 4 = $ ■.

Practice

Add. Use a number line.

1. $^-2 + 5$ **2.** $3 + {}^-7$ **3.** $^-8 + 5$

4. $^-5 + {}^-5$ **5.** $4 + 6$ **6.** $^-7 + 7$

7. $8 + {}^-1$ **8.** $^-7 + 8$ **9.** $^-8 + 1$

10. $5 + {}^-6$ **11.** $4 + {}^-4$ **12.** $^-4 + 8$

13. $6 + {}^-5$ **14.** $^-5 + 6$ **15.** $1 + {}^-1$

Cooperative Learning

16. Explain to a partner how you use a number line to add the integers in number **10** in **Practice**.

17. Ask a partner to add two integers using a number line. Check the work.

11·4 ▶ Adding and Absolute Value

In the last lesson, you added integers by using a number line. You can also add integers by using absolute value.

To add two negative integers or two positive integers, add their absolute values. The sum is negative if the integers are negative. The sum is positive if the integers are positive.

▶ **EXAMPLE 1**

Add. $^-10 + ^-12$

Find the absolute value of each. $|^-10| = 10$ $|^-12| = 12$

Add the absolute values. $10 + 12 = 22$

$^-10$ and $^-12$ are both negative.

The sum is negative.

$^-10 + ^-12 = ^-22$

To find the sum of a positive integer and a negative integer, subtract the smaller absolute value from the larger. Use the sign of the integer with the larger absolute value as the sign of the sum.

▶ **EXAMPLE 2**

Add. $17 + ^-22$

Find the absolute value of each. $|17| = 17$ $|^-22| = 22$

Subtract the smaller from the larger. $22 - 17 = 5$

$^-22$ has the larger absolute value.

The sum is negative.

$^-22 + 17 = ^-5$

▶ **EXAMPLE 3**

Add. $30 + ^-20$

Find the absolute value of each. $|30| = 30$ $|^-20| = 20$

Subtract the smaller from the larger. $30 - 20 = 10$

30 has the larger absolute value.

The sum is positive.

$30 + ^-20 = 10$

Try These

Add.

1. $^-25 + 20$

    The signs are different.

    Find the absolute values. $|^-25| = \blacksquare$
                                      $|20| = 20$

    Subtract the smaller. $\quad \blacksquare - 20 = \blacksquare$

    $^-25$ has the larger absolute value.

    The sum is negative.

    $^-25 + 20 = \blacksquare$.

2. $^-18 + {}^-5$

    The signs are the same.

    Find the absolute values. $|^-18| = 18$
                                        $|^-5| = \blacksquare$

    Add the absolute values. $18 + \blacksquare = \blacksquare$

    $^-18$ and $^-5$ are both negative.

    The sum is $\blacksquare$.

    $^-18 + {}^-5 = \blacksquare$.

Practice

Add.

1. $^-11 + 17$ **2.** $^-13 + 6$ **3.** $17 + 10$

4. $^-20 + 20$ **5.** $^-14 + {}^-18$ **6.** $^-16 + {}^-12$

7. $8 + {}^-15$ **8.** $^-20 + {}^-18$ **9.** $^-32 + 20$

10. $^-25 + 22$ **11.** $21 + {}^-30$ **12.** $^-10 + 14$

13. $^-16 + 20$ **14.** $16 + {}^-24$ **15.** $18 + {}^-9$

Cooperative Learning

16. Explain to a partner how you add the integers in number **11** in **Practice**.

17. Write two integers. Ask a partner to find their sum. Check the work.

11-5 Subtracting Integers

You can use a number line to see how subtracting integers is like adding integers.

This shows the addition: $^-2 + {}^-3 = {}^-5$
This shows the subtraction: $^-2 - 3 = {}^-5$
Subtracting 3 is just like adding $^-3$.
Subtracting an integer is just like adding its opposite.
So, you can follow the rules you know for adding integers.

EXAMPLE 1

Subtract. $^-4 - {}^-5$

Change to adding the opposite of $^-5$. $^-4 + 5$

Find the absolute values. $|{}^-4| = 4$ $|5| = 5$

Subtract the smaller from the larger. $5 - 4 = 1$

5 has the larger absolute value.

5 is positive, so the answer is positive.

$^-4 - {}^-5 = 1$

EXAMPLE 2

Subtract. $^-7 - 3$

Change to adding the opposite of 3. $^-7 + {}^-3$

Find the absolute values. $|{}^-7| = 7$ $|{}^-3| = 3$

Add the absolute values. $7 + 3 = 10$

$^-7$ and $^-3$ are both negative.

So, the answer is negative.

$^-7 - 3 = {}^-10$

Try These

Subtract.

1. $5 - {}^-10$

Change to adding the opposite of $^-10$.

$5 + \blacksquare$

$|5| = 5 \quad |\blacksquare| = \blacksquare$

$5 + \blacksquare = \blacksquare$

5 and 10 are both positive.
So, the answer is positive.

$5 - {}^-10 = \blacksquare$.

2. $^-3 - 8$

Change to adding the opposite of 8.

$\blacksquare + {}^-8$

$|^-3| = \blacksquare \quad |^-8| = 8$

$3 + 8 = 11$

$^-3$ and $^-8$ are both negative.
So, the answer is negative.

$^-3 - 8 = \blacksquare$.

Practice

Subtract.

1. $^-2 - {}^-3$

2. $5 - {}^-1$

3. $^-4 - 1$

4. $^-3 - {}^-4$

5. $^-8 - {}^-8$

6. $^-4 - 5$

7. $^-9 - 4$

8. $6 - {}^-2$

9. $^-5 - {}^-2$

10. $1 - 1$

11. $^-10 - 14$

12. $^-7 - {}^-10$

13. $^-16 - {}^-20$

14. $10 - {}^-20$

15. $20 - {}^-10$

Cooperative Learning

16. Explain to a partner how you subtract the integers in number **12** in **Practice**.

17. Write any two integers. Have a partner subtract them. Check the work.

Multiplying Integers

Multiplication is a way of doing addition when the addends are the same. This can be used to find out how to multiply integers.

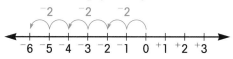

Addition: $^-2 + {}^-2 + {}^-2 = {}^-6$

Multiplication: $(3)(^-2) = {}^-6$

Math Fact
$(2)(3) = (6)$ is another way to write $(^+2)(^+3) = (^+6)$.

This shows that the product of a positive integer and a negative integer is negative. The product of two positive integers is positive. $(2)(3) = 6$

▶ **EXAMPLE 1**

Multiply. $(^-5)(4)$

Find the absolute values. $|^-5| = 5$ $|4| = 4$

Multiply the absolute values. $5 \cdot 4 = 20$

The product of a positive integer
and a negative integer is negative. $(^-5)(4) = {}^-20$

Look at these products to find out the sign of the product of two negative integers.

$(^-3)(2) = {}^-6$ $(^-3)(1) = {}^-3$ $(^-3)(0) = 0$
$(^-3)(^-1) = ?$ $(^-3)(^-2) = ?$

To continue the pattern:

$(^-3)(^-1) = {}^+3$ and $(^-3)(^-2) = {}^+6$

The product of two negative integers is positive.

▶ **EXAMPLE 2**

Multiply. $(^-2)(^-8)$

Find the absolute values. $|^-2| = 2$ $|^-8| = 8$

Multiply the absolute values. $2 \cdot 8 = 16$

The product of two negative
integers is positive. $(^-2)(^-8) = 16$

Try These

Multiply.

1. (4)($^-$8)

Find the absolute value of each.	$\|4\| = 4$ $|^-8| = $ ■
Multiply the absolute values.	4 • ■ = ■
The product of a positive integer and a negative integer is ■.	(4)($^-$8) = ■

2. ($^-$6)($^-$1)

Find the absolute value of each.	$|^-6| = $ ■ $\|^-1\| = 1$
Multiply the absolute values.	■ • 1 = ■
The product of two negative integers is ■.	($^-$6)($^-$1) = ■

Practice

Multiply.

1. ($^-$2)($^-$3)

2. (3)(2)

3. ($^-$4)(7)

4. (6)($^-$3)

5. (5)($^-$1)

6. ($^-$5)($^-$8)

7. ($^-$6)($^-$2)

8. (4)(7)

9. ($^-$9)(0)

10. (9)($^-$3)

11. ($^-$5)($^-$3)

12. (9)($^-$5)

13. (1)($^-$8)

14. ($^-$1)($^-$8)

15. ($^-$10)(10)

16. ($^-$10)($^-$10)

17. ($^-$7)(10)

18. (5)($^-$10)

Cooperative Learning

19. Explain to a partner how you find the product of the integers in number **14** in **Practice**.

20. Write any two negative integers. Have a partner find their product. Then, write a positive integer and a negative integer. Have a partner find the product. Check the work.

Dividing Integers

From your work with whole numbers, you know that multiplication is related to division. The factors of a product divide the product evenly.

$$2 \times 3 = 6 \quad \rightarrow \quad 6 \div 3 = 2$$
$$6 \div 2 = 3$$

You can use this and what you know about multiplying integers to divide integers.

$$(^+2)(^+3) = (^+6) \quad \rightarrow \quad (^+6) \div (^+2) = {}^+3$$
$$(^-2)(^+3) = (^-6) \quad \rightarrow \quad (^-6) \div (^-2) = {}^+3$$

The quotient of two positive or two negative integers is positive.

▶ EXAMPLE 1

Divide. $^-10 \div {}^-2$

Find the absolute values.　　　　$|{}^-10| = 10 \quad |{}^-2| = 2$

Divide the absolute values.　　　　$10 \div 2 = 5$

The quotient of two negative integers is positive.　　　$^-10 \div {}^-2 = 5$

Here are products of positive and negative integers. You can see how they relate to division.

$$(^-2)(^-3) = {}^+6 \quad \rightarrow \quad {}^+6 \div (^-3) = {}^-2$$
$$(^+2)(^-3) = {}^-6 \quad \rightarrow \quad {}^-6 \div (2) = {}^-3$$

The quotient of a positive integer and a negative integer is negative.

▶ EXAMPLE 2

Divide. $^-18 \div 2$

Find the absolute values.　　　　$|{}^-18| = 18 \quad |2| = 2$

Divide the absolute values.　　　　$18 \div 2 = 9$

The quotient of a positive integer and a negative integer is negative.　　　$^-18 \div 2 = {}^-9$

Try These

Divide.

1. $9 \div {}^-3$

Find the absolute values.	$\|9\| = 9$ $\|{}^-3\| = \blacksquare$
Divide the absolute values.	$9 \div \blacksquare = \blacksquare$

The quotient of a positive integer and a negative integer is $\blacksquare$.

$9 \div \blacksquare = \blacksquare$

2. $^-14 \div {}^-2$

Find the absolute values.	$\|{}^-14\| = \blacksquare$ $\|{}^-2\| = 2$
Divide the absolute values.	$\blacksquare \div 2 = \blacksquare$

The quotient of two negative integers is $\blacksquare$.

$^-14 \div {}^-2 = \blacksquare$

Practice

Divide.

1. $32 \div 2$

2. $16 \div {}^-8$

3. $^-2 \div {}^-2$

4. $21 \div {}^-3$

5. $^-21 \div 3$

6. $^-45 \div 5$

7. $^-15 \div {}^-5$

8. $0 \div {}^-10$

9. $^-60 \div {}^-20$

10. $20 \div {}^-4$

11. $^-20 \div 5$

12. $72 \div 9$

13. $^-48 \div 8$

14. $^-100 \div 10$

15. $^-21 \div {}^-3$

16. $63 \div 7$

17. $^-32 \div {}^-4$

18. $^-15 \div 15$

Cooperative Learning

19. Explain to a partner how you find the quotient in number **11** in **Practice.**

20. Use different signs for the divisor and dividend in number **14** in **Practice.** Ask a partner to find the quotient. Check the work.

11·8 ▶ Calculator: Operations with Integers

You can use a calculator to solve problems with negative numbers. Remember to follow the rules for doing operations with integers.

▶ **EXAMPLE 1**

Find the sum of ⁻19 and ⁺25.

The signs are different.

Find the absolute values. $|^-19| = 19$ $|25| = 25$

Subtract the smaller absolute value from the larger.

		Display
Enter 25 by pressing:	[2] [5]	25
Then, subtract 19 by pressing:	[−] [1] [9]	19
	[=]	6

The sign of the number with the larger absolute value is positive.

The sum of ⁻19 and ⁺25 is ⁺6.

▶ **EXAMPLE 2**

Find the sum of ⁻37 and ⁻54.

Add the absolute values. $|^-37| = 37$

$|^-54| = 54$

		Display
Enter 37 by pressing:	[3] [7]	37
Then, add 54 by pressing:	[+] [5] [4]	54
	[=]	91

The sign of both numbers is negative, so the sum is negative.

The sum of ⁻37 and ⁻54 is ⁻91.

Practice

1. $^-89 + {^-13}$

2. $27 + {^-53}$

3. $^-82 + 14$

4. $^-102 - 62$

5. $28 - 33$

6. $(^-19)(^-21)$

7. $(11)(^-13)$

8. $^-212 \div 4$

Math Connection

WIND CHILL

Have you ever noticed that you feel much colder outside on a windy day than on a calm day with the same outdoor temperature? The combination of temperature and wind can make you feel colder than the actual temperature reading. Wind chill is the estimate of how cold the wind makes a person feel under the existing conditions.

Wind Chill Table					
Wind Speed (mph)	Outdoor Temperature (°F)				
0	0	10	20	30	40
5	$^-5$	6	16	27	37
10	$^-22$	$^-9$	3	16	28
15	$^-31$	$^-18$	$^-5$	9	23
20	$^-39$	$^-24$	$^-10$	4	19
25	$^-44$	$^-29$	$^-15$	1	16

The National Weather Service publishes a table for estimating wind chill. Part of that chart is shown on this page.

It is important to understand positive and negative integers before you can read and understand the chart. If the temperature is 10°F and the wind speed is 15 mph, the wind chill is $^-18$°F. This means that the temperature outside feels like it is 18°F below zero.

It is important to consider wind chill, especially during the cold months. Extremely cold weather is dangerous to people who are not prepared for its effect. You need to dress warmly in such weather.

11·9 ▸ Problem Solving: Small Groups

You can make small groups from large groups to solve problems.

▶ **EXAMPLE**

Taylor, Steve, and Lucia are working on a school fund raiser. Two of the students must make phone calls for the fund raiser. How many different pairs can be made from Taylor, Steve, and Lucia?

READ **What do you need to find out?**
You need to find the number of different pairs that can be made from the three people.

PLAN **What do you need to do?**
You need to take each person and pair him or her with the other two.

DO **Follow the plan.**

Use Taylor with the other two: Taylor with Steve
Taylor with Lucia

Use Steve with the other two: Steve with Taylor
Steve with Lucia

Use Lucia with the other two: Lucia with Taylor
Lucia with Steve

There are six pairs, but some are the same. Taylor with Steve is the same as Steve with Taylor. There are only three different pairs: Taylor with Steve, Taylor with Lucia, and Steve with Lucia.

CHECK **Does your answer make sense**
There are six pairs.
Look back.
Cross off the pairs that are repeated.
This leaves three different pairs. ✓

There are three different pairs to make phone calls for the fund raiser.

Try These

1. How many different groups of two letters can you make from A, B, and C?

Use A with the other two. A B, ■ C

Use B with the other two. B ■, B C

Use C with the other two. C A, C ■

There are 6 groups of two letters. ■ groups are the same. Count them once. The 3 different groups that can be formed are: A B, ■ C, and ■ ■.

2. How many different groups of 3 letters can be formed from C, D, E, and F?

Start with C: C D E, C D ■, C E ■

Start with D: D C E, D C ■, D E ■

Start with E: E ■ D, E ■ F, E C ■

Start with F: F C ■, F C ■, F ■ E

There are 12 groups.
The 4 different groups that can be formed are:
C D E, C D ■, C E ■, D ■ F.

Practice

Find the small groups from the large groups.

1. How many different groups of three people can you make from Louis, Juan, Anita, and Harriet?

2. How many different groups of two letters can you make from A, B, C, D, and E?

3. How many different groups of three letters can you make from A, B, C, D, and E?

Cooperative Learning

4. Explain to a partner how you find the groups in number **2** in **Practice.**

5. Work with a partner. How many different groups of two letters can you make from A, B, C, D, E, and F? Take turns writing the pairs. Check each other's work.

A **number scale** shows positive numbers above 0 and negative numbers below 0. Number scales are used in many ways. They show temperatures above and below 0. They show **altitudes,** or heights, above and below 0.

▶ **EXAMPLE 1**

In the morning, the temperature on the Celsius thermometer was ⁻3°C. The temperature went up to 20°C. What was the change in temperature?

100°	--- Water ---	212°
80°	boils	180°
60°		150°
		120°
40°		90°
20°		60°
0°	--- Water ---	32°
	freezes	
⁻20°		0°

Celsius   Fahrenheit

Subtract to find the change in temperature. To subtract, change to adding the opposite of ⁻3.

20°C − ⁻3°C
20 + 3
$|20| = 20$ $|3| = 3$

20°C − ⁻3°C = 23°C

The change in temperature is 23°C.

▶ **EXAMPLE 2**

Heights (in meters)

6,194 m ── Mt. McKinley

4,418 m ── Mt. Whitney

1,917 m ── Mt. Washington

0 m ── Sea Level
⁻86 m ── Death Valley
⁻340 m ── Dead Sea

This number scale shows the heights of mountains and other places above and below sea level. Sea level is at 0 meters. The Dead Sea is at ⁻340 m. This means the Dead Sea is 340 m lower than sea level. What is the difference in altitude between the Dead Sea and Mt. Whitney?

Subtract to find the difference. To subtract, change to adding the opposite of ⁻340.

4,418 m − ⁻340 m
4,418 + 340
$|4,418| = 4,418$ $|340| = 340$

4,418 + 340 = 4,758
4,418 m − ⁻340 m = 4,758 m

The difference in the altitudes is 4,758 m.

1. What is the difference between the boiling and freezing points on the Celsius number scale?

    Subtract. $100°C - ■°C$

    $100°C - ■°C = ■°C$

    The difference between the boiling and freezing point is ■°C.

2. How much lower is the Dead Sea than Death Valley?

    Subtract. $^-86 \text{ m} - {}^-340 \text{ m}$

    $^-86 \text{ m} + 340 \text{ m}$

    $^-86 \text{ m} + 340 \text{ m} = ■ \text{ m}$

    The Dead Sea is ■ m lower than Death Valley.

Practice

Look at the number scales. Then, answer the questions.

1. The temperature changed $^-10°C$ to $^-2°C$. What was the temperature before the change?

2. The temperature went from $^-4°F$ to $32°F$. What was the change in temperature?

3. The temperature of hot water is $185°F$. How much warmer must the water get to boil?

4. How much higher is Mt. Whitney than Mt. Washington?

5. How much lower is Death Valley than Mt. McKinley?

6. A countdown to a race is at $^-3$ seconds. How many seconds are there to the start of the race?

Cooperative Learning

7. Explain to a partner how you find the time in number 6 in **Practice**.

8. Ask a partner a question about temperature using number scales and subtraction. Check the work.

Summary

You can use a number line to compare positive and negative integers.
The absolute value of any positive or negative integer is positive.
To add a positive integer, move right on a number line. Move left to add a negative integer.
To add two negative integers or two positive integers, add their absolute values. The sum is negative if the integers are negative. The sum is positive if the integers are positive.
To find the sum of a positive integer and a negative integer, subtract the smaller absolute value from the larger. Use the sign of the integer with the larger absolute value as the sign of the sum.
To subtract one integer from another, add the opposite of the integer to be subtracted.
The product of a positive integer and a negative integer is negative. The product of two negative integers or two positive integers is positive.
The quotient of two negative integers or two positive integers is positive. The quotient of a positive integer and a negative integer is negative.

integers

positive integers

negative integers

opposites

absolute value

number scale

Celsius

Vocabulary Review

Complete the sentences with words from the box.

1. Integers to the right of zero on a number line are called _____.

2. Numbers such as ...$^-3$, $^-2$, $^-1$, 0 1, 2, 3,... are called _____.

3. _____ are the same whole numbers, one with a positive sign and one with a negative sign.

4. The distance between 0 and an integer on the number line is its _____.

5. _____ is a temperature scale that has the freezing point of water as 0°C and the boiling point as 100°C.

6. A _____ shows numbers above and below zero.

7. Integers to the left of zero on a number line are called _____.

Chapter Quiz

Compare. Use >, <, or = for •.

1. 6 • 1 0

2. ⁻4 • ⁻5

3. ⁻7 • 8

Find the opposite of each integer.

4. ⁻18

5. 27

6. ⁻28

Find the absolute value of each integer.

7. |⁻9|

8. |4|

9. |⁻22|

Add. Use a number line.

10. ⁻6 + ⁻3

11. ⁻3 + 2

12. ⁻5 + 4

Add.

13. ⁻13 + 20

14. ⁻15 + 8

15. ⁻12 + 10

Subtract.

16. ⁻5 − ⁻7

17. 9 − ⁻2

18. ⁻14 − 11

Multiply.

19. (⁻12)(⁻3)

20. (⁻3)(2)

21. (⁻6)(10)

Divide.

22. 30 ÷ ⁻2

23. 18 ÷ ⁻9

24. ⁻3 ÷ ⁻3

Find the small groups from the large groups.

25. How many different groups of three letters can you make from A, B, C, D, E, and F?

Answer the question.

26. A countdown to the launch of a space shuttle is at ⁻10 hours. How many hours are there to the launch?

Chapter 12

Integers and Algebra

During a thunderstorm, the top part of a cloud has a positive electrical charge. The bottom part of the cloud has a negative electrical charge. What is the word for the spark that results?

Learning Objectives

- Evaluate expressions with integers.
- Simplify expressions with integers.
- Solve equations with integers.
- Graph equations and inequalities.
- Solve inequalities.
- Use a calculator to evaluate expressions with integers.
- Solve probability problems.
- Apply concepts and skills to graphing a range on a number line.

Words to Know

graph of a solution   points on the number line that show the solution

number line   shows positive numbers to the right of 0, negative numbers to the left of 0, and 0

inequality   greater than, greater than or equal to, less than, less than or equal to

probability   the chance of something happening

Temperature Comparison Project

Look in a newspaper each day for a week to find the day's predicted high and low temperatures. On two separate number lines, graph the day's temperatures, one for the predicted high and one for the predicted low temperature. Then, in the evening, listen to a weather report or surf the Net for the actual high and low temperatures. Graph those temperatures on the same number lines in a second color. Compare the predicted temperatures with the actual temperatures.

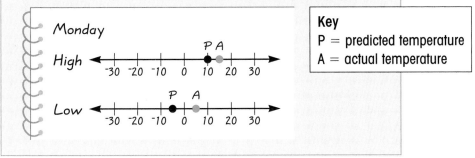

Key
P = predicted temperature
A = actual temperature

You know that to simplify variable expressions, you combine like terms. Combining like terms means adding or subtracting their coefficients. When the coefficients are integers, add or subtract carefully.

▶ **EXAMPLE 1**

Simplify. $^-11a + 9a$

Remember
Think: $^-11 + 9 = ^-2$

$^-11a + 9a$

Combine like terms. ^-2a

▶ **EXAMPLE 2**

Simplify. $^-4x - ^-6x$

Remember
Think: $^-4 - ^-6 = ^-4 + ^+6$
       $= ^+2$

$^-4x - ^-6x$

Rewrite as addition. $^-4x + ^+6x$

Combine like terms. $2x$

You may have to change the order of terms so that like terms are together.

▶ **EXAMPLE 3**

Simplify. $^-2a - 11 - ^-3a + 15$

$^-2a - 11 - ^-3a + 15$

Rewrite subtractions as additions. $^-2a + (^-11) + (^+3a) + 15$

Math Fact
1a can be written as a.

Change the order. $^-2a + (^+3a) + (^-11) + 15$

Combine like terms. $1a \quad + \quad 4$

$a + 4$

▶ **EXAMPLE 4**

Simplify. $6c - ^-9d + 2c + ^-4d$

$6c - ^-9d + 2c + ^-4d$

Rewrite subtraction as addition. $6c + (^+9d) + 2c + (^-4d)$

Change the order. $6c + 2c + (^+9d) + (^-4d)$

Combine like terms. $8c \quad + \quad 5d$

Practice

Simplify.

1. $3r + {}^-2r$

2. $^-3t - 2t - 5 - 4$

3. $5 - {}^-8 + 2t$

4. $^-7 + 2h - 5 - 8h$

5. $3 + 9x - x$

6. $^-4g + 8 - 3g + {}^-5$

7. $^-3a + 2a - {}^-5a$

8. $^-4b + 8b - 9c + 2c$

9. $5z - 4 + 2y - 8y$

10. $xy - 4x + 2 - 7xy$

11. $s - {}^-3 + 5 - 4t - 9$

12. $^-2t + 4s + 10t - 7$

Cooperative Learning

13. Explain to a partner how you simplify the expression in number **10** in **Practice**.

14. Write a variable expression with integers as coefficients. Have a partner simplify the expression.

12·2 Evaluating Expressions with Integers

You can find the value of a variable expression by replacing the variables with integers. This will give you a number expression. Perform the operations in the number expression. Be sure to follow the order of operations.

▶ **EXAMPLE 1**

Evaluate $8 - {}^-2x$ when $x = {}^-3$.

Remember
Order of Operations
1. First, multiply and divide.
2. Then, add and subtract.

Rewrite as addition.
Replace x with ${}^-3$.

$$8 - {}^-2x$$
$$8 + ({}^+2x)$$
$$8 + ({}^+2 \bullet x)$$
$$8 + ({}^+2 \bullet {}^-3)$$

Multiply first.

$$8 + ({}^-6)$$

Then, add.

$$2$$

The value of $8 - {}^-2x$ is 2 when $x = {}^-3$.

▶ **EXAMPLE 2**

Find the value of $5y \div {}^-3$ when $y = {}^-6$.

Math Fact
The quotient of two negative integers is positive.

Replace y with ${}^-6$.

$$5y \div {}^-3$$
$$5 \bullet y \div {}^-3$$
$$5({}^-6) \div {}^-3$$

Multiply.

$${}^-30 \div {}^-3$$

Then, divide.

$$10$$

The value of $5y \div {}^-3$ is 10 when $y = {}^-6$.

▶ **EXAMPLE 3**

Find the value of ${}^-6(r + s)$ when $r = {}^-4$ and $s = {}^-2$.

Replace r with ${}^-4$.
Replace s with ${}^-2$.

$${}^-6(r + s)$$
$${}^-6({}^-4 + {}^-2)$$

Work in parentheses first.
Multiply.

$${}^-6({}^-6)$$
$$36$$

The value of ${}^-6(r + s)$ is 36 when $r = {}^-4$ and $s = {}^-2$.

Try These

Evaluate each expression.

1. $x^2 + 6$ when $x = {}^-5$

Replace x with ${}^-5$.

$$x^2 + 6$$
$$(\blacksquare)(\blacksquare) + 6$$

Multiply first.

$$\blacksquare + 6$$

Then, add.

$$\blacksquare$$

The value of $x^2 + 6$ is $\blacksquare$ when $x = {}^-5$.

2. $3a + 2b$ when $a = 2$ and $b = {}^-4$

Replace a with 2 and b with ${}^-4$.

$$3a + 2b$$
$$(3)(2) + 2(\blacksquare)$$

Multiply first.

$$6 + \blacksquare$$

Then, add.

$$\blacksquare$$

The value of $3a + 2b$ is $\blacksquare$ when $a = 2$ and $b = {}^-4$.

Practice

Evaluate each expression.

1. $5r - 6$ when $r = {}^-4$

2. $5 + j \div {}^-2$ when $j = 30$

3. ${}^-8x + 25$ when $x = 5$

4. $r + 3s$ when $r = 7$ and $s = {}^-1$

5. $a^2 + 2$ when $a = 3$

6. $4h \div {}^-2$ when $h = {}^-6$

7. $2x + 5y$ when $x = {}^-8$ and $y = {}^-8$

8. $ab + 1$ when $a = 9$ and $b = {}^-2$

9. $8 \div q - 6r$ when $q = {}^-4$ and $r = 11$

10. $3 - y + {}^-8x$ when $y = {}^-12$ and $x = 1$

11. $5(a + b)$ when $a = {}^-10$ and $b = 10$

12. $a(1 + b)$ when $a = {}^-1$ and $b = {}^-2$

Cooperative Learning

13. Explain to a partner how to find the value of the expression in number **12** in **Practice**.

14. Pick three integers for w and three for v. Ask a partner to find the value of $2w + 2v$. Check the work.

Solving Equations with Integers

You can solve equations with integers just as you do with other numbers. Find an equivalent equation that you can solve just by looking at it.

► EXAMPLE 1

Solve. $^-2x = 6$

Divide both sides by $^-2$.

$$^-2 \cdot x \div ^-2 = 6 \div ^-2$$
$$\frac{^-2}{^-2} \cdot x = ^-3$$
$$x = ^-3$$

Solution: $^-3$

Check:
$$^-2(^-3) = 6$$
$$6 = 6 \quad \text{true}$$

► EXAMPLE 2

Solve. $3y - ^-1 = ^-8$

Add $^-1$ to both sides.
Simplify both sides.
Divide both sides by 3.

$$3y - ^-1 + ^-1 = ^-8 + ^-1$$
$$3y = ^-9$$
$$3 \cdot y \div 3 = ^-9 \div 3$$
$$\frac{3}{3} \cdot y = ^-3$$
$$1y = ^-3$$
$$y = ^-3$$

Solution: $^-3$

Check:
$$3(^-3) - ^-1 = ^-8$$
$$^-9 - ^-1 = ^-8$$
$$^-8 = ^-8 \quad \text{true}$$

► EXAMPLE 3

Solve. $^-7a = ^-8a + 10$

Add $8a$ to both sides.
Group like terms together.
Simplify each side.

$$^-7a + 8a = ^-8a + 10 + 8a$$
$$^-7a + 8a = ^-8a + 8a + 10$$
$$1a = 0 + 10$$
$$a = 10$$

Solution: 10

Check:
$$^-7(10) = ^-8(10) + 10$$
$$^-70 = ^-80 + 10$$
$$^-70 = ^-70 \quad \text{true}$$

Try These

Solve.

1. $\frac{x}{^-5} = {}^-7$

   $x \div {}^-5 = {}^-7$

Multiply both sides by ■. $x \div {}^-5(■) = {}^-7(■)$

Simplify both sides. $x = ■$

Solution: ■

Check: $\frac{■}{^-5} = {}^-7$

         $■ = {}^-7$ true

2. $y + {}^-3 = 1$

Subtract $^-3$ from both sides. $y + {}^-3 - ■ = 1 - ■$

Simplify both sides. $y = ■$

Solution: ■

Check: $■ + {}^-3 = 1$

         $■ = 1$ true

Practice

Solve.

1. $^-5r = 45$

2. $y + {}^-9 = 13$

3. $m - {}^-12 = {}^-5$

4. $\frac{y}{2} = {}^-10$

5. $a - 9 = {}^-5$

6. $b + {}^-10 = 0$

7. $^-4x = {}^-20$

8. $9y = {}^-18$

9. $2 + {}^-3j = 8$

10. $5v - {}^-13 = 28$

Cooperative Learning

11. Explain to a partner how to solve the equation in number **10** in **Practice**.

12. Ask a partner to solve $^-2x + 7 = {}^-9$. Check the work. Then write a new equation. Ask a partner to solve this new equation.

12-4 Graphing Inequalities

You can show a **graph of a solution** to an equation on a **number line.** The graph shows a point for the number that is the solution.

▶ **EXAMPLE 1**

Graph the solution of $x = {}^-2$.

$x = {}^-2$.

Solution: $^-2$

Place at dot at $^-2$.

You can also graph the solution of an **inequality.** Just remember what the signs mean.
> means "is greater than."
< means "is less than."
≥ means "is greater than or equal to."
≤ means "is less than or equal to."

▶ **EXAMPLE 2**

Graph the solution of $y \geq {}^-1$.

$y \geq {}^-1$

y is greater than or equal to $^-1$.

Place a dot at $^-1$ because $y = {}^-1$.

"Is greater than" means go to the right.

Shade the number line to the right of $^-1$.

▶ **EXAMPLE 3**

Graph the solution of $x < 2$.

$x < 2$.

x is less than 2.

Place an open dot at 2 because 2 is not part of the solution.

"Is less than" means go to the left.

Shade the number line to the left of 2.

Try These

1. Graph the solution of $x > {}^-4$.

   $x > {}^-4$

   x is greater than $^-4$.

   Place an open dot at ■.

   "Is greater than" means go to the ■.

   Shade the number line to the ■ of ■.

2. Graph the solution of $y \leq 0$.

   $y \leq 0$

   y is less than or equal to 0.

   Place a dot at ■.

   "Is less than" means go to the ■.

   Shade the number line to the ■ of ■.

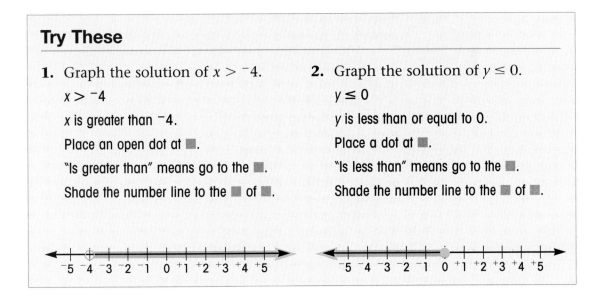

Practice

Graph each solution on a number line.

1. $x \leq {}^-4$ 2. $x = 2$ 3. $x \geq 1$

4. $x < 3$ 5. $x > 3$ 6. $x \geq 3$

7. $y > 6$ 8. $z = 3$ 9. $a = 4$

10. $a < 4$ 11. $a > 4$ 12. $x < {}^-2$

13. $x = 8$ 14. $x > {}^-8$ 15. $x \leq {}^-8$

Cooperative Learning

16. Explain to a partner how you graph the solution of the inequality in number **12** in **Practice**.

17. Write an inequality using integers. Ask a partner to graph the solution of the inequality. Check the work.

Solving Inequalities by Adding or Subtracting

The inequality $x < 2$ is easy to solve. Just by looking at it, you know the graph of this solution is all numbers to the left of 2 on the number line.

The inequality $x + 2 < 6$ is not so easy to solve. You can solve it the way you solve equations. Add or subtract the same number from both sides. This will give you an inequality that is easy to solve.

▶ **EXAMPLE 1**

Solve $x + 2 < 6$.   Graph the solution.

$$x + 2 < 6$$

Subtract 2 from both sides. $x + 2 - 2 < 6 - 2$

Simplify both sides. $x + 0 < 4$

$$x < 4$$

$x < 4$

x is less than 4.

Place an open dot at 4.

Shade the number line to the left of 4.

▶ **EXAMPLE 2**

Solve $y - 1 \geq {}^{-}1$.   Graph the solution.

$$y - 1 \geq {}^{-}1$$

Add 1 to both sides. $y - 1 + 1 \geq {}^{-}1 + 1$

Simplify both sides. $y + 0 \geq 0$

$$y \geq 0$$

$y \geq 0$

y is greater than or equal to 0.

Place a dot at 0.

Shade the number line to the right of 0.

Try These

Solve each inequality. Graph each solution.

1. $x + {}^-3 > {}^-2$

   Subtract $^-3$ from both sides.

   $x + {}^-3 - \blacksquare > {}^-2 - \blacksquare$

   Simplify both sides.

   $x + \blacksquare > {}^-2 + \blacksquare$

   $x > \blacksquare$

2. $y - 2 \leq 4$

   Add $\blacksquare$ to both sides.

   $y - 2 + \blacksquare \leq 4 + \blacksquare$

   Simplify both sides.

   $y - \blacksquare \leq \blacksquare$

   $y \leq \blacksquare$

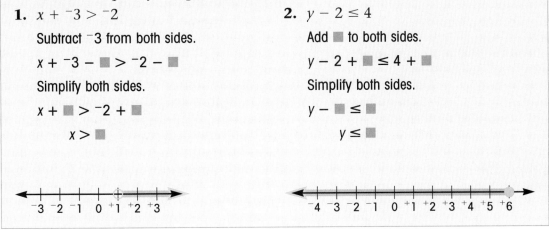

Practice

Solve each inequality. Graph each solution.

1. $x - 2 < 4$

2. $x + 1 \geq {}^-3$

3. $y + {}^-2 > 1$

4. $x - {}^-3 \geq 8$

5. $x + {}^-6 < {}^-3$

6. $y + {}^-2 \leq {}^-1$

7. $x + 8 > 4$

8. $x - 1 \leq 3$

9. $x - {}^-5 < 3$

10. $x + 4 \geq {}^-2$

Cooperative Learning

11. Explain to a partner how you solve the inequality in number 8 in **Practice**.

12. Write an inequality that contains integers. Use addition and subtraction in the inequality. Have a partner solve the inequality. Check the work.

Solving Inequalities by Multiplying or Dividing

You multiply or divide both sides of an equation by the same number to solve it. You can also multiply or divide both sides of an inequality to solve it. When you do this, you must watch for a change in the inequality.

$2 < 4$

Multiply both sides by 3.
$2(3) \, ? \, 4(3)$
$6 < 12$
The inequality stays "is less than."

$2 < 4$

Multiply both sides by $^-3$.
$2(^-3) \, ? \, 4(^-3)$
$^-6 > ^-12$
The inequality changes to "is greater than."

When you multiply both sides of an inequality by the same negative number, the inequality changes. The inequality also changes when you divide both sides by the same negative number.

▶ **EXAMPLE 1**

Solve $\dfrac{x}{^-3} \geq 2$.

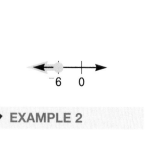

Multiply both sides by $^-3$ and change the inequality.

$$\dfrac{x}{^-3} \geq 2$$
$$\left(\dfrac{x}{^-3}\right)(^-3) \leq 2\,(^-3)$$
$$\dfrac{^-3}{^-3} \bullet x \leq ^-6$$
$$x \leq ^-6$$

▶ **EXAMPLE 2**

Solve $4y > 12$.

Divide both sides by 4.

The inequality stays the same.

$$4y > 12$$
$$4y \div 4 > 12 \div 4$$
$$\dfrac{4}{4} \bullet y > 3$$
$$y > 3$$

Try These

Solve each inequality. Graph each solution.

1. $4y \le 20$

   Divide both sides by ■.

   The inequality stays the same.

   $(4 \cdot y) \div ■ \le 20 \div ■$

   Simplify both sides.

   $\frac{■}{■}y \le ■.$

   $y \le ■.$

2. $^-6y < ^-24$

   Divide both sides by ■.

   The inequality changes.

   $^-6 \cdot y \div ■ > ^-24 \div ■.$

   Simplify both sides.

   $\frac{■}{■}y > ■.$

   $y > ■.$

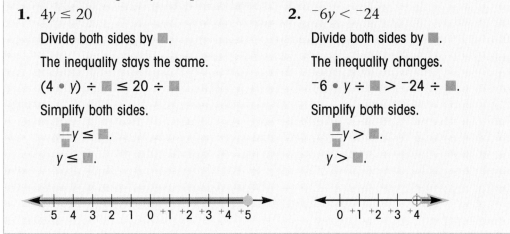

Practice

Solve each inequality. Graph each solution.

1. $\frac{x}{5} < 4$

2. $^-2y > 6$

3. $3x \le ^-9$

4. $\frac{x}{^-4} \ge 5$

5. $^-5x < ^-10$

6. $7x < 14$

7. $2y < ^-16$

8. $4y \le 28$

9. $\frac{y}{2} > 10$

10. $10x \ge 100$

11. $\frac{x}{3} \le ^-5$

12. $\frac{x}{^-5} \le 2$

Cooperative Learning

13. Explain to a partner how you solve the inequality in number **4** in **Practice**.

14. Make up an inequality with numbers. Use it to show a partner that dividing both sides of your inequality by the same negative number changes the inequality.

Calculator: Evaluating Expressions

You can use a calculator to evaluate an expression with negative numbers.

► **EXAMPLE**

Evaluate. $12x + 16 + 21y$ when x is $^-3$ and y is 2.

Replace x with $^-3$ and y with 2. $12 \bullet {}^-3 + 16 + 21 \bullet 2$

Display

Remember
Follow The Order of Operations.

Multiply 12 and 3 first.
Enter 12 by pressing: [1] [2] | 12 |

Multiply by 3 by pressing: [×] [3] | 3 |

[=] | 36 |

The signs are different, so the product
is negative. $^-36$

Now, multiply 21 and 2.
Enter 21 by pressing: [2] [1] | 21 |

Multiply by 2 by pressing: [×] [2] | 2 |

[=] | 42 |

The expression becomes $^-36 + 16 + 42$.

Math Fact
Add. $^-36 + 16$

Enter 36 by pressing: [3] [6] | 36 |

Subtract 16 by pressing: [−] [1] [6] | 16 |

[=] | 20 |

The sign of the number with the larger absolute value
is negative. So, subtract 20 from 42.

Enter 42 by pressing: [4] [2] | 42 |

Subtract 20 by pressing: [−] [2] [0] | 20 |

[=] | 22 |

The sign of the number with the larger absolute value
is positive.

The value of $12x + 16 + 21y$ is 22 when x is $^-3$ and y is 2.

Practice

Use your calculator to evaluate each expression.

1. $13k + r + 26$ when k is $^-3$ and r is 42

2. $4j - 8p$ when j is 12 and p is $^-5$

3. $6m + 32 \div g$ when m is 4 and g is $^-8$

4. $48 - x - 15y$ when x is 11 and y is $^-2$

5. $3s + 15r$ when s is $^-12$ and r is 3

6. $z + 9t \div 3$ when z is 15 and t is $^-2$

7. $f \div 9 - 14c$ when f is $^-27$ and c is 3

8. $s - 16d + 31$ when s is 40 and d is $^-3$

Math Connection

HURRICANE WARNING

A hurricane is a powerful storm. It can cause great damage. A hurricane has high winds and heavy rain that often cause flooding. Many people have lost their lives during hurricanes by drowning in floods.

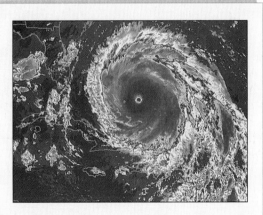

Hurricanes happen mostly in the fall season. They sometimes strike cities and towns along the Atlantic Ocean. Thousands of people live where these hurricanes hit. They need to know when a hurricane is coming so they can move to a safer place.

Who warns people that a hurricane is coming? Weather specialists at the National Weather Service keep a close watch on the Atlantic Ocean during hurricane season. They use weather satellites to collect information. The satellites send pictures taken from space. This photo shows where a hurricane is forming. Weather specialists use grids and number scales to find the exact location of the hurricane. They issue warnings to people to keep them safe.

Problem Solving: Using a Number Line

You can use a number line to show a range of numbers.

▶ **EXAMPLE**

Last winter, the coldest temperature in Eastgate was ⁻10°F. The warmest temperature was 45°F. Show this range of temperatures on the number line.

READ **What do you need to find out?**
You need to find the temperature range.

PLAN **What do you need to do?**
You need to draw a number line and show the range.

DO **Follow the plan.**

Draw a number line.

Place a dot at ⁻10 for the coldest temperature.

Place a dot at 45 for the warmest temperature.

Shade the number line between ⁻10 and 45.

The graph shows ⁻10°F and 45°F. It also shows all temperatures between ⁻10°F and 45°F.

CHECK **Does your answer make sense?**
The graph begins at ⁻10°F and ends at 45°F. ✓

The graph shows ⁻10°F and 45°F. It also shows all temperatures between ⁻10°F and 45°F.

Try These

1. A serving of peanut butter can have as few as 90 calories. It can also have as many as 130 calories. Show the range of calories.

   Place a dot at ■.

   Place a dot at ■.

   Shade in the number line between ■ and ■.

2. The coldest winter temperature in Northgate was ⁻5°F. The warmest was 40°F. Show the temperature range that did not set the cold record last winter.

   Place an open dot at ■.

   Place a dot at ■.

   Shade in the number line between ■ and ■.

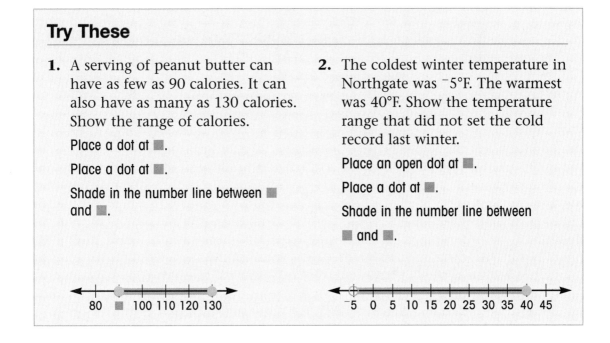

Practice

Use a number line.

1. An adult Canada goose can be as short as 25 inches or as long as 45 inches. Show this range in length on a number line.

2. When spread, the wings of the falcon can cover as little as 36 inches or as much as 44 inches. Show this range on a number line.

3. The lowest temperature recorded in Gateport last winter was 0°F. The warmest temperature was 80°F. Show this temperature range on a number line.

Cooperative Learning

4. Explain to a partner how you graph the range in number 3 in **Practice**.

5. Work with a partner. Ask ten students their scores on their last math test. Show the range of scores on a number line.

Here is a jar. It holds five tags. There is a letter written on each tag. You can select a tag from the jar. Each tag has the same chance of being selected. 1 of the 5 tags is marked A. There is 1 chance out of 5 of selecting an A. The probability of selecting an A is $\frac{1}{5}$.

Probability is the chance that something will happen. To find probability, divide the choice that you want by the total number of choices.

▶ **EXAMPLE 1**

What is the probability of selecting a C?

There is 1 tag marked C in the jar.	1
There are 5 choices in all.	5
Divide.	$\frac{1}{5}$

The probability of selecting a C is $\frac{1}{5}$.

▶ **EXAMPLE 2**

What is the probability of selecting a G?

There are 2 tags marked G.	2
There are 5 choices in all.	5
Divide.	$\frac{2}{5}$

The probability of selecting a G is $\frac{2}{5}$.

▶ **EXAMPLE 3**

What is the probability of selecting an F?

There are 3 tags marked F.	3
There are 5 choices in all.	5
Divide.	$\frac{3}{5}$

The probability of selecting an F is $\frac{3}{5}$.

Try These

Find each probability.

1. What is the probability of getting a 5 on this game spinner?

There are ▥ parts marked 5.

There are ▥ choices in all.

Divide. $\dfrac{▥}{▥}$

The probability of spinning a 5 is $\dfrac{▥}{▥}$.

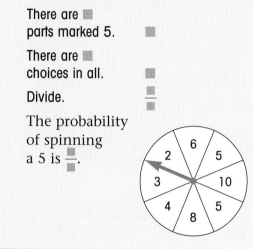

2. What is the probability of getting an even number on this game spinner?

There are 5 parts marked with an even number.

There are ▥ choices in all.

Divide. $\dfrac{▥}{▥}$

The probability of spinning an even number is $\dfrac{▥}{▥}$.

Practice

Use this jar to find the probabilities.

1. What is the probability of selecting a letter?

2. What is the probability of selecting an A?

3. What is the probability of selecting a number?

4. What is the probability of selecting a 7?

5. What is the probability of selecting an odd number?

Cooperative Learning

6. Explain to a partner how you find the probability in number **1** in **Practice**.

7. Write different numbers and letters in a picture jar. Ask a partner different probability questions about selecting a number or a letter.

Summary

Replacing variables with integers gives you a number expression.
You can simplify variable expressions with integers by combining like terms.
You can solve equations with integers just as you do with other numbers.
A graph can show the point for the number that is the solution.
Inequalities can be solved in the same way you solve equations.
When you multiply or divide both sides of an inequality by the same negative number, the inequality changes.
You can use a number line to show a range and group of numbers to solve a problem.
To find probability, divide the choice that you want by the total number of choices.

graph of a solution

number line

inequality

probability

Vocabulary Review

Complete the sentences with words from the box.

1. You can show a _____ to an equation on a number line.

2. The chance that something will happen is called a _____ .

3. A _____ shows positive numbers to the right of 0, negative numbers to the left of 0, and 0.

4. An _____ is greater than, greater than or equal to, less than, or less than or equal to.

Chapter Quiz

Simplify.

1. $a^2 + {}^-5a^2 - a^2 - a$

2. $6lw - 9lw + w - {}^-2w$

3. $cd + c - d$

4. $10cd - {}^-10cd + d^2 - d^2$

Evaluate each expression.

5. ${}^-6a \div {}^-3b$ when $a = {}^-1$ and $b = {}^-1$

6. $b^2 - c^2$ when $b = 4$ and $c = {}^-2$

7. $a - b$ when $a = {}^-1$ and $b = {}^-1$

8. $9c - 5d$ when $c = 3$ and $d = {}^-2$

Solve.

9. ${}^-2g + {}^-6 = 10$

10. ${}^-4 = 8 + 3y$

11. $\frac{x}{-3} = {}^-12$

12. $3x - {}^-4 = 25$

Graph each solution on a number line.

13. $a = {}^-5$

14. $a = 5$

15. $a < {}^-5$

Solve each inequality. Graph each solution.

16. $y - 2 < {}^-2$

17. $x + 1 \geq 8$

Solve each inequality. Graph each solution.

18. ${}^-8x < {}^-16$

19. $9x < 27$

People in many professions use the formulas and tools of mathematics to help them solve problems. What professions can you think of that use math?

Learning Objectives

- Give the location of a point on the coordinate plane.
- Graph an ordered pair.
- Find ordered pairs from equations.
- Graph equations.
- Use a calculator to find ordered pairs.
- Use information from a graph to solve problems.
- Apply skills and concepts to find the slope of a line.

Words to Know

plane	a flat surface
coordinate plane	a plane with coordinate axes drawn on it
coordinate axes	two perpendicular number lines
horizontal	left to right
vertical	up and down
***x*-axis**	horizontal axis
***y*-axis**	vertical axis
origin	the point where the coordinate axes cross each other
ordered pair	a pair of numbers in a special order; the numbers help locate points
graph of an ordered pair	a dot that shows the location of an ordered pair
graph of an equation	a line made with graphs of ordered pairs from the equation
broken-line graph	a graph made up of different pieces of straight lines
slope	the steepness of a straight line
rise	the change between two points on a line in an up-and-down direction
run	the change between two points on a line in a left-to-right direction

Plant Project

Place a bean seed on a damp paper towel in a clear plastic cup. Then insert a few toothpicks into a potato and rest it on top of another cup so half the potato is in water. Place the cups side by side. Draw a coordinate plane, and plot both plants' growth as a function of time (*x*-axis shows growth in cm; *y*-axis shows time in days). Describe the slope of each graph. What does the slope tell you?

13·1 Coordinate Axes

A **plane** is a flat surface. A **coordinate plane** has two perpendicular number lines. These are called **coordinate axes.** One axis is **horizontal.** It goes from left to right. Sometimes, it is labeled with an x. The other axis is **vertical.** It goes up and down. Sometimes, it

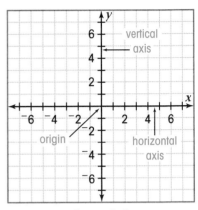

Math Fact

Negative numbers are to the left of the origin on the x-axis. Negative numbers are below the origin on the y-axis.

is labeled with a y. The axes cross at the **origin. Ordered pairs** are used to give the location of points.

► EXAMPLE 1

Remember

Move in the x direction first. This is right or left. Move in the y direction next. This is up or down.

Give the location of A at (2, 3).

Begin at the origin. Move right 2 units. Next, move up 3 units.

A is 2 units to the right of the origin. Then, up 3 units.

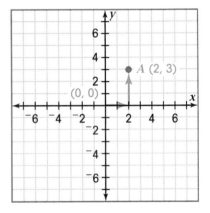

► EXAMPLE 2

Give the location of B at (⁻3, 4).

Begin at the origin. Move 3 units to the left. Next move up 4 units.

B is 3 units to the left of the origin. Then, up 4 units.

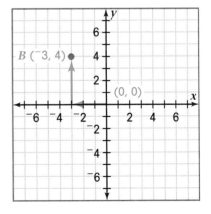

Try These

Give the location of these points.

1. A (3, 4)

    ■ units to the right of the origin.
Then up 4 units.

2. B (5, ⁻3)

    ■ units to the right of the origin.
Then down 3 units.

3. C (⁻2, ⁻2)

    2 units to the ■ of the origin.
Then down ■ units .

4. D (0, 4)

    Up ■ units from the origin.

Practice

Give the location of each point.

1. A (4, 4)   **2.** B (4, 5)

3. C (⁻2, 2)   **4.** D (2, ⁻2)

5. E (⁻5, ⁻1)   **6.** F (0, 5)

7. G (0, ⁻3)   **8.** H (2, ⁻6)

9. I (⁻4, 0)   **10.** J (⁻1, ⁻1)

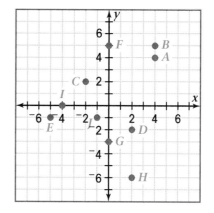

Cooperative Learning

11. Explain to a partner how you give the location of the point in number 7 of **Practice**.

12. Ask a partner to tell why K (⁻3, 3) and L (3, ⁻3) are not the same location without looking at the points.

Graphing Ordered Pairs

You have just learned how to give the location of a point by using an ordered pair. Now you will **graph an ordered pair** on a coordinate plane. The graph of an ordered pair is a point.

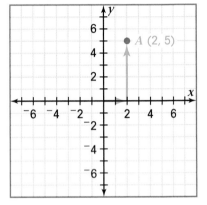

▶ **EXAMPLE 1**

Graph point A at (2, 5).

(2, 5)

Start at the origin.
Move 2 units to the right.

Next, move 5 units up.
Draw a dot at this spot.

Label it as A (2, 5).

▶ **EXAMPLE 2**

Remember
⁻5 means left 5 units.
⁻4 means down 4 units.

Graph point B at (⁻5, ⁻4).

(⁻5, ⁻4)

Start at the origin.
Move 5 units to the left.

Next, move 4 units down.
Draw a dot at this spot.

Label it as B (⁻5, ⁻4).

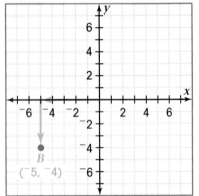

▶ **EXAMPLE 3**

Remember
0 means no units left or right.
3 means 3 units up.

Graph point C at (0, 3).

(0, 3)

Start at the origin.
Don't move left or right.

Next, move 3 places up.
Draw a dot at this spot.

Label it as C (0, 3).

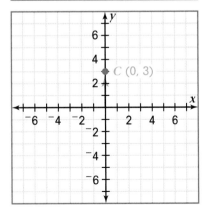

Try These

Use graph paper. Draw coordinate axes. Graph and label each point on the same pair of axes.

1. A at (3, ⁻6)

Start at the origin.

Move ▦ units to the right.

Move 6 units ▦. Draw a dot.

Label it A (3, ⁻6).

2. B at (⁻1, 5)

Start at the origin.

Move 1 unit to the left.

Move ▦ units ▦. Draw a dot.

Label it B (⁻1, 5).

Practice

Use graph paper. Draw coordinate axes. Graph and label each point on the same pair of axes.

1. A at (⁻3, ⁻6)

2. B at (0, 0)

3. C at (1, ⁻1)

4. D at (⁻1, 0)

5. E at (2, 2)

6. F at (⁻5, ⁻5)

7. G at (⁻2, ⁻3)

8. H at (0, ⁻1)

9. I at (1, 4)

10. J at (6, 0)

11. K at (1, 8)

12. L at (⁻2, 6)

13. M at (8, 8)

14. N at (0, ⁻7)

15. O at (8, 6)

16. P at (⁻1, 7)

Cooperative Learning

17. Explain to a partner how you graphed the point in number **12** of **Practice**.

18. Write four ordered pairs. Have a partner graph each pair. Check the work.

You can find ordered pairs from equations with two variables. Later, you will use these ordered pairs for graphing the equation. If the equation contains x and y, pick any value for x. Then find the value for y. These two numbers become the numbers of the ordered pair. The number you picked for x is the first number in the ordered pair. The number you find for y is the second number in the ordered pair.

▶ **EXAMPLE 1**

Find three ordered pairs for $y = x + 2$.

Let $x = 0$. Then $y = 0 + 2 = 2$ ⟶ $(0, 2)$

Let $x = {}^-1$. Then $y = {}^-1 + 2 = 1$ ⟶ $({}^-1, 1)$

Let $x = 1$. Then $y = 1 + 2 = 3$ ⟶ $(1, 3)$

Three ordered pairs for $y = x + 2$ are $(0, 2)$, $({}^-1, 1)$, and $(1, 3)$.

Math Fact
The first number of the ordered pair is on the top. The second is on the bottom.

You can arrange these ordered pairs in a table.

x	0	$^-1$	1
$y = x + 2$	2	1	3

▶ **EXAMPLE 2**

Find three ordered pairs for $y = 1 - 2x$.

Let $x = 0$. Then $y = 1 - 2 \bullet 0 = 1 - 0 = 1$ ⟶ $(0, 1)$

Let $x = 1$. Then $y = 1 - 2\,(1) = 1 - 2 = {}^-1$ ⟶ $(1, {}^-1)$

Let $x = {}^-1$. Then $y = 1 - 2\,({}^-1) = 1 + 2 = 3$ ⟶ $({}^-1, 3)$

Three ordered pairs for $y = 1 - 2x$ are $(0, 1)$, $(1, {}^-1)$, and $({}^-1, 3)$.

Here is a table showing the three ordered pairs.

x	0	1	$^-1$
$y = 1 - 2x$	1	$^-1$	3

Try These

Find three ordered pairs for each equation.

1. $y = x - 5$

Let $x = 1$ $y = 1 - 5 = \blacksquare$
$(1, \blacksquare)$

Let $x = 0$ $y = \blacksquare - 5 = \blacksquare$
$(\blacksquare, \blacksquare)$

Let $x = {}^-1$ $y = {}^-1 - 5 = \blacksquare$
$({}^-1, \blacksquare)$

x	1	$\blacksquare$	$\blacksquare$
$y = x - 5$	$\blacksquare$	$\blacksquare$	$\blacksquare$

2. $y = 4x$

Let $x = 0$ $y = 4 \bullet 0 = \blacksquare$
$(0, \blacksquare)$

Let $x = 1$ $y = 4 \bullet 1 = \blacksquare$
$(\blacksquare, \blacksquare)$

Let $x = {}^-1$ $y = 4\,({}^-1) = \blacksquare$
$({}^-1, \blacksquare)$

x	0	$\blacksquare$	${}^-1$
$y = 4x$	$\blacksquare$	$\blacksquare$	$\blacksquare$

Practice

Find three ordered pairs for each equation.

1. $y = x + 5$

2. $y = {}^-2x$

3. $y = 3x + 1$

4. $y = 2x - 3$

5. $y = 1 - x$

6. $y = 5 - 2x$

Copy and complete each table.

7.

x	${}^-2$	${}^-1$	0	1	2
$y = 4x + 1$	?	?	?	?	?

8.

x	1	2	0	${}^-1$
$y = x - 2x$	?	?	?	?

Cooperative Learning

9. Explain to a partner how you find the three ordered pairs for number 6 in **Practice**.

10. Write an equation containing x and y. Have a partner find three ordered pairs for the equation. Check the work.

Graphing Equations

To **graph an equation** with two variables, use the equation to find ordered pairs. Then, graph these ordered pairs. Connect these points with a straight line. The straight line is a graph of the equation.

► EXAMPLE 1

Graph $y = 2x + 2$.

First, find the ordered pairs.

Let $x = 0$.
Then, $y = 2 \cdot 0 + 2 = 2$
Ordered pair: $(0, 2)$

Let $x = 1$.
Then, $y = 2 \cdot 1 + 2 = 4$
Ordered pair: $(1, 4)$

Let $x = {}^-1$.
Then, $y = 2\,({}^-1) + 2 = 0$
Ordered pair: $({}^-1, 0)$

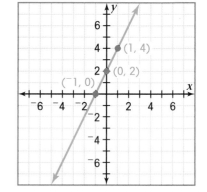

Graph the ordered pairs $(0, 2)$, $(1, 4)$, and $({}^-1, 0)$. Connect them with a straight line.

x	0	1	$^-1$
y	2	4	0

► EXAMPLE 2

Graph $y = 4 - x$.

Let $x = 0$.
Then, $y = 4 - 0 = 4$
Ordered pair: $(0, 4)$

Let $x = 1$.
Then, $y = 4 - 1 = 3$
Ordered pair: $(1, 3)$

Let $x = 4$.
Then, $y = 4 - 4 = 0$
Ordered pair: $(4, 0)$

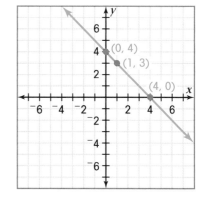

Graph the ordered pairs $(0, 4)$, $(1, 3)$ and $(4, 0)$. Connect them with a straight line.

x	0	1	4
y	4	3	0

Try These

Graph each equation.

1. $y = x + 1$

$x = 1$	$y = 1 + 1$	
	$y = \blacksquare$	$\rightarrow$ (1, $\blacksquare$)
$x = 0$	$y = 0 + 1$	
	$y = 1$	$\rightarrow$ (0, $\blacksquare$)
$x = {}^-1$	$y = {}^-1 + 1$	
	$y = \blacksquare$	$\rightarrow$ ($^-1$, $\blacksquare$)

2. $y = {}^-2x$

$x = 1$	$y = {}^-2(1)$	
	$y = \blacksquare$	$\rightarrow$ (1, $\blacksquare$)
$x = 0$	$y = {}^-2(0)$	
	$y = \blacksquare$	$\rightarrow$ (0, $\blacksquare$)
$x = {}^-1$	$y = {}^-2({}^-1)$	
	$y = \blacksquare$	$\rightarrow$ ($^-1$, $\blacksquare$)

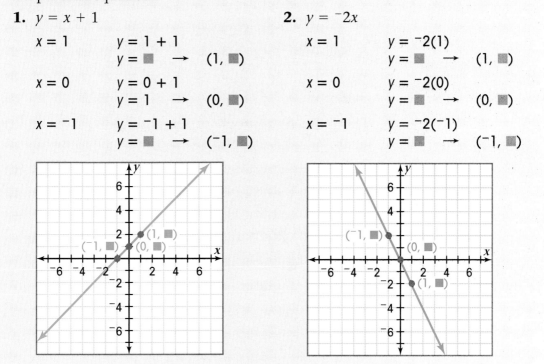

Practice

Use graph paper. Graph each equation. Use the values of x: $^-2$, $^-1$, 0, 1, 2.

1. $y = 3x + 1$ **2.** $y = 4 - x$ **3.** $y = x$

4. $y = 2x$ **5.** $y = {}^-3x$ **6.** $y = {}^-3x + 1$

7. $y = 5x - 3$ **8.** $y = 7 - x$ **9.** $y = 4x - 2$

Cooperative Learning

10. Explain to a partner how to graph the equation in number **3** of **Practice**.

11. Write an equation containing x and y. Work with a partner to graph the equation. Take turns finding ordered pairs. Check the work.

Calculator: Finding Ordered Pairs

You can use your calculator to complete a table of ordered pairs.

▶ **EXAMPLE**

Complete the table of ordered pairs for the equation $y = 15x - 18$.

x	1	2	3	4	5
$y = 15x - 18$	⁻3	12	?	?	?

Enter 1.

	Display
Enter 1.	1	ꞁ

Multiply by 15 by pressing: × 1 5 = **ꞁ5**

Subtract 18 by pressing: − 1 8 = **-3**

The first ordered pair is (1, ⁻3). Write ⁻3 in the table below 1.

Then use 2.

Display

Enter 2. 2 **2**

Multiply by 15 by pressing: × 1 5 = **30**

Subtract 18 by pressing: − 1 8 = **ꞁ2**

The second ordered pair is (2, 12). Write 12 in the table below 2.

Then use 3, 4, and 5.

Practice

Complete each table of ordered pairs.

1. $y = 14x - 26$

x	1	2	3	4	5
$y = 14x - 26$	?	?	?	?	?

2. $y = 50x + 12$

x	1	2	3	4	5
$y = 50x + 12$	?	?	?	?	?

3. $y = 34x - 14$

x	1	2	3	4	5
$y = 34x - 14$	?	?	?	?	?

4. $y = 27x + 16$

x	1	2	3	4	5
$y = 27x + 16$	?	?	?	?	?

On-the-Job Math

DR. MAE JEMISON: ASTRONAUT

Mae Jemison always believed that someday she would travel in space. As a child, she looked up at the stars and wondered what it would be like. Years later, her dream came true. She was the first African-American woman to travel in space.

Mae Jemison had to work hard to make her dream come true. She read books about space. She took many science and math classes. Mae studied algebra, statistics, and calculus. Later, she earned a degree in medicine.

After medical school, Dr. Jemison joined the Peace Corps. She worked as a doctor in West Africa. Then, she was chosen by NASA to become an astronaut. She traveled through space on a space shuttle flight in 1991. While in space, she conducted experiments.

Mae Jemison was happy because her dream came true. She traveled in space among the stars.

Problem Solving: Using Line Graphs

Information from graphs can be used to solve problems. The ordered pairs may contain words and numbers. Here is a **broken-line graph** showing monthly calculator sales for January through July of last year. 300 calculators were sold in January. This is shown by (Jan., 300).

Monthly Calculator Sales

EXAMPLE

Which month had the highest sales? How many calculators were sold that month? Describe this with an ordered pair.

READ **What do you need to find out?**
You need to find which month had the highest sales and its ordered pair.

PLAN **What do you need to do?**
You need to look for the highest point on the broken-line graph.

DO **Follow the plan.**
The highest point of the graph is above June.
From the origin: Move right to June. Move up to 500.

CHECK **Does your answer make sense?**
Look at the graph again. The highest point is above June. ✓

The highest sales were in June. 500 calculators were sold. The point is at (June, 500).

Try These

Use the graph on monthly calculator sales to answer each question.

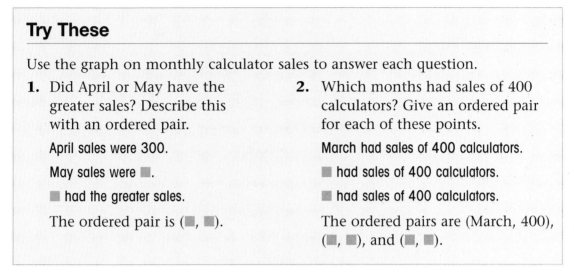

1. Did April or May have the greater sales? Describe this with an ordered pair.

   April sales were 300.

   May sales were ■.

   ■ had the greater sales.

   The ordered pair is (■, ■).

2. Which months had sales of 400 calculators? Give an ordered pair for each of these points.

   March had sales of 400 calculators.

   ■ had sales of 400 calculators.

   ■ had sales of 400 calculators.

   The ordered pairs are (March, 400), (■, ■), and (■, ■).

Practice

Use this graph to answer the questions.

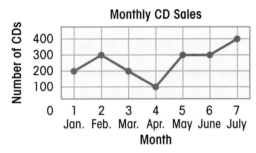

1. Which month had the highest sales? Describe this with an ordered pair.

2. Did February or March have the greater sales? Describe this with an ordered pair.

3. Which months had sales of 300? Give an ordered pair for each of these points.

Cooperative Learning

4. Explain to a partner how you use the graph to answer number 2 in **Practice**.

5. Ask a partner to find the total sales for January through July. Check the work.

Application: Slope of a Line

The **slope** of a line is the steepness of the line. A line with a greater slope is more steep. You can find the slope of a line using the rise and the run.

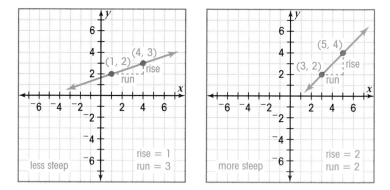

less steep   rise = 1
                  run = 3

more steep   rise = 2
                  run = 2

The **rise** is the change between two points of a line in an up or down direction. The **run** is the change in two points of a line from left to right. You can find the rise by finding the difference between the *y* parts of the ordered pairs. You can find the run by finding the difference in the *x* parts of the ordered pairs. The ratio of the rise to the run is the slope of the line.

 **EXAMPLE 1**

Remember
Subtract the *y* parts in the same order as you subtract the *x* parts.

Find the slope of a line that contains (4, 3) and (1, 2).

Find the rise. Subtract the *y* parts. $3 - 2 = 1$

Find the run. Subtract the *x* parts. $4 - 1 = 3$

Divide the rise by the run. $\dfrac{1}{3}$

The slope of the line that contains (4, 3) and (1, 2) is $\frac{1}{3}$.

 EXAMPLE 2

Find the slope of a line that contains (3, 2) and (5, 4).

Find the rise. Subtract the *y* parts. $2 - 4 = {}^-2$

Find the run. Subtract the *x* parts. $3 - 5 = {}^-2$

Divide the rise by the run. $\dfrac{{}^-2}{{}^-2} = 1$

The slope of the line that contains (3, 2) and (5, 4) is 1.

Try These

Find the slope of each line that contains these pairs of points.

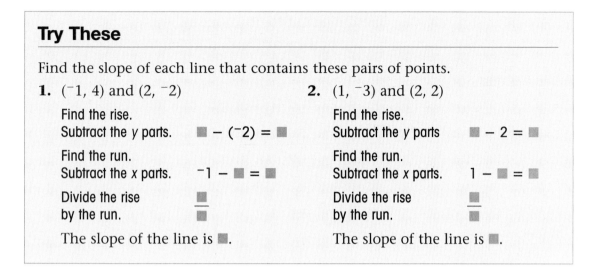

1. ($^-1$, 4) and (2, $^-2$)

Find the rise.
Subtract the y parts.   ▨ $-$ ($^-2$) $=$ ▨

Find the run.
Subtract the x parts. $^-1 -$ ▨ $=$ ▨

Divide the rise   ▨
by the run.   ▬▬
           ▨

The slope of the line is ▨.

2. (1, $^-3$) and (2, 2)

Find the rise.
Subtract the y parts   ▨ $- 2 =$ ▨

Find the run.
Subtract the x parts. $1 -$ ▨ $=$ ▨

Divide the rise   ▨
by the run.   ▬▬
           ▨

The slope of the line is ▨.

Practice

Find the slope of each line that contains these pairs of points.

1. (2, 6) and (3, 4)

2. ($^-1$, 2) and (4, 1)

3. ($^-2$, 5) and (2, $^-3$)

4. (0, 3) and (8, $^-3$)

5. (3, 2) and (5, $^-1$)

6. ($^-3$, 4) and (1, $^-2$)

7. ($^-4$, $^-3$) and (2, 2)

8. (7, 0) and ($^-5$, $^-5$)

Cooperative Learning

9. Explain to a partner how you find the slope of the line for number 8 in **Practice**.

10. Write two ordered pairs. Have a partner find the slope of the line that contains the two points. Check the work.

Summary

You can use coordinate axes to find the location of ordered pairs.

Coordinate axes are used to graph the locations of ordered pairs.

You can find ordered pairs from equations with two variables.

Equations with two variables can be graphed on coordinate axes.

Line graphs can be used to solve problems.

You can apply your skills and find the slope of a line using the rise and run.

plane

coordinate axes

coordinate plane

horizontal

vertical

x-axis

y-axis

origin

ordered pair

graph of an ordered pair

graph of an equation

slope

run

Vocabulary Review

Complete the sentences with words from the box.

1. Two perpendicular number lines are called _____ .

2. A flat surface is called a _____ .

3. Left to right means _____ .

4. Up and down means _____ .

5. The horizontal axis is called the _____ .

6. The _____ is the point where the coordinate axes cross each other.

7. A _____ is a plane with coordinate axes drawn on it.

8. A pair of numbers in a special order is called an _____ .

9. The steepness of a straight line is the _____ .

10. The change between two points on a line in a left to right direction is called the _____ .

11. A dot that shows the location of an ordered pair is called a _____ .

12. The vertical axis is called the _____ .

13. A line made with graphs of ordered pairs from an equation is the _____ .

Chapter Quiz

Use graph paper. Draw coordinate axes. Graph and label each point on the same pair of axes.

1. A at (6, ⁻9)

2. B at (2, 5)

3. C at (⁻8, ⁻8)

4. D at (⁻4, 0)

Copy and complete each table.

5.

x	⁻2	⁻1	0	1	2
$y = 3x + 4$	?	?	?	?	?

6.

x	1	2	0	⁻1
$y = 4x - 2x$	?	?	?	?

Use graph paper. Graph each equation. Use the values of x: ⁻2, ⁻1, 0, 1, 2.

7. $y = 3x - 1$

8. $y = 4 + x$

9. $y = 9 + x$

10. $y = 3x - 5$

11. $y = 10 - x$

12. $y = 5x - 2$

Find the slope of each line containing these pairs of points.

13. (3, 7) and (2, 3)

14. (⁻4, 2) and (6, 3)

15. (0, ⁻5) and (5, 3)

16. (0, 6) and (5, ⁻6)

Unit 5 **Review**

Choose the letter for the correct answer.

Use the broken-line graph to answer Questions 1 and 2.

Pamela's Distance

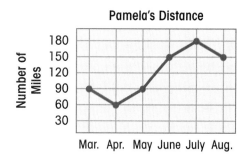

1. What is the greatest number of miles Pamela ran in one month?

A. 90 B. 120
C. 150 D. 180

2. During one of these months, Pamela was injured. She ran the least number of miles during this month. Which month was this?

A. April B. June
C. July D. March

3. A jar contains 10 marbles numbered 1, 2, 3, 4, 5, 6, 7, 8, 9, 10. What is the probability of selecting an odd number?

A. $\frac{2}{5}$ B. $\frac{3}{10}$
C. $\frac{1}{2}$ D. $\frac{9}{10}$

4. A line contains the points $(-2, 1)$ and $(3, 3)$. What is the slope of the line?

A. $\frac{5}{2}$ B. 0
C. $\frac{1}{2}$ D. $\frac{2}{5}$

5. How many groups of two people can be made from Angel, Ben, Carlos, Drew, Emily?

A. 20
B. 10
C. 15
D. 5

6. What is the value of $-2x + 3y$ when $x = -3$ and $y = -2$?

A. 12
B. 9
C. 0
D. Not given

Critical Thinking

Graph the equations $y = 2x - 1$ and $y = 2x + 3$ on the same coordinate axes. For each line, choose any two points. Then, find the slope. What do you notice about the slopes?

CHALLENGE Look at the equation $2x + 1$. What do you think will be the slope of the line? Graph the equation. Then find the slope.

ADDITIONAL PRACTICE
Chapter 1: Review of Whole Numbers

Find the value of the digit in the number.

1. What is the value of 6 in 263,195?

2. What is the value of 8 in 1,862,167?

3. Compare 3,617 and 3,017.

4. Compare 210 and 2,010.

Round to the nearest hundred.

5. 429

6. 689

7. 1,201

Round to the nearest thousand.

8. 7,839

9. 6,322

10. 36,917

Add or subtract.

11.   178
        $-$ 65

12.   362
        $+$ 48

13.   23,162
        $+$ 5,314

Round each number to the hundreds place. Then, estimate the sum or difference.

14. 682 + 319

15. 1,238 − 599

16. 1,628 + 429

Multiply or divide.

17.   72
        $\times$ 48

18.   638
        $\times$ 53

19. $23\overline{)4,765}$

Find the power.

20. 16^2

21. 8^3

22. 4^4

Find the perimeter.

23.

8 ft   5 ft
9 ft

24.

11 in.
10 in.
13 in.
15 in.

Chapter 2: Number Expressions, Equations, Properties

Simplify.

1. $18 \div 3$

2. $17 + 21$

3. $6 \cdot 8$

4. $12 - 2 \cdot 3$

5. $8 - 3 + 7$

6. $24 \div 3 \cdot 8$

7. $13 + 6 - 5 - 7$

8. $32 - 15$

9. $2 \cdot 7 - 5$

10. $3(10 + 2)$

11. $17 - (5 + 2)$

12. $(2 + 3)2 - 9$

Tell whether the expressions are equivalent.

13. $3 \cdot 8$ and $4(6)$

14. 23 and 32

15. $3 + (2 + 6)$ and $(3 + 2) + 6$

Tell whether the equation is true or false.

16. $16 = 8 \cdot 2$

17. $15 + 30 = 3(15)$

18. $82 = 8 \cdot 2$

Name the property shown.

19. $3 + 10 = 10 + 3$

20. $6 \cdot (2 \cdot 5) = (6 \cdot 2) \cdot 5$

21. $5(4 + 7) = 5 \cdot 4 + 5 \cdot 7$

22. $15 \cdot 0 = 0$

Use a property to complete.

23. $8 + (5 + 3) = (8 + \blacksquare) + 3$

24. $13 \cdot 6 = \blacksquare \cdot 13$

25. $9(3 + 7) = 9 \cdot \blacksquare + 9 \cdot \blacksquare$

26. $16 \cdot \blacksquare = 16$

Find the area.

27. 6 m, 5 m

28. 4 in., 8 in.

ADDITIONAL PRACTICE
Chapter 3: Variable Expressions

Name the variable or variables in each expression.

1. $3xy$

2. $3(a + 2)$

3. $4n^2 - 6m$

Are the terms like or unlike?

4. $2x$ and $5xy$

5. $3a$ and a

6. $6xy^2$ and $4x^2y$

Simplify.

7. $7x + 12x$

8. $3a^2 + 9a^2 - 4a$

9. $4y^2 + 6y + 2y^2 - 3y$

Evaluate each variable expression.

10. $6n$, when $n = 5$.

11. $16 - c$, when $c = 10$.

12. $x \div 4$, when $x = 32$.

13. $5x - 2y$, when $x = 5$ and $y = 3$.

14. $2ab$, when $a = 6$ and $b = 3$.

15. $t^2 + 3$, when $t = 3$.

16. $4x^2 + 2x$, when $x = 3$.

Solve the problem.

17. How much rope is needed to close in a garden that is 50 ft wide and 25 ft long?

Find the volume of each cube.

18.

3 m
2 m
1 m

19.

4 ft
4 ft
2 ft

ADDITIONAL PRACTICE
Chapter 4: Variable Equations

Tell whether the number is the solution to
the equation.

1. $6; n + 14 = 20$

2. $4; 5a = 30$

3. $4; 6x - 3 = 21$

4. $10; 2(c - 6) = 8$

Solve. Then, check the solution.

5. $x + 5 = 25$

6. $13 = y - 9$

7. $2n = 14$

8. $8 + n = 16$

9. $\frac{c}{3} = 12$

10. $24 = 3x$

11. $y \div 6 = 2$

12. $3x - 5 = 13$

13. $13 = 2x + 7$

14. $n \div 4 + 3 = 7$

15. $12t - 6 = 30$

16. $\frac{x}{5} - 15 = 5$

Find the pattern. Then, find the next two numbers.

17. 2, 7, 6, 11, 10, _?_, _?_

18. 3, 0, 6, 0, 9, _?_, _?_

Use a formula to solve the problem.

19. Find the width of a rectangle with an area of 65 cm^2
and a length of 13 cm.

20. Find the volume of a box with a height of 4 in.,
a width of 2 in., and a length of 10 in.

ADDITIONAL PRACTICE
Chapter 5: Decimals and Algebra

Give the value of each digit.

1. 21.05

2. 1.67

3. .318

Compare the numbers.

4. 3.1 and 3.01

5. 12.7 and 12.70

6. 1.167 and 1.2

Round to the nearest hundredth.

7. 19.112

8. .879

9. 1.209

Round to the nearest tenth.

10. 8.82

11. 10.097

12. .55

Add or subtract.

13. $2 + 3.87$

14. $6 - 1.08$

15. $6.782 + 3.41$

Multiply or divide.

16. $.8 \times .62$

17. 1.2×3.61

18. $.9 \div .15$

Multiply or divide by moving the decimal point.

19. 1.38×10

20. 16.7×100

21. $12 \div 100$

Write each number in scientific notation.

22. 1,420

23. 304

24. 5,600

Simplify the expression.

25. $.3x + 1.2x - .4x$

26. $7.2a^2 + 5a - 6a^2 - 2.5a$

Evaluate the expression.

27. $6a$, when $a = 1.2$

28. $3n - 4.2$, when $n = 2.7$

1. Tell whether 4 is a factor of 96. **2.** Tell whether 6 is a factor of 86.

3. Tell whether 75 is divisible by 3. **4.** Tell whether 48 is divisible by 16.

Find the common factors and the greatest common factor for each pair of numbers.

5. 18 and 27 **6.** 11 and 20 **7.** 48 and 60

8. 6 and 5 **9.** 3 and 12 **10.** 16 and 24

Find the least common multiple of each pair of numbers. Remember that zero is not the least common multiple.

11. 3 and 6 **12.** 5 and 12 **13.** 4 and 6

14. 4 and 9 **15.** 8 and 12 **16.** 9 and 30

Find the prime factorization of each number. Write your answer using exponents.

17. 48 **18.** 68 **19.** 84

Use the bar graph to answer the questions.

20. On which day did it rain the most?

21. On which days did it rain 2 in.?

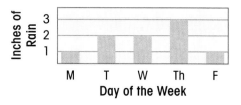

ADDITIONAL PRACTICE
Chapter 7: Fractions and Mixed Numbers

Write a fraction for the shaded part.

1. 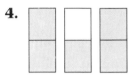 **2.** 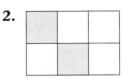 **3.**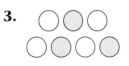

Write a fraction and a whole number or mixed number
for the shaded strips.

4.   **5.**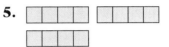

Write a whole number or mixed number for each
fraction.

6. $\frac{9}{4}$ **7.** $\frac{40}{3}$ **8.** $\frac{13}{5}$ **9.** $\frac{27}{9}$

Multiply each numerator and denominator by 3 to find
an equivalent fraction.

10. $\frac{2}{3}$ **11.** $\frac{4}{5}$ **12.** $\frac{7}{9}$ **13.** $\frac{10}{11}$

Write each fraction in lowest terms.

14. $\frac{10}{12}$ **15.** $\frac{6}{18}$ **16.** $\frac{11}{15}$ **17.** $\frac{15}{25}$

Write a decimal for each fraction.

18. $\frac{7}{10}$ **19.** $\frac{8}{10}$ **20.** $\frac{59}{100}$ **21.** $\frac{4}{100}$

Write a fraction or mixed number for each decimal.

22. .67 **23.** 2.08 **24.** 1.4 **25.** .42

Find the average.

26. 5, 5, 17 **27.** 12, 15, 31, 36, 41 **28.** 2.4, 2.4, 2.5, 3.1

ADDITIONAL PRACTICE
Chapter 8: Adding and Subtracting Fractions

Find the equivalent fractions with the least common denominator.

1. $\frac{2}{3}$ and $\frac{7}{10}$

2. $\frac{3}{8}$ and $\frac{5}{12}$

3. $\frac{1}{2}$ and $\frac{7}{8}$

Add or subtract.

4. $\frac{5}{13} + \frac{6}{13}$

5. $\frac{14}{15} - \frac{8}{15}$

6. $\frac{7}{12} - \frac{1}{3}$

7. $\frac{1}{7} + \frac{1}{2}$

8. $3\frac{1}{2} + 2\frac{1}{6}$

9. $1\frac{7}{8} + 5\frac{1}{4}$

10. $5 - \frac{2}{3}$

11. $12\frac{1}{10} - 2\frac{1}{3}$

12. $\frac{3}{4} - \frac{1}{8}$

Evaluate each expression.

13. $n + 1\frac{1}{4}$ when $n = \frac{3}{4}$

14. $r - \frac{3}{7}$ when $r = \frac{4}{5}$

15. $x + y$ when $x = 3$ and $y = 2\frac{1}{6}$

16. $a - b$ when $a = 5\frac{1}{2}$ and $b = 2\frac{7}{9}$

Solve. Then, check.

17. $c - \frac{1}{3} = 5$

18. $x + 1\frac{2}{5} = 6\frac{3}{5}$

19. $2\frac{5}{12} + n = 4\frac{1}{6}$

20. $3\frac{1}{2} = y - \frac{1}{4}$

Solve the problem if you can. Tell whether there is too much or too little information.

21. Stewart went to the store to buy clothes. He bought 3 pairs of socks for $2 each, a shirt for $12, and a pair of pants for $20. How much money did he have left over?

Chapter 9: Multiplying and Dividing Fractions

Find the reciprocal.

1. $\frac{4}{5}$ **2.** $\frac{1}{6}$ **3.** $\frac{9}{2}$ **4.** 3

Multiply or divide.

5. $\frac{2}{5} \times \frac{1}{4}$ **6.** $\frac{3}{4} \times \frac{8}{9}$ **7.** $\frac{1}{2} \div 2$ **8.** $\frac{4}{5} \div \frac{4}{5}$

9. $3\frac{1}{2} \div 2\frac{1}{3}$ **10.** $6\frac{2}{5} \div \frac{4}{5}$ **11.** $4 \times 3\frac{1}{4}$ **12.** $1 \div \frac{3}{4}$

Simplify.

13. $\frac{n}{5} + \frac{2n}{5}$ **14.** $\frac{x}{3} + \frac{x}{4}$

15. $4c + \frac{3}{8}c^2 + \frac{1}{2}c$ **16.** $\frac{2}{7}a + \frac{b}{7} + \frac{3}{7}a$

Evaluate.

17. $3x + \frac{1}{2}$ when $x = \frac{1}{2}$ **18.** $2n - 3m$ when $n = \frac{3}{4}$ and $m = \frac{1}{4}$

19. $x \div 4$ when $x = \frac{4}{8}$ **20.** c^3 when $c = 2$

Solve. Then, check.

21. $2a + \frac{1}{4} = \frac{3}{4}$ **22.** $\frac{1}{3}x - 3 = 2$

23. $7 = \frac{2}{5}x - 3$ **24.** $\frac{n}{2} + 7 = 10$

ADDITIONAL PRACTICE
Chapter 10: Ratio, Proportion, and Percent

Write the ratio.

1. Cheese costs $5 for 2 pounds. Write the ratio of pounds to cost.

Solve the proportion.

2. $\dfrac{3}{5} = \dfrac{x}{20}$

3. $\dfrac{n}{12} = \dfrac{25}{60}$

4. $\dfrac{6}{x} = \dfrac{8}{4}$

5. $\dfrac{7}{10} = \dfrac{70}{x}$

Write a percent for each ratio.

6. 12 to 100

7. 85 to 100

8. 1 to 100

Write a decimal for each percent.

9. 8%

10. 12%

11. 204%

Write a percent for each decimal.

12. .25

13. 1.5

14. .96

Write a fraction for each percent.

15. 75%

16. 122%

17. 10%

Write a number equation for each percent fact.

18. 20% of 60 is 12

19. 56 is 80% of 70

Solve the percent problem.

20. 6 is 5% of what number?

21. 24 is what percent of 48?

22. 2% of 50 is what number?

23. 50 is what percent of 75?

Find the percent increase or decrease.

24. A number changes from 5 to 4.

25. A number changes from 4 to 5.

Compare. Use >, <, or = for •.

1. $^-3 • ^-19$ **2.** $^-11 • 0$ **3.** $5 • ^-12$ **4.** $^-16 • ^-16$

Find the opposite of each integer.

5. $^-16$ **6.** $^+23$ **7.** $^-10$ **8.** 4

Find the absolute value of an integer.

9. $|^-16|$ **10.** $|^+8|$ **11.** $|5|$ **12.** $|^-39|$

Add. Use a number line.

13. $^-8 + 4$ **14.** $^-3 + ^-3$ **15.** $3 + ^-7$ **16.** $^-6 + 6$

Add.

17. $^-12 + ^-6$ **18.** $4 + ^-16$ **19.** $^-10 + ^-11$ **20.** $^-15 + 5$

Subtract.

21. $^-4 - ^-9$ **22.** $3 - 16$ **23.** $^-5 - 17$ **24.** $^-12 - ^-9$

Multiply.

25. $(^+6)(^-3)$ **26.** $(^-4)(^-7)$ **27.** $(^-7)(12)$ **28.** $(^+4)(^+12)$

Divide.

29. $^-36 \div ^-12$ **30.** $49 \div ^-7$ **31.** $^-50 \div 2$ **32.** $81 \div 3$

Simplify.

1. $^-7x + {}^-6x$

2. $^-4a - 8a + 6a$

3. $5r - 9 - 6r + 4$

4. $3ab + 6 - {}^-4ab - 10$

Evaluate each expression.

5. ^-6x, when $x = {}^-3$

6. ^-4n, when $n = {}^-9$

7. y^2, when $y = {}^-4$

8. $3x - 5y$, when $x = {}^-7$ and $y = 4$

9. $a - b$, when $a = 4$ and $b = {}^-2$

10. $n \div 5$, when $n = {}^-25$

Solve.

11. $^-2x + 4 = {}^-10$

12. $3a + {}^-7 = 20$

13. $3 = \frac{{}^-x}{4} + 2$

14. $^-5x - {}^-3 = 33$

Graph each solution on a number line.

15. $x \le {}^-1$

16. $x > 5$

17. $x = 3$

Solve each inequality. Graph each solution.

18. $y + 5 > 0$

19. $x + 3 \le {}^-4$

20. $c - 7 < {}^-5$

Solve each inequality. Graph each solution.

21. $4x \le {}^-20$

22. $\frac{n}{{}^-3} > {}^-5$

23. $^-2x < 12$

ADDITIONAL PRACTICE
Chapter 13: The Coordinate Plane

Use graph paper. Draw coordinate axes. Graph and label each point on the same set of axes.

1. A (3, $^-$5)

2. B (0, $^-$4)

3. C ($^-$1, 2)

4. D ($^-$4, $^-$3)

Copy and complete each table.

5.

x	-2	-1	0	1	2
$y = 2x + 3$	?	?	?	?	?

6.

x	-2	-1	0	1	2
$y = -2x - 1$	?	?	?	?	?

Use graph paper. Graph each equation. Use the values of x: $^-$2, $^-$1, 0, 1, 2.

7. $y = x + 3$

8. $y = {}^-x$

9. $y = 2x - 4$

10. $y = {}^-x + 1$

11. $y = 3 - 2x$

12. $y = 3x - 2$

Find the slope of each line containing these pairs of points.

13. (5, 2) (1, 1)

14. (3, 1) (4, 2)

15. ($^-$3, $^-$2) (0, 4)

16. (1,3) ($^-$3, 2)

Glossary

absolute value   the distance between 0 and an integer on the number line

addends   numbers added together

area   the number of squares needed to cover a closed figure

altitudes   height above and below 0

Associative Property   more than two numbers can be added or multiplied in groups of two. The way the numbers are grouped does not matter.

average   a number that tells you something about a group of numbers

bar graph   a way of showing information by using bars

base   a factor; in 3^2, 3 is the base; it is used as a factor 2 times.

broken-line graph   a graph made up of different pieces of straight lines

Celsius   a temperature scale that has the freezing point of water as 0°C and the boiling point as 100°C

coefficient   a number that multiplies a variable

combine like terms   add or subtract the coefficients of the variables

common denominator   a common multiple of the denominators

common factor   a factor of two or more different numbers

common multiple   a multiple of two or more different numbers

composite number   a number that has three or more factors

Commutative Properties   two numbers can be added in any order; two numbers can be multiplied in any order

constant   a term that is a number

coordinate axes   two perpendicular number lines

coordinate plane   a plane with coordinate axes drawn on it

cross product   the product of numbers across from each other in a proportion; in $\frac{3}{6} = \frac{4}{8}$ the cross products are 3×8 and 6×4.

decimal   a number written with a dot; values of places to the left of the dot are greater than 1. Values of places to the right are less than 1.

decimal point   the dot in a decimal; it separates the part greater than 1 from the part less than 1.

denominator   the bottom number of a fraction

difference   the answer in subtraction

digits   the ten basic numbers (0, 1, 2, 3, 4, 5, 6, 7, 8, 9)

discount   the amount or percent a price is reduced

Distributive Property   to multiply a sum or difference by a number, multiply each number of the sum or difference

dividend the number being divided

divisible able to be divided by a number giving a 0 remainder; one number is divisible by another.

Division Properties a number divided by itself is 1; a number divided by 1 is the same number; 0 divided by any number that is not 0 is 0

divisor the number used to divide

equivalent having the same value

equivalent equations variable equations with the same solutions

equivalent fractions fractions with different numerators and denominators that name the same amount

estimate tells you about how large a sum or difference will be

evaluate a variable expression find the value by substituting numbers for the variables

exponent tells how many times the base is used as a factor

factors numbers multiplied to give a product; the product divided by the factor gives a 0 remainder

Fahrenheit a temperature scale that has the freezing point of water as 32°F and the boiling point as 212°F

fraction a number that names part of a whole or part of an object

frequency table a table that shows counts of items in different groups

graph of an equation a line made with graphs of ordered pairs from the equation

graph of an ordered pair a dot that shows the location of an ordered pair

graph of a solution points on the number line that show the solution

greatest common factor (GCF) the largest common factor of two or more numbers

horizontal left to right

horizontal axis the line on a bar graph that goes in the left-to-right direction

identity properties adding 0 to a number does not change the number; multiplying a number by 1 does not change the number

improper fraction a fraction in which the numerator is larger than or equal to the denominator

inequality greater than, greater than or equal to, less than, less than or equal to

integers numbers in the set ..., $^-3$, $^-2$, $^-1$, 0, 1, 2, 3,...

inverse operations operations that "undo" each other; addition and subtraction are inverse operations, and multiplication and division are inverse operations.

least common denominator the smallest common denominator

least common multiple the smallest common multiple of two or more numbers that is not 0

like fractions fractions with the same denominators

like terms   numbers or terms that have the same variable with the same exponent

lowest terms fraction   when the greatest common factor of the numerator and denominator is 1

maximum   the largest number in a group of numbers

median   the middle number in a group of numbers when the numbers are in order from smallest to largest.

minimum   the smallest number in a group of numbers

mixed number   a number with a whole number part and a fraction part

mode   the number that appears most often in a group of numbers

multiple   the product of a number and a whole number

negative integers   integers to the left of zero on the number line

number line   shows positive numbers to the right of 0, negative numbers to the left of 0, and 0

number equation   a statement that two number expressions are equal

number expression   a number or numbers together with operation symbols

number property   a fact that is true for all numbers

number scale   shows numbers above and below zero

numerator   the top number of a fraction

opposites   two whole numbers that are the same distance from zero on the number line, but are on opposite sides of zero.

ordered pair   a pair of numbers in a special order; the numbers help locate points.

origin   the point where the coordinate axes cross each other

parentheses   a pair of grouping symbols ( ); may also mean multiplication

percent   a ratio of a number to 100

percent decrease   the percent change when a number decreases

percent increase   the percent change when a number increases

perimeter   the sum of the lengths of the sides of a polygon

place value   the value of a place within a number

plane   a flat surface

polygon   a closed figure with three or more sides

positive integers   integers to the right of zero on the number line

power   the result of multiplying when factors are the same

prime factorization   a number written as the product of its prime factors

prime number   a number that has only 1 and itself as factors

probability   the chance of something happening

product   the answer in multiplication

proper fraction a fraction in which the numerator is less than the denominator

properties of equality adding, subtracting, multiplying, or dividing both sides of an equation by the same number gives an equivalent equation

proportion a statement that two ratios are equal

quotient the answer in division

range the difference between the largest and smallest number in a group of numbers

ratio a comparison of two numbers or quantities

reciprocal of a fraction the fraction you get when you exchange the numerator and denominator

remainder the number left over in division

revise change; change a guess when you know more information

rise the change between two points on a line in an up-and-down direction

run the change between two points on a line in a left-to-right direction

scientific notation a number written as the product of two factors; the first factor is a decimal and the second factor is a power of ten.

simplify carry out the operations; find the value

simplify a variable expression combine like terms

slope the steepness of a straight line

solution a value of the variable that makes a variable equation true

solve find the solution of an equation

solving a proportion finding a number in a proportion when the other three numbers are known

substitute replace a variable with a number

sum the answer in addition

tally a way to keep a count

terms parts of an expression separated by a $+$ or $-$ sign

unlike fractions fractions with different denominators

variable a letter that represents a number

variable equation an equation containing a variable

variable expression an expression containing operations with variables or with variables and numbers

vertical up and down

vertical axis the line on a bar graph that goes in the up-and-down direction

volume the number of cubes needed to fill a space

x–axis horizontal axis

y–axis vertical axis

Zero Property a number multiplied by 0 is 0

Index

Percents, 243, 248, 249
  and decimals, 250, 251
  decrease, 243, 262, 263
  and equations, 254, 255
  and fractions, 252, 253
  increase, 243, 262, 263
  solving equations for, 256, 260, 261
  using calculator in writing, for fractions,
    264, 265
Perfect number, 157
Perimeter, 3, 28, 29
  of rectangle, 106
Pharmacy assistants, 51
Picture taking, 265
Place value, 3, 4, 5
  in comparing numbers, 6, 7
  of decimals, 112, 113
  in rounding numbers, 8, 9
Plane, 321, 323
  coordinate, 322
Polygons, 3, 28, 29
Positive integers, 275, 276
Power, 3, 18
Prices, discount, 268, 269
Prime factorization, 145, 154, 155
  finding, with calculator, 156, 157
Prime number, 145, 152, 153
Probability, 299, 316, 317
Problem solving
  amount of information in, 212, 213
  counting in, 184, 185
  finding patterns in, 158, 159
  grouping in, 292, 293
  guessing, checking, and revising in,
    26, 27
  line graphs in, 332, 333
  number line in, 314, 315
  number patterns in, 104, 105
  numbers for words in, 52, 53
  proportions in, 266, 267
  tables in, 236, 237
  working backward in, 136, 137

Problem solving, drawing pictures in,
  76, 77
Products, 3, 16
  estimating, 22, 23
Proper fraction, 165, 166
Properties of equality, 83, 88, 89
Proportions, 243, 246, 247
  using, in problem solving, 266, 267

Q
Quadrilateral, 28
Quotients, 3, 20
  estimating, 22, 23

R
Range, 219, 238, 239
Ratios, 243, 244, 245
Reciprocals, 220
  of fraction, 219
Rectangle
  area of, 54, 55, 106
  perimeter of, 106
  volume of, 106
Remainder, 3, 20
Revise, 3, 26
Richter scale, 25
Rise, 321
Rounding
  of decimals, 114, 115
  in estimating, 14
  of numbers, 8, 9
Run, 321

S
Scientific notation, 111, 126, 127
Simplification
  of number expressions, 33, 36, 37
  of variable expressions, 61, 66, 67,
    128, 129
  with calculator, 50, 51
Slope of a line, 321, 334, 335

Solutions, 83, 84
    checking, with calculator, 102, 103
    for proportions, 243, 246
Solve, 83, 84
Stock, 291
Substituting, 61, 68
Subtraction, 12, 13
    on calculator, 24, 25
    of decimals, 116, 117
    estimating differences in, 14, 15
    of fractions, on calculator, 210, 211
    of integers, 284, 285
    of like fractions, 194, 195
    of mixed numbers, 204, 205
    solving equations by, 92, 93
    solving inequalities with, 308, 309
    of unlike fractions, 200, 201
Sum, 3, 10
    estimating, 14, 15

T

Table
    place-value, 4, 5
    in problem solving, 236, 237
Tally, 111, 138
Terms, 61
    combining, 61, 66, 67
    like, 64, 65
    unlike, 64, 65
Triangle, 28

U

Unlike fractions, 165, 178, 179
    addition of, 198, 199
    subtraction of, 200, 201

V

Variable, 61, 62
Variable equations, 82
Variable expressions, 61, 62, 63
    calculators in evaluating, 74, 75
    evaluating, 130, 131, 206, 207, 230, 231
        by substitution, 68, 69

simplifying, 300, 301
    with calculator, 50, 51
    by combining like terms, 66, 67,
        128, 129
    with fractions for coefficients, 228, 229
    using more than one operation in, 70, 71
    using more variables in, 72, 73
Variables, using more, in variable
    expressions, 72, 73
Vertical axis, 145, 160, 321, 322
Volume, 61, 78, 79
    of rectangle, 106

W

Whole numbers, 2, 31
    addition of, 10, 11
    comparing, 6, 7
    division of, 20, 21
    estimating products and quotients,
        22, 23
    estimating sums and differences, 14, 15
    multiplication of, 16, 17
    perimeters, 28, 29
    place value foe, 4, 5
    problem solving with, 26, 27
    rounding of, 8, 9
    subtraction of, 12, 13
    using calculator with, 24, 25
    using exponents in, 18, 19
Word statements, writing number
    equations for, 52, 53

X

x-axis, 321, 322

Y

y-axis, 321, 322

Z

Zero property of multiplication, 33, 46

Photo Credits